Eastern European Economies

Eastern European Economies

A Region in Transition

Marcus Goncalves and Erika Cornelius Smith

BEP BUSINESS EXPERT PRESS

Eastern European Economies: A Region in Transition

First published in 2016 by
Business Expert Press, LLC
222 East 46th Street, New York, NY 10017
www.businessexpertpress.com

ISBN-13: 978-1-63157-399-6 (paperback)
ISBN-13: 978-1-63157-400-9 (e-book)

Business Expert Press Economics Collection

Collection ISSN: 2163-761X (print)
Collection ISSN: 2163-7628 (electronic)

Cover and interior design by Exeter Premedia Services Private Ltd., Chennai, India

First edition: 2016

10 9 8 7 6 5 4 3 2 1

Printed in the United States of America.

For my International Business students at Nichols College, for the great discussions about these markets and the global markets as a whole, and for keeping me on my toes; for my beloved wife Carla, always patient and caring with me during these intense projects; for my son Samir, who brings me so much pride; and for my other two children, Andrea and Joshua (in memory), also treasures in my life, for which I count the days to be reunited with. To God be the glory!

Marcus Goncalves
Spring 2016

For my students at Nichols College, who inspire me with their humor and grit; for my muses, Sophie and Phoebe, who inspire me with their curiosity and moments of pure joy; and for Andrew, who inspires me with his generosity and an abundant supply of strawberry licorice. For all of this and more, I am truly blessed.

Erika Cornelius Smith
Spring 2016

Abstract

Nearly seven decades ago, six countries in Western Europe (Belgium, France, West Germany, Italy, Luxembourg, and the Netherlands) decided to take economic cooperation to the next level. The vision of the European Union (EU) founding states, epitomized by the Schuman Declaration in 1950, was to tie their economies—including the reemerging West German economy—so closely together that war would become impossible.

Europe will not be made all at once, or according to a single plan. It will be built through concrete achievements which first create a de facto solidarity—Robert Schuman. In 1973, Denmark, Ireland, and the United Kingdom joined what was then referred to as the "European Community." The 1970s were also a decade of deep social and political transformations in Greece, Portugal, and Spain, where military regimes and dictatorships were overthrown. Inspired by the prosperity and stability of the European Community, these countries joined the European project within 10 years, strengthening their emerging democracies. The countries benefited enormously from free trade and common economic policies, in particular structural funds designed to foster convergence by funding infrastructure and investments in poorer regions.

The Maastricht Treaty established convergence criteria to ensure that countries joining the new common currency would be sufficiently similar, and it also gave market forces a significant role in disciplining member states, by establishing the "no bailout" clause. To dispel skepticism and preserve fiscal discipline after the common currency was introduced, member countries signed the Stability and Growth Pact in 1997, which was designed to tie policies to fiscal balance and debt targets. In sum, the euro's architecture was built on the premise that market forces, combined with minimal coordination of policies, would sufficiently align economies, discipline fiscal policies, and allow countries to withstand idiosyncratic shocks.

This book examines how these larger trends were experienced in individual member states throughout the Eastern European states. This book also scans the regional block of Central and Eastern Europe (CEE), South East Europe (SEE), and the Commonwealth of Independent States (CIS), and the macroeconomic dynamics of these states and the EU.

Keywords

CEE, CIS, Eastern European Economies, EU, European Union, Eurozone, Maastricht Treaty, Schuman Declaration, SEE, Western Europe

Contents

Preface

This book is divided into seven chapters, each addressing a significant aspect of the economic, political, and social transition in central and eastern Europe over the last several decades. We integrate historical data with the most recent political and economic reporting in our analysis, including our assessments, opinions, and experience (where appropriate) as scholars, researchers, consultants, and global citizens.

Chapter 1 provides the reader with an introduction to the historical context for European integration, including the political structures and economic relationships forged in the post-World War II period. We pay close attention to the impact of nationalist histories and geography on the politics of integration, and include brief introductions to each country included in later chapters of this publication.

Chapter 2 focuses more specifically on the relationship between the European Union (EU) and the economies of states in central and eastern Europe. We examine the political, economic, and security considerations that complicated the federalist relationship in each state, and end with a brief discussion of the adoption of the euro.

Chapter 3 provides an overview of these eastern European countries in transition from a state-centered economy to a free market, decentralized one. We provide an overview of the geopolitical and economic challenges of both, the Central and Eastern European (CEE) bloc and the Commonwealth of Independent States (CIS) blocs. We also discuss the economic challenges faced by these economies regionally, as well as in consequence of external forces brought by advanced economies, such as the global financial contagion resulted of the economic crisis that started in 2007, and the currency wars and their consequences to local and global economies.

Chapter 4 discusses the economic impact of integration of CEE countries as they attempt to make their economic transition and to integrate with the EU and other free-market economies. We look at the economic growth and challenges these countries face, as well as how the indebtedness of the advanced economies is impacting these economies and prompting them to launch economic countermeasure to protect their own economies.

Chapter 5 discusses the many challenges for foreign investors and multinational corporations (MNCs) in entering eastern European markets, from skill mismatches and educational systems, to the impact of economic restructuring, legal framework, and trading policies. This chapter also provides an overview as to the main reasons why MNCs fail in eastern Europe markets.

Chapter 6 introduces multiple frameworks for the study of political risk, and provides an overview of this important field for the reader. The chapter proceeds with country-based case studies that include *Freedom House* scores, electoral results, and in-depth political analysis to assess the potential risk created by stable or reforming political institutions in each CEE state.

Chapter 7 concludes with an overview of the CEE region in 2015, including economic progress and potential geopolitical threats to stability in the region. We then examine recently published economic data and forecasts for 2016, and provide a brief analysis of the outlook for the region.

Extensive, user-friendly appendices that provide additional country-specific case studies and analysis for the reader follow these chapters. Our hope is that this work will provide an introduction to the historical and political context of the culturally rich, vibrant, and rapidly changing region of CEE. We have balanced this introduction with breadth and depth for the international business professional who desires to engage in the significant opportunities available to those willing to explore this very important region in transition.

Acknowledgments

There were many people who helped us during the process of writing this book. It would be impossible to keep track of them all. Therefore, to all that we have forgotten to list, please don't hold it against us!

We would like to thank Dr. Patrick Barron, professor at the Graduate School of Banking at the University of Wisconsin, Madison, and of Austrian economics at the University of Iowa, in Iowa City, for his contributions on the issue of currency wars in Chapter 4.

We also would like to thank Mr. Bo-Young Lin, from the Graduate Institute of International and Development Studies and United Nations Conference on Trade and Development (UNCTAD) for his support and insights. We would also like to express our appreciation to many corporate leaders who shared their views and experiences with us in the eastern European region. Our special thanks go to the following leaders and great friends: Jörgen Eriksson, founding partner at Bearing Group Ltd, in London, UK; Ewelina Kroll, public relations manager at East Europe Consulting; Piotr Kozicki, business information security officer at Citigroup Global Fund Services in Warsaw, Poland; Julius Niedvaras, director of international business school at Vilnius University, Lithuania; Luc Jalllois Sr. vice president at LJL Consulting, Kiev, Ukraine; Galyna Konto, investment manager, Kiev, Ukraine; Markéta Remišovská, principal at Rizzo Associates, Praga, Czech Republic; and Dmitriy Lisenkov, hedge fund manager at The Russian Technology Fund, St. Petersburg, Russia.

CHAPTER 1

The European Context for Integration and Accession

Europe will not be made all at once, or according to a single plan. It will be built through concrete achievements, which first create a de facto solidarity.

—Robert Schuman

Overview

Nearly seven decades ago, six countries in Western Europe (Belgium, France, West Germany, Italy, Luxembourg, and the Netherlands) decided to take economic cooperation to the next level. The vision of the European Union (EU) founding states, epitomized by the Schuman Declaration in 1950, was to tie their economies—including the re-emerging West German economy—so closely together that war would become impossible.

In 1973, Denmark, Ireland, and the United Kingdom joined what was then referred to as the "European Community." The period of 1970s was also a decade of deep social and political transformations in Greece, Portugal, and Spain, where military regimes and dictatorships were overthrown. Inspired by the prosperity and stability of the European Community, these countries joined the European project within 10 years, strengthening their emerging democracies. The countries benefited enormously from free trade and common economic policies, in particular structural funds designed to foster convergence by funding infrastructure and investments in poorer regions.

Despite these significant cooperative achievements, the most significant episode in Europe's postwar political and economic integration was symbolized by the fall of the Berlin Wall. A defining moment in the collapse of the centrally planned economic systems of the 1980s, the collapse of the Wall and the Soviet Union ushered in a multifaceted process of liberalization.

On one hand, the fall of communism broke countries apart, with the dissolution of the Soviet Union and Yugoslavia, followed in 1993 by the "Velvet Divorce" of the Czech and Slovak Republics. On the other hand, less than a year after the Berlin Wall came down, East and West Germany reunified. More than 20 countries emerged from communism in a new, more democratic Europe. The integration of these states presented the greatest opportunities and also the greatest challenges of the post-World War II era. In this context, this chapter provides the reader with an introduction to the broader context of European integration and accession, with special attentions to economic, political, and social challenges across the region. It concludes with a series of short case studies that introduce the reader to the process of transition in the individual Central and Eastern European (CEE) states.

The Effects of History and Geography on Regional Identity

As depicted in Figure 1.1, several scholars writing about the CEE regions are faced with the unique challenge of identifying and "naming" a series of states in the process of "a return to Europe." Some who study the region suggest that the "English language lacks an appropriate and widely acceptable collective name" for the regions that form the Balkans and East Central Europe.[1] In German language, for example, they are referred to as *Zwischeneuropa* (in between Europe). Global political and economic integration, as well as redefined political communities within each state, present new opportunities to construct communities of belonging. Katalin Fábián[2] writes,

> The Baltic states of Estonia, Latvia, and Lithuania, as well as several stateless people, divided sub-regions, and ethnic, linguistic, and religious minorities (the Russian territory between Ukraine,

---

[1] Bideleux and Jeffries (2007, xiii).

[2] Fábián (2007, 6).

Figure 1.1 CEE political bloc

Source: Kubilius (2016).

Poland, Slovakia, Hungary, or Muslims in Bulgaria, for example) keenly illustrate how previously submerged political and cultural identities can re-emerge and create themselves.

As a consequence of these shifting identities and politics, scholars who focus on the study of CEE states struggle with how or what to call this region, given the historical context and changing political affiliations.[3] Use of the term "Central Europe" typically refers to Germany and Austria (formally the "Central Powers") and excludes the Baltic States and the South Eastern European countries that can be included in an analysis of transition and accession. Use of the term "East Europe" delineates the states from the "West" of Europe in the post-World War II Cold War context and aligns them more closely with the Soviet sphere of influence.

---

[3] Kubilius (2016).

Historians, political scientists, economists, and other researchers writing about the region emphasize one or the other signifier as a matter of political choice. Geography has very little to do with the choice to employ Central or Eastern Europe. It is a matter of selective inclusion and exclusion.

With these considerations in mind, our study will cast a broader net by referring to the collective region as CEE, unless referencing a specific organization or regional alliance. This includes: the Baltic States (Estonia, Latvia, Lithuania), Poland, the Czech Republic, Slovakia, Hungary, Romania, Slovenia, Croatia, Bosnia and Herzegovina, Serbia and Montenegro, Bulgaria, Macedonia, and Albania. Other studies of the region integrated the Baltic countries alongside Poland, Hungary, and former Czechoslovakia as part of their analysis of CEE economics and politics because the two areas achieved independent statehood within the eastern zone of Europe between 1918 and 1940.[4]

Global Influences on the Transition

The distinctions in the history and geography that impact "naming" also signal that these states each had very different relationships to communism. Slovenian scholars, for example, protest the use of "post-communism" to describe their state, arguing that the ruling regime was clearly not a true communist system. Rather, "it relied on oppression and never reached the level of material abundance required for this stage of development according to Marxist theory."[5] For this reason, it is important to discuss the broad economic and political trends that influenced the transition of CEE states beyond the fall of the Berlin Wall.

The End of National Planning

Many of the "national economic" models employed after World War II began to pull apart by the 1970s. This included Soviet-style state capitalism, national planning in the West, and import-substitution industrialization

---

[4] For examples of these inclusive studies see Crampton (1994) and Rothschild (1974).

[5] Humer (2007).

in developing countries. The decade witnessed a "loosening" of capital controls in the United States and Britain, and a deregulation of stock exchanges. These changes "facilitated a spectacular growth and centralization of international banking, insurance, and securities markets."[6] The restructuring of finance capital and the deregulation of national capital markets created the first "wave" of the demise of the national planning systems.

It should be noted that from 1973 to 1978, while the Western world experienced economic recession in response to the staggering increases in oil prices of Organization of the Petroleum Exporting Countries (OPEC), the CEE and eastern Balkan states continued to grow. In some cases, this growth was even faster than the previous decade.[7] Increasing dependency on the Soviet market and imports of underpriced Soviet oil, gas, power-generating equipment, and technology were accompanied by exports of agricultural and manufactured goods back to the Soviet Union. This type of Soviet "assistance" insulated these economies against adverse trading trends and the potentially damaging effects of recession and higher oil prices, but impaired their future capacity to export successfully to the West.

Despite continuing reliance on the Soviet Union, the 1970s East-West détente did facilitate an increase in the flow of Western capital and technology into the CEE economies. Many of the states "eagerly accepted" Western investments, joint ventures, loans, industrial installations, and "technology transfers" as substitutes for fundamentally altering their economic systems.[8] Economic historians note that excessive reliance on increased Western capital technology and firms had two significant consequences for the CEE states: (1) increased contact with Western visitors

---

[6] Dale (2011, 11).

[7] Bideleux and Jeffries (2007, 511–12). Two notable exceptions existed at this time: the increasingly nationalist Albanian and Romania communist regimes were denied Soviet "assistance," despite their rapidly diminishing domestic mineral resources. Albania began receiving significant support from China in return for its support of that state during the Sino-Soviet disputes of the 1960s and early 1970s, and at that point no longer participated as an active member in Comecon.

[8] Bideleux and Jeffries (2007, 513).

and products helped to diffuse Western values, consumerism, and pop culture, particularly among younger generations; and (2) reliance on these transfers created equally serious economic hazards.[9] The Westernization of CEE values, dress, leisure activities, and worldviews among young people living in the region contributed as much to the demise of the communist system as systemic reforms. Through their clumsy attempts to curb the grown influence of rock concerts, Western pop music, blue jeans, and consumerism, the ageing dictators made them seem increasingly old fashioned, puritanical, out of touch, and ridiculous, especially in the eyes of the young.[10]

Further, capital and technology transfers created serious economic problems. Debt-service payments were burdensome and drained much-needed resources for infrastructure. As CEE credit ratings fell in the 1970s, the states had difficulty continuing to import goods, including materials needed for existing Western projects within their states. Jeff Sommers, Jānis Bērzinš, and Adam Fabry[11] argue that financialization and economic globalization were linked as a response to the crises of the mid-1970s.

These factors were further complicated by another slowdown of global economic growth and return of crises in the 1980s. From 1979 to 1983, the economies of the CEE states suffered acute economic recessions. Whereas economists noted per capita annual global growth in the 1960s and 1970s at a rate of roughly 3 percent, the 1980s and beyond have seen a rate of nearly half that amount. In the more extreme cases of Romania and Poland, the economies experienced severe economic contractions and significant reductions in living standards.

The Rise of Neoliberalism

Daniel Gros and Alfred Steinherr[12] championed the progress of CEE states in the mid-1990s, writing, "Like Western Europe after World War II, Eastern European countries now have the historic opportunity to

---

[9] Stokes (1991).

[10] Bideleux and Jeffries (2007, 513).

[11] Sommers and Bērzinš (2011, 119–42).

[12] Gros and Steinherr (1995, 86).

create *ex nova* optimal economic and social institutions and thereby free their latent energies."[13] Persuaded by the merits of neoliberal ideology, the scholars championed CEE countries potential to "leapfrog those Western countries whose oligarchic and inward-looing politico-institutional framework [had] not had the chance to be dynamited away."[14] By the mid-1990s, most CEE countries had liberalized prices and witnessed the collapse of intra-Comecon trading. But with outdated technology, poorer quality commodities, few established marketing connections, and facing the protectionist policies of major powers, CEE manufacturers found it difficult, if not nearly impossible, to break into external markets. The comparison to Western Europe also neglected the important historic context of the post-1945 political and economic world—economic boom and Marshall Aid that overwhelmingly benefitted Western European states, as well as infrastructure development and tariff protection for industries in those states. Nearly 90 percent of Marshall Aid was issued in grant form, yet only 10 percent of that aid was received by post-communist European states, in part because Stalin prevented many states from receiving this assistance.[15] Historians note that only Poland received significant support from Western allies in the form of debt cancellation to both public and private creditors and EU assistance with a preferential status for agricultural imports.[16] Jan Drahokoupil[17] writes that Hungary, on the other hand, possessed the world's highest per capita debt and was obligated to earmark revenue raised by privatizing state-owned corporations.

The Expansion of Liberal-Democratic Government

Beginning in the mid-1970s, a significant number of states around the globe, including Southern Europe, adopted parliamentary government. In terms of the Second and Third Worlds, John Walton and David

---

[13] Gros and Steinherr (1995, 86).

[14] Gros and Steinherr (1995, 86).

[15] Outhwaite (2010, 92).

[16] Dal (2011, 11).

[17] Drahokoupil (2009, 102).

Seddon identify three potential pragmatic explanations for these shifts.[18] First, democracy provides a relatively stable environment for business. Second, the neoliberal ideology noted above is promoted by international financial organizations and favors noninterventionist states. Liberal democratic governments fulfill this role because they "dilute state power to a level acceptable to diverse coalitions, just as they give greater power to the free play of markets."[19] Finally, debt and austerity can lead to "partial state breakdown," as the measures required by structural adjustment programs impede the ability of authoritarian governments to extend patronage, and austerity policies require the support of large portions of the polity.

One of the major potential impediments to mature liberal democracy in the CEE countries during the early 1990s was the fact that independent and impartial political and civil institutions barely existed (with the exception of the Czech lands). As Robert Bideleux and Ian Jeffries[20] write,

> Even those [institutions] that did emerge had been largely destroyed by the combined effects of intolerant "ethnic" nationalism and authoritarianism, the 1930s Great Depression, fascism, the Second World War, the Holocaust and neo-Stalinist dictatorship, all of which had helped to decimate, emasculate, or drive abroad the ethnic and social groups that were most capable of producing or recreating autonomous, pluralistic and liberal-minded "civil societies."

In other words, "No bourgeoisie, no democracy."[21] An example of this in the CEE context of transition is Poland in 1989. As General Jaruzelski noted, after initial steps toward democracy were taken "we tried economic reforms time and again. But we always met with public resistance and

---

[18] Walton and Seddon (1994, 334–35). See also Hoogvelt (1997) and Derluguian (2005).

[19] Walton and Seddon (1994, 334–35). See also Hoogvelt (1997) and Derluguian (2005).

[20] Bideleux and Jeffries (2007, 540–41).

[21] Moore (1969).

explosions. It is very different now. Now, with a government that enjoys public confidence, it has become possible to demand sacrifices."[22]

The Collapse of Labor and the Left

Another trend impacting the transition of CEE countries was the global downturn and the effect on the labor movement and social movements of the political Left. Control over industrial production shifted toward full-time officials, and as their industrial strength waned, labor groups turned to leftist political parties for assistance. G.M. Tamás and Stuart Shields argue that both groups "accepted" the present defeat of their vision for political and economic life and the idealization of Western institutions that would shape the post-1989 global environment.[23] In parts of CEE, democratic reformers promoted a market-fundamentalist agenda, encouraged by Western foundations and governments.[24]

Post-Communist Economic Transformations

Economists and historians studying the transformations argue that it is misleading to label the post-communist economic transformations as moving from "socialism" to "capitalism."[25] Rather, they should be understood as movements from "state capitalism" to more liberalized and marketized versions of capitalism. Those changes involved major shifts from effectively "vertical" economic power structures to more "horizontal" relationships in which parties interacted more with one another than the state bureaucratic organizations. The broad steps to shifting the economies in this direction included emphasizing (and sometimes introducing) the rule of law, encouraging stricter fiscal discipline, creating market institutions, encouraging greater competition and a more "level playing field," and investing in new infrastructure and technology, all while supporting privatization.

---

[22] Quoted in Haynes and Hasan (1998). See also Dale (2004, 274–75).

[23] Tamás (2011) and Shields (2011).

[24] Bandelj (2008, 115).

[25] See Sachs (1994); Sjöberg and Wyzan (1991); Taras (1992).

Essentially, the change from centrally planned command economies to more market-oriented economies required "not only proper macro-economic policies and institutions but also well-defined behavioral rules for integrating the decisions of decentralized agents… Perhaps of utmost importance is rule certainty for all economic agents."[26]

In each state, the initial challenge for the transition was stabilization. High hopes in late-1989 and the early-1990s were quickly deflated by realities of falling output, soaring inflation, rising unemployment, fiscal retrenchment, infrastructure decay, and simmering interethnic tensions, particularly in the Balkans and Slovakia. Many economists and politicians advocated mobilizing Western aid to the CEE states on a scale of the Marshall Plan and rejected the notion by skeptically contending that these countries were incapable of using it effectively. They argued that the CEE states could become Europe's "tiger economies," possessing substantial reserves of cheap, underemployed, skilled, and educated labor with a "strong drive to prosper." Jeffrey Sachs, who served as an economic advisor to Poland between 1989 and 1991, argued that Western aid could help sustain political support for the reforms long enough for them to take hold. The Marshall Plan did not provide Europe with the funds for economic recovery. It provided governments with enough financial backing to achieve economic and political stability, give hope to the population, and thus make economic recovery possible.[27] Economists, such as Sachs, warned that if the West failed to provide short-term assistance, it would be faced with the choice of having to "do business" with lackluster states and economies, rife with corruption.

Western states did not provide large-scale grants of aid, however, and CEE states felt the impact of this almost immediately in their attempts to recover from the early-1990s economic collapse. According to reports by economic historians and global institutions, such as the World Bank,

---

[26] van Brabant (1989).

[27] "Crossing the Valley of Tears in East European Reform," *Challenge*, September October 1991; "Jeffrey Sachs: My Plan for Poland," in The *International Economy*, December 1989/January 1990, Volume III, Number 6; "Eastern Europe's Economies—What is to be done?" in The *Economist*, January 13, 1990. PDFs of all articles are available at: www.earth.columbia.edu/articles/view/1023

the collapse of traditional trade and investment links and dislocation of domestic demand contributed to large output collapses in the early years of transition, ranging from about 10 percent in Poland and Hungary to some 40 percent in countries such as Latvia and Lithuania. As prices were liberalized, they tended to skyrocket, partly as relative prices were set by supply and demand rather than central planning, but with especially steep increases, where state revenues dried up and governments had few sources of finance other than turning to central banks to print money. In 1994, the United Nations Children's Fund (UNICEF) released a report claiming the collapse of European command economies had precipitated a slump in birth rates and major increases in poverty, death rates, morbidity rates, malnutrition, truancy, family breakdown, and violent crime. The result was such that by 1993, conditions in the eastern half of the European continents were worse than those in Latin America during the "lost decade" of the 1980s or in Western Europe during the 1930s depression.[28]

According to Bideleux and Jeffries, partially reconstructed ex-communists continued to operate Romania until 1996, Slovakia and Bulgaria until 1998, Croatia until 1999, and Serbia until 2000. Similar problems were evident in Poland and Hungary, while large sectors of the economies of Serbia, Montenegro, Bulgaria, Macedonia, Bosnia, and Albania fell under the control of "organized criminal networks, black marketeers, armed thugs, and traffickers in fuel, drugs, arms, cigarettes, and prostitutes."[29]

In many ways, the post-1989 political and economic transformations of the CEE countries were even more fraught with difficulties than the post-1918 and post-1945 efforts. Although the Balkan and CEE economies suffered severe human losses, war damage and dislocation in both of the prior postwar periods, they were comparably less industrialized than in 1989 and did not have to contend with "extensive closures of industrial capacity."[30] Historians note that even if they were subject to wartime controls, they were still already market economies. This prevented them

---

[28] *The Independen* (1994, 10).

[29] Bideleux and Jeffries (2007, 551).

[30] Bideleux and Jeffries (2007, 554).

from undergoing simultaneous economic reconstruction, stabilization programs, and the profound reordering of their economic systems.

When CEE countries began their post-1989 transformations, most of them were already burdened with large foreign debts (see Table 1.1) and heavy debt-service payments inherited from the outgoing communist regimes. In 1918 and 1945, they had the opportunity to begin their new states with relatively clean slates.

Despite the many challenges outlined in the 1994 UNICEF report, the CEE post-communist states, with the exceptions of Bosnia and Macedonia, were achieving significant economic growth. Their efforts to establish market economies were more or less effective, again with the exception of Bosnia. As discussed in more detail in the subsequent country case studies, the initially high levels of inflation were largely brought under control through monetary policy by most CEE states in 1993, in Latvia and Albania by 1994, in Estonia, Romania, Croatia, Bosnia, and Macedonia in 1995, in Lithuania by 1996, and in Serbia-Montenegro and Bulgaria by 1998.

Even with measurable progress in the 1990s, the figures presented in the tables below illustrate the significance of the technical and economic gap between the EU-15 and CEE states.[31] Table 1.2 presents data on the

Table 1.1 Hard-currency debts of European communist states, 1979 (in $)

	Total ($ billion)	$ per inhabitant
Yugoslavia	17	780
Hungary	7.5	700
Poland	19.5	557
Romania	7	320
Bulgaria	4	455
Czechoslovakia	3.5	233
USSR	10.2	39

Source: Bideleux (1987, 270).

---

[31] The EU-15 is composed of Austria, Belgium, Denmark, Finland, France, Germany, Greece, Ireland, Italy, Luxembourg, the Netherlands, Portugal, Spain, Sweden, and the United Kingdom.

Table 1.2 Cars, personal computers, and computer linked to Internet per 100 inhabitants (1999 to 2000)

	Cars	PCs	PCs linked to Internet
EU-15 average	46.1	24.8	2.3
Slovenia	42.6	25.3	1.2
Estonia	33.9	13.5	2.1
Czech Republic	36.2	10.7	1.2
Latvia	23.5	8.2	0.8
Hungary	23.5	7.4	1.2
Slovakia	23.6	7.4	0.5
Poland	25.9	6.2	0.4
Lithuania	31.7	5.9	0.4
Bulgaria	24.4	2.7	0.2
Romania	13.9	2.7	0.2

Source: European Commission. December 13, 2003. Press Release, State/01/129, p. 4.

numbers of cars, personal computers, and computers connected to the Internet per 100 inhabitants as of 1999.

Table 1.3 provides figures on the percentage of the workforce employed in "knowledge-intensive services" and tech manufacturing. Finally, the data on disparities in hourly labor costs between the EU-15 states and the accession states, as depicted in Table 1.4, reveals the extent of the gap between the two regions in a way not fully captured by others studies utilizing per capita gross domestic product (GDP).

Foreign Direct Investment

Foreign direct investment (FDI) entails investing directly in production in another country, either by buying a company there or establishing new operations of an existing business. This is done mostly by companies as opposed to financial institutions, which prefer indirect investment abroad such as buying small parcels of a country's supply of shares or bonds. FDI grew rapidly during the 1990s before slowing a bit, along with the global economy, in the early years of the 21st century. Most of this investment went from one member-country of the OECD to

Table 1.3 Percentage of workforce employment in knowledge-intensive services and medium- or high-tech manufacturing (2002)

	Knowledge-intensive services	Medium- and high-tech manufacturing
EU-15 average	33.3	7.4
Estonia	30.9	3.4
Hungary	26.4	8.5
Lithuania	24.7	2.6
Latvia	24.7	1.9
Slovakia	24.0	8.2
Czech Republic	23.9	8.9
Slovenia	22.8	9.2
Bulgaria	22.2	5.3
Romania	12.8	5.5

Source: European Commission. November 7, 2003. Press Release, STAT/03/127, pp. 1–2. No data available for Poland.

Table 1.4 Hourly labor costs in industry and services (2000)[32]

EU-15 average[33]	22.70	Accession states' average	4.21
Sweden	28.56	Cyprus	10.74
Denmark	27.10	Slovenia	8.98
Germany	26.54	Poland	4.48
France	24.39	Czech Republic	3.90
United Kingdom	23.85	Hungary	3.83
Austria	23.60	Slovakia	3.06
Netherlands	22.99	Estonia	3.03
Ireland	17.34	Lithuania	2.71
Spain	14.22	Latvia	2.42
Greece	10.40	Romania	1.51
Portugal	8.13	Bulgaria	1.35

Source: EU Press Release. March 3, 2003. STAT/03/23, p. 2.

---

[32] Note: The average hourly labor costs are total annual labor costs divided by the total number of hours worked during the year.

[33] Excluding Italy and Belgium, no available data.

another, but the share going to developing countries, especially in Asia, increased steadily.[34]

There was a time when economists considered FDI a substitute for trade. Building factories in foreign countries was one way of jumping tariff barriers. Now economists typically regard FDI and trade as complementary. For example, a firm can use a factory in one country to supply neighboring markets. Some investments, especially in services industries, are essential prerequisites for selling to foreigners. Who would buy a Whopper in London if it had to be sent from Chicago?

Governments used to be highly suspicious of FDI, often regarding it as corporate imperialism. Nowadays they are more likely to court it. They hope that investors will create jobs, and bring expertise and technology that will be passed on to local firms and workers, helping to sharpen up their whole economy. Furthermore, unlike financial investors, multinationals generally invest directly in plant and equipment. Since it is hard to uproot a chemical factory, these investments, once made, are far more enduring than the flows of money that whisk in and out of emerging markets.

Although FDI was restricted before 1989, foreign investors started entering the region after the fall of the communist regimes and it has been considered particularly important to CEE economies.[35] Economists and international financial organizations have cited FDI as "an engine for transition" to a market-based economy and a "powerful force for integration" of this region into the larger global economy.[36] Absent "massive inflows of foreign capital," they believed "successful transition [from planned to market economies] in CEE is unlikely."[37] Many believed that FDI would prove to be the catalyst in a transition away from socialist economies and

---

[34] For more information on studying foreign direct investment (FDI), see www.economist.com/economics-a-to-z#2DI6CRzKPkRSqArm.99

[35] Along with efforts to reform their socialist regimes, Hungary, Poland, and Yugoslavia allowed joint ventures with foreign investors prior to 1989. The provisions, however, only really began to see the effects of FDI beginning in 1989, as demonstrated by the data in Table 1.5, "Foreign Direct Investment Trends."

[36] IMF (1997); UNCTAD (1998).

[37] Schmidt (1995).

positively affect macroeconomic indicators such as balance of payment and unemployment. Foreign investors would introduce technological and managerial resources, along with financial capital, and encourage corporate restructuring and privatization of state-owned firms.[38]

As Table 1.5 shows, the initial FDI inflows were minimal, but rapidly grew after 1995. Between 1995 and 2004, average FDI stock as percent share in GDP for CEE countries has been higher than the world average.

Table 1.5 FDI Trends During the Transition (1970 to 2004)

	FDI inflows ($ billion)		Average FDI stock as % GDP	
	CEE	World	CEE	World
1970	0	13	0	-
1980	0	55	0	5
1989	<1	193	0	8
1990	<1	208	0	8
1991	2	161	2	8
1992	3	169	5	8
1993	4	228	7	9
1994	4	259	9	9
1995	10	341	10	9
1996	9	393	12	10
1997	10	488	16	12
1998	18	701	19	14
1999	19	1,092	23	16
2000	21	1,397	27	18
2001	22	826	31	20
2002	25	716	35	21
2003	17	633	37	22
2004	28	648	39	22

Note: CEE in this table includes Bulgaria, Croatia, Czech Republic, Estonia, Hungary, Latvia, Lithuania, Poland, Romania, Slovakia, and Slovenia.
Source: UNCTAD (2006).[39]

---

[38] Meyer (1995); Meyer (1998); Lankes and Venables (1996); OECD (1998); Bevin and Estrin (2014).

[39] http://unctadstat.unctad.org/EN/Index.html

By 2004, it was almost twice as high, contributing on average to 39 percent GDP. This placed the CEE among the world's top regions in terms of foreign capital penetration at that time.[40]

Although these inflows formed a significant portion of the CEE economy, for the entire CEE region, FDI between 1989 and 1994 amounted to only two-fifths of the flow to China in 1993 alone. These differences in regional FDI are partially explained by differences in investor countries of both the regions. As displayed in Table 1.6, the primary regional investors in the CEE countries during the transition were not identical to the top worldwide investors.

Germany and the Netherlands rank higher than the United States based on total stock of investment in the region as of 2000, while France and the United Kingdom had a much less significant presence. Austria and Sweden, although ranked 23rd and 13th respectively, were much more prominent investors.

These relationships are further complicated when one examines the presence of significant worldwide investors in individual CEE countries during the transition. Table 1.7 highlights these disparities in percent share of total FDI stock across the CEE region nearly 10 years after the fall of the communist regimes. The Czech Republic and Poland received

Table 1.6 Top investor countries in 2000

	World	CEE
1.	United States	Germany
2.	United Kingdom	Netherlands (#7 in the world)
3.	France	United States
4.	Germany	Austria (#23 in the world)
5.	Hong Kong	Sweden (#13 in the world)

Note: Rankings are based on outward FDI stock as of 2000.
Source: UNCTAD (2001).

---

[40] According to the The United Nations Conference on Trade and Development (UNCTAD) (2006), data for the period revealed only one other region higher in FDI stock as percent of GDP, "Developing America, other." This category by their definition included island states of Central America where FDI stock as percent of GDP was 43.

Table 1.7 Investments by Significant Worldwide Investor Countries in CEE (Percent Share of Total FDI Stock in Host in 2000)

World Ranking	Investor Country	Bulgaria	Croatia	Czech Republic	Estonia	Hungary	Latvia	Lithuania	Poland	Slovakia	Slovenia
1	US	12	21	6	5	8	9	10	10	7	4
2	UK	11	2	3	2	1	5	7	3	3	4
3	France	3	2	4	1	7	<1	1	12	3	11
4	Germany	19	22	26	3	26	11	7	19	28	12
5	Hong Kong	0	0	0	<1	0	1	<1	<1	0	<1
6	Belgium/Luxembourg	6	6	5	<1	5	<1	4	2	2	<1
7	Netherlands	4	4	30	2	23	3	1	25	24	3
8	Japan	<1	0	<1	<1	2	0	<1	<1	0	<1
9	Switzerland	3	1	4	1	2	2	5	2	<1	4
10	Canada	<1	<1	<1	<1	<1	<1	<1	<1	<1	<1
11	Italy	2	2	<1	<1	3	<1	<1	4	2	5
12	Spain	3	<1	<1	<1	<1	<1	<1	2	<1	0
13	Sweden	<1	2	<1	40	<1	13	17	3	<1	<1
14	Australia	<1	1	<1	0	0	0	<1	<1	0	<1
15	Singapore	<1	0	0	1	<1	1	0	<1	0	<1

16	Finland	<1	<1	<1	30	<1	6	6	<1	<1	<1
17	Taiwan	0	0	<1	0	0	0	0	<1	0	0
18	Denmark	<1	1	4	<1	10	18	2	<1	1
19	Norway	<1	<1	4	<1	6	4	<1	<1	0
20	South Africa	0	0	0	0	0	<1	<1	0	0
21	China	0	<1	<1	<1	0	<1	<1	0	0
22	South Korea	0	<1	0	<1	<1	<1	<1	0	0
23	Austria	25	11	<1	12	<1	<1	3	14	46
24	Argentina	0	0	0	0	0	0	<1	0	0
25	Malaysia	0	<1	0	0	0	0	0	0	0

Source: UNCTAD (2001, 2006), percentages tabulated manually.

the greatest share of investment to CEE states. German corporations were heavily invested throughout the central part of Europe, (Czech Republic, Hungary, Poland, Romania, and Slovakia) more so than the Baltic states of Estonia, Latvia, and Lithuania. Comparing the latter, Estonia received the greatest investment from Finland, while Denmark and Sweden invested in Lithuania and Latvia. In 2000, the U.S. investment amounted to nearly 20 percent of FDI stock in Croatia, but less than 5 percent in nearby Slovenia. Investments by Latin American, South African, and Asia countries were negligible across the region.

How do we explain the difference in investment patterns across the region? Scholars writing in economic sociology argue that the pre-existing social and cultural relationships shared across these regions facilitated these economic patterns.[41] Nina Bandelj writes,

> In cases where uncertainty surrounding economic transactions is high, such as in post-communist Europe during the transition period, the role of social relations and pre-existing knowledge of potential partners in facilitating FDI transactions is even more pronounced.[42]

Bandelj argues that scholars can trace the inflows of FDI to pre-existing international relations and cultural affinities between investor and recipient countries, even when measured against geographic proximity.[43]

Despite the optimism surrounding the power of FDI by economic advisors, when examining the transition period between 1990 and 2010 as a whole, economic data reveals that a significant portion of the CEE region experienced a regional Great Depression. Currencies across the region devalued rapidly and banking crises were widespread. In terms of GDP, nearly two decades were lost.[44] In some cases, where there was adequate political and institutional support for fiscal and monetary discipline, stabilization was achieved within a couple of years; others faced

---

[41] Smith-Doerr and Powell (2005).

[42] Bandelj (2007, 45).

[43] Bandelj (2008).

[44] Dale (2011, 11).

longer or multiple attempts to establish low inflation and sustainable public finances.

Following a period of stabilization, the new member states focused on institution building to improve the functioning of the economies, using Western Europe and other democratic states as models. Many of these countries, however, faced significant challenges in privatization, public sector reform, and establishment of an environment conducive to reform. Scholars credit the creation of credible monetary and exchange rate frameworks—whether involving floating or different types of fixed-rate arrangements—as key to the success of transition. Reza Moghadam, Director of the International Monetary Fund (IMF's) European Department, argues, "integration has been particularly evident in the financial sector, with western European banks dominating in most of the transition countries."[45] This relationship has had both positive and negative consequences for transitioning states. On one hand, it brought critical expertise in financing. On the other hand, the unrestricted flow of capital into the region in the early- to mid-2000s inflated bubbles that burst in the ensuing global financial crisis.

Many experts take the position that integration has also contributed to strong convergence of incomes. Average GDP per capita across emerging Europe relative to advanced economies in Europe rose by about 50 percent between 1995 and 2013, despite the recent crisis. Sizable trade and investment links with western Europe were key to the growth and convergence progress that brought emerging Europe's income levels to just under half of those in their advanced economy neighbors.

Conclusion

The CEE states experienced several significant periods of transition in the 20th century, marked by the events of 1918, 1945, and 1989. In both 1918 and 1945, the CEE and Balkan economies were suffering from devastating losses, destruction, and dislocation. Although they needed to focus on economic restructuring and stabilization, they did not have to profoundly reinvent their economic and political systems. The post-1989

---

[45] www.imf.org/external/pubs/ft/fandd/2014/03/moghadam.htm

transformations, however, were complicated by large foreign debts and debt-service payments inherited from the outgoing communist regimes. They were not in the process of recovering from a World War, but did struggle to recover from a state of economic collapse, high levels of inflation, severe infrastructure neglect and decay, environmental crises, the political anxieties of the Cold War, and in some cases, internal ethnic conflict.

This chapter concludes with a brief introduction to each state explored in the text. Chapter 2 will proceed with an analysis of the role of the EU and economic integration in CEE economies, followed by a discussion of current market trends in each of the regional blocks in Chapter 3. Chapter 4 examines the integration of East and West through the establishment of supply chains and manufacturing satellites in the region, while Chapter 5 will assess the economic impact of the recent global economic crises on the CEE economies. Finally, the text will conclude with a discussion of the challenges and divergence among the CEE, Southeastern Europe (SEE), and Commonwealth of Independent State (CIS) countries, including individual case studies analyzing political risk within each state.

Brief Country Introductions

Bosnia and Herzegovina

Bosnia and Herzegovina is a country in SEE on the Balkan Peninsula. A mountainous country, it borders Croatia, Serbia, and Montenegro and has a small Adriatic Sea coastline. The government system is an emerging federal democratic republic. Three members (one Bosniak, one Croat, and one Serb) make up the presidency but the chief of state is the chairman of the presidency, a rotating position between the three. The head of government is the chairman of the council of ministers. Formally a planned economy, Bosnia and Herzegovina, member of the Central European Free Trade Agreement (CEFTA), is transitioning to an economic system built on private-enterprise and combined government regulation.

Bulgaria

Bulgaria, located in Southern Europe situated on the eastern Balkan Peninsula, is a mostly mountainous country surrounded by Greece,

Macedonia, Romania, Serbia, and the Black Sea. With strategic access to Turkish Straits, it also controls key land routes to Europe and the Middle East. The government system is a parliamentary democracy. The chief of state in the president and the head of government is the prime minister. Bulgaria has transitioned to a market economic system and is a member of both the EU and the Black Sea Economic Cooperation (BSEC).

Croatia

Croatia is a country in Central Europe and SEE on the Adriatic Sea and members of CEFTA. With a combination of flat plains, mountains and small islands, the country also shared borders with Bosnia and Herzegovina, Hungary, Montenegro, Serbia, and Slovenia. It controls most land routes from Western Europe to the Aegean Sea and Turkish Straits. The government system is a presidential or parliamentary democracy. The chief of state is the president and the head of government is the prime minister. Croatia has a mixed economic system in which the economy includes private enterprise, centralized economic planning, and government regulation.

Czech Republic

The Czech Republic, strategically located along some of the oldest land routes in Central Europe, is a landlocked country with rolling hills and plains that borders Poland, Germany, Austria, and Slovakia. The government system is a parliamentary democracy. The chief of state is the president and the head of government is the prime minister. Czech Republic has successfully transformed from a centrally planned economy to a market economy in which the prices of goods and services are determined in a free price system. The Czech Republic is a member of the EU.

Estonia

Estonia is a country located in Eastern Europe that includes bays, straits, inlets, and an estimated 1,500 islands. Bordered by Russia, Latvia, the Gulf of Finland, and the Baltic Sea, the mainland is flat and heavily forested. The government system is a parliamentary republic. The chief of state is the president and the head of government is the prime minister. Estonia has a market-based economy in which the prices of goods and services are determined in a free price system. Estonia is a member of the EU.

Hungary

Hungary, an EU member, is located in Central Europe bordering Austria, Croatia, Romania, Serbia, Slovakia, Slovenia, and Ukraine. A landlocked state, Hungary's landscape consists of flat to rolling plains divided in two by its main waterway, the Danube. The government system is a parliamentary democracy. The chief of state is the president and the head of government is the prime minister. Hungary has made the transition from a centrally planned economic system to a market economy.

Latvia

Latvia, located in the Baltic region of Northern Europe, is bordered by Estonia, Lithuania, Russia, Belarus, and the Baltic Sea. Across the Baltic Sea lies Sweden. The government system is a parliamentary democracy. The chief of state is the president and the head of government is the prime minister. Latvia has transitioned to a market-oriented economy and is a member of the EU.

Lithuania

Lithuania, also located in Northern Europe, is situated on the southeastern shore of the Baltic Sea. It shares a border with Latvia, Belarus, Poland, and the Russian enclave of Kaliningrad. Across the Baltic Sea lies Sweden and Denmark. The government system is a parliamentary democracy. The chief of state is the president and the head of government is the prime minister. Lithuania has transitioned from a command economy to a market economy, with the private sector accounting for the majority of GDP. Government regulation is transparent and efficient, and Lithuania is a member of the EU.

Montenegro

Montenegro, with both mountainous and coastal plain regions, is a country located in SEE. It has a coast on the Adriatic Sea and is bordered by Croatia, Bosnia and Herzegovina, Serbia, Kosovo, and Albania. The government system is a republic. The chief of state is the president and the head of government is the prime minister. Montenegro has a service-based market economy and it is a member of the CEFTA.

Poland

Located in Central Europe, Poland is bordered by Belarus, Czech Republic, Germany, Lithuania, Russia, Slovakia, and Ukraine. The government system is a republic. The chief of state is the president and the head of government is the prime minister. Poland has a mixed economic system in which the economy includes a variety of individual liberties, combined with centralized economic planning and government regulation. Poland is a member of the EU.

Romania

Located at the crossroads of Central and SEE, Romania has a coastline on the Black Sea and borders Bulgaria, Hungary, Moldova, Serbia, and Ukraine. Mountain ranges running from north and west in the interior, collectively known as the Carpathians, form a significant portion of the state's geography. The government system is a republic. The chief of state is the president and the head of government is the prime minister. Romania has a mixed economy and is a member of the BSEC.

Serbia

As part of the central Balkans, Serbia is a landlocked country located at the crossroads of Central and SEE. It shares borders with Bosnia and Herzegovina, Bulgaria, Croatia, Hungary, Kosovo, Macedonia, Montenegro, and Romania. The geography of Serbia is varied and includes fertile plains, limestone ranges, and in the southeast, the Dinaric Alps and on its border with Romania, the Carpathian Mountain range. The government system is a republic. The chief of state is the president and the head of government is the prime minister. A member of CEFTA, Serbia has a mixed economic system in which the presence of the state in the economy is still considerable, but there is limited private sector freedom.

Slovakia

Known for its beautiful mountains, Slovakia is a landlocked country in Central Europe that shares borders with Austria, Czech Republic, Hungary, Poland, and Ukraine. The government system is a parliamentary democracy. The chief of state is the president and the head of government is the prime minister. A member of the EU, Slovakia has a mixed economic system in which there is political liberty, combined with centralized economic planning and government regulation.

Slovenia

Bordering the Mediterranean Sea, Slovenia is a country in Central Europe. The Alps dominate the northern portion of the state and numerous rivers lie in the east, while it shares borders with Austria, Croatia, Hungary, and Italy. Despite its small size, Slovenia controls some of Europe's major transit routes. The government system is a parliamentary republic. The chief of state is the president and the head of government is the prime minister. A member of the EU, Slovenia has a mixed economic system in which the state is considerably involved in centralized planning, but there is private-sector freedom.

CHAPTER 2

The Role of the European Union in Eastern European Economies

The European Union plays important roles in diplomacy, trade, development aid and work with global organizations.

—European Union External Action

Historians, economists, and political scientists have described the transition process following the post-1989 collapse of communist regimes throughout the Central and Eastern European (CEE) states as a "return to Europe."[1] The task of "reconnecting" with Europe reflected a desire on the part of the elites and a significant portion of the public in these states to (re)claim a heritage or identity that, in political terms, entailed the creation of liberal democratic institutions and, in economic terms, a move toward the creation of market economies. Many believed this would be achieved gradually through participation in European integration and a single market. This chapter will provide the reader with information on the gradual integration of the CEE post-communist states into the European Union (EU), including how the process was influenced by, and how it in turn influenced, the political and economic transformations taking place in those states.

Accession, Negotiation, and the EU

By May 2007, most CEE states had become member states of the EU, leaving only the western Balkans and several former-Soviet Union states

---

[1] For just a few examples of the use of "return to Europe," see: Smith (2000); Bideleux and Jeffries (2007); Wolchik and Curry (2011); Jacoby (2004).

outside the EU. In outlining the process for EU accession, the Treaty on European Union states that any European country may apply for membership if it respects the democratic values of the EU and is committed to promoting them. The country must meet the key criteria for accession, as defined at the European Council in Copenhagen in 1993 and referred to as "Copenhagen criteria."[2] The criteria, in essence, state that countries need to possess (1) stable institutions guaranteeing democracy, the rule of law, human rights, and respect for and protection of minorities; (2) a functioning market economy and the capacity to cope with competition and market forces in the EU; and (3) the ability to take on and implement effectively the obligations of membership, including adherence to the aims of political, economic, and monetary union.[3] The process for states proceeds in three steps:

1. When a country is ready, it becomes an official candidate for membership—but this does not necessarily mean that formal negotiations have been opened.
2. The candidate moves on to formal membership negotiations, a process that involves the adoption of established EU law, preparations to be in a position to properly apply and enforce it, and implementation of judicial, administrative, economic, and other reforms necessary for the country to meet the conditions for joining, known as accession criteria.
3. When the negotiations and accompanying reforms have been completed to the satisfaction of both sides, the country can join the EU.[4]

Some elements of the process of accession are subject to negotiation, such as *financial arrangements*—how much the new member is likely to pay into and receive from the EU budget (in the form of transfers) or *transitional arrangements*—sometimes certain rules are phased in gradually, to give the new or existing members time to adapt.[5]

---

[2] See the European Commission (1993).
[3] European Commission (2015).
[4] European Commission (2015a).
[5] European Commission (2015).

The elements of this process are reflected in the series of transitions experienced by the EU in the 20th century. Historians of the EU mark the decade of the 1990s for Europe as one "without frontiers."[6] The signing of the Single European Act of 1986, which provided the basis for a six-year program aimed at liberalizing free trade across the EU borders in a single market, was completed with the adoption of the "four freedoms in 1993, the movement of goods, services, people, and money." The formation of the single market was also complemented by the creation of the "Maastricht" Treaty on EU in 1993 and the Treaty of Amsterdam in 1999.

The Maastricht Treaty and the Euro

Europe's core countries continued to grow closer in the transition and accession processes. In the early stages, exchange rate variability between member states was reduced through the European Exchange Rate Mechanism (ERM), which allowed currencies to fluctuate around parities within predefined bands. In 1990, exchange controls within the European Economic Community were abolished, allowing for the free flow of capital. Although there were crises under the ERM—for example, the United Kingdom was forced out in 1992 when the value of the pound sterling fell below ERM limits—realignments became less frequent over time as monetary policies and inflation rates converged.[7]

The idea of a common currency slowly gained traction, but it was not until the Maastricht Treaty of 1992 that the "Economic and Monetary Union," and with it a common currency and monetary policy, truly began to take shape. While creation of a single currency was rooted in Europe's integration and facilitating economic transactions within the EU, it also helped place the unified Germany that emerged at the end of the Cold War solidly within a common European institutional framework.[8]

The Maastricht Treaty established convergence criteria to ensure that countries joining the new common currency would be sufficiently similar,

---

[6] European Commission (2015d).

[7] *BBC News: World Edition* (2001).

[8] Treaty of Maastricht on European Union (n.d.).

and it also gave market forces a significant role in disciplining member states, by establishing the "no bailout" clause.[9] To dispel skepticism and preserve fiscal discipline after the common currency was introduced, member countries signed the Stability and Growth Pact in 1997, which was designed to tie policies to fiscal balance and debt targets.[10]

During the initial stages of CEE accession, external economic assistance came mainly from other countries and international institutions such as the International Monetary Fund (IMF), the World Bank, and the new European Bank for Reconstruction and Development. But as the process of accession gained steam, the EU became a critical force in developing institutions, guiding economic policy, and financing infrastructure for the transitioning states. The process culminated in EU accession for 11 countries (4 of them already euro area members), and candidate status for an additional 3 countries. Reza Moghadam and others argue that this achievement was "inconceivable" 25 years prior and brought tremendous benefits both to the transition countries and to the existing EU members through increased trade, capital, and labor flows.

The Complexities of Accession for CEE States

The path to EU membership, however, was longer and more complex for the CEE states than many of those in neighboring regions (Southern Europe, for example).[11] The CEE states varied significantly both in their preparedness for EU membership and with respect to the "political effort" they were willing to undertake to move closer to accession.[12] EU accession was a broadly, not universally shared aspiration, as evidenced by the domestic political, social, and economic debates that emerged within the CEE states. Parties who feared themselves "transition losers" included workers in state-subsidized heavy industries, the public sector, small farmers, and individuals on fixed incomes. Social groups emerged

---

[9] Treaty of Maastricht on European Union (n.d.).

[10] Resolution of the European Council on the Stability and Growth Pact Amsterdam (1997).

[11] Heinisch and Landsberger (n.d.).

[12] Heinisch and Landsberger (n.d.).

with objections to accession on religious, cultural, or ideological grounds. Eager political entrepreneurs took advantage of potential social discord and momentary setbacks to consolidate and boost their own domestic political power. Some parties within the CEE states expressed concerns about the general transition to a market economy and the impact of globalization, political corruption, or bureaucratic incompetence, expressing fears that extended beyond accession. After the collapse of communism, CEE countries found themselves in a potential security vacuum and feared the possibility of returning to totalitarianism, secessionist movements, nationalist movements, or paralyzing political fragmentation that could jeopardize their potential future security, stability, and economic growth. This led to a push for "quick accession to the EU... to ensure this region remained on the path of growth."[13]

With the opening of accession negotiations, public debate shifted; the public and political elites become more aware of possible consequences of accession and the debate moved from generalities to specifics.[14] Further, the exclusion of the CEE states from the European integration process until their official membership in 2004 and 2007 and the long accession negotiation periods undermined the initially strong enthusiasm among the public.[15] What began as a "euro enthusiastic" process of accession and the "return to Europe," quickly transitioned to "euro scepticism," and a realization of the complexity of reform measures that needed adoption.[16] Cecile Leconte and others argue that in countries where such processes are lengthy and drawn-out, the "perception of a link between the processes can be eroded."[17]

Nonetheless, the CEE countries adopted some form of economic liberalization, including changes to monetary policy, elimination of hyperinflation, independence of the central banks, and unification of exchange rates.[18] The reforms and EU accession led to positive social, economic,

---

[13] deCrombruggle, Minton-Beddoes, and Sachs (1996, 3).

[14] Whitefield and Rohrschneider (2006).

[15] Medrano (2003).

[16] Taggart (1998).

[17] Leconte (2010, 73).

[18] Tupy (2003).

and political benefits for most of the CEE states. Broadly speaking, the EU enlargement to include CEE states provided the "needed impetus for their political and economic modernization."[19] It united Europe in a common vision of democracy, stability, prosperity, and a growing internal market with over 500 million people. For this reason, the 2004 and 2007 enlargements were unique "due to the number of acceding countries, their size, their comparatively low levels of economic development, the predominance of their agrarian sector, and their post-communist past."[20]

Security Considerations

The enlargement, in many ways, complemented the North Atlantic Treaty Organization (NATO) in "filling the security vacuum resulting from the dismantling of the Soviet empire."[21] Following the signing of the Balladue Pact in 1993, the EU could help diffuse threats posed by the collapse of communism or any border disputes. In the case of Poland and Romania, for example, "the EU could minimize the inflow of migrants, drugs, arms, and human trafficking," which constituted important security concerns for both the countries in the post-communist transition period.[22]

Economic Considerations

CEE accession to the EU opened the way for people to freely travel across national boundaries, reconnect with friends and family in other states, and more easily relocate to other member states, if desired. With the support of the Erasmus Programme, students from CEE countries could complete their education at Western universities and the possibility of study abroad was viewed positively by nearly 84 percent of EU citizens.[23] In the case of Romania, for example, university students and faculty received scholarships to study at Western EU member's states to

---

[19] Serbos (2008).

[20] Anne Faber (2009).

[21] Stoian (2005, 12).

[22] Stoian (2005, 13).

[23] BIS: Department of Business, Innovation, and Skills (2010).

address a chronic shortage of investment in education and research in the Romania state.[24] This was not an isolated case. According to a report produced by the European Commission in 2010, more than 15 million citizens have moved to other EU countries to work or enjoy retirement, benefitting from social benefit transferability and the enlargement of the Schengen Area.[25]

These positive social changes also illustrate the strength of the EU as an economic unit. The EU is one of the strongest and largest economic and free trade areas in the world. As noted previously, the Treaty of Rome of 1957 based Europe's reconstruction on the gradual development of a borderless common market involving the free movement of goods, services, people, and capital between participating countries.[26] This early vision evolved into the European Monetary System, a precursor to the economic and monetary union launched in 1979, and the 1992 Maastricht Treaty, establishing the European Central Bank.

Despite the rises and falls of the transition period for most CEE states, the process of economic reform and accession led to strong convergence with the western side of Europe. Even before they achieved full member status, Poland, the Czech Republic, and Hungary experienced strong initial growth in gross domestic product (GDP).[27] In Poland, between May and August 2007, economic growth was nearly 6.5 percent and unemployment declined from 20 (2003) to nearly 11.4 percent.[28] In Hungary, imports from other new member states increased from €4 billion in 2003 to €13.7 billion in 2007.[29] After EU accession, a wider financial market in Slovenia opened access to capital that stimulated import-export activity across small, medium, and large enterprises.[30] Foreign direct investments sharply increased in Bulgaria, along

---

[24] Guyader (2009).

[25] BIS: Department of Business, Innovation, and Skills (2010).

[26] For more information, see: *The European Union Explained: Economic and Monetary Union and the Euro* (2014).

[27] BIS: Department of Business, Innovation, and Skills (2010).

[28] Karasinka-Fendler (2009, 122).

[29] Szemler (2009, 36).

[30] Kajne (2009, 42).

with GDP—which grew from nearly 35 million BGN (Bulgarian Lev) in 2003 to nearly 57 million BGN in 2007.[31] On average, income per capita rose from about 30 percent of EU15 levels in the mid-1990s to that of around 50 percent in 2014.[32] That average, noted in 2014 IMF Report, does not include the difference between CEE countries, with some states, such as the Baltics, making huge advances; and others, such as Bosnia and Herzegovina, Moldova, and Ukraine, getting increasingly left behind. On the whole, however, price levels and wages have risen as part of the convergence process.

Political Considerations

In addition to incentives for growth and economic reform, accession to the EU required substantial political reforms in CEE countries. The EU standards imposed criteria for democratization that "aimed at minimizing the danger of a return to authoritarian regimes and centrally planned economies."[33] Following the guidelines of the Copenhagen Criteria and the adoption of the EU *acquis*, most CEE countries underwent extensive political reform between 1992 and 2002. Many adopted a parliamentary system of government similar to the states in Western Europe, as opposed to the presidential system favored by members of the former Soviet bloc.[34] Since that time, most states consciously adopt reforms that bring their governing institutions in closer alignment with western liberal democracies. In Poland, for example, the state's commitment to EU accession led to changes in the Polish constitution, which diminished the ability for an authoritarian regime to emerge. In Romania, the 1996 election of the Romanian Democratic Convention removed communists from power. This is not to say that politics and institutions are perfectly aligned in the CEE states, and this will be discussed in more detail in Chapter 8, "Political Risk in Eastern Europe."

---

[31] Krassimir and Kaloyan (2009, 29).

[32] Roaf et al. (2014, 5).

[33] Stoian (2005, 8).

[34] For more on this, see Beachain, Sheridan, and Stan (2012).

The Adoption of the Euro

Before the adoption of the euro and the post-communist transition, CEE states experienced price distortions, with prices detached from market forces. Trading took place primarily among Comecon members, with limited trade with the rest of the world. To integrate the post-communist economies into the international monetary and trading systems, several reforms were needed: liberalization of prices, establishment of currencies as units of exchange, and the establishment of functioning, autonomous, accountable central banks.

CEE states varied widely in their experiences with these reforms. For example, Poland's new central bank law in 1989 established the independence of the governor, distributed previous commercial banking activities to nine commercial banks, and set a central goal of "strengthening of the Polish currency." Czechoslovakia adopted similar reforms in 1990. Countries that were not able to adopt these types of reforms (i.e., Bulgaria, Romania, Russia, and Ukraine) were forced to undergo more than one round of stabilization.[35]

For CEE countries, multiple rounds of accession, negotiation, and reform also mark membership in the EU. The euro area includes those EU member states that have adopted the single currency. But the euro area is not static—under the Treaty, all EU member states have to join the euro area once the necessary conditions are fulfilled, except Denmark and the United Kingdom which have negotiated an "opt-out" clause that allows them to remain outside the euro area.[36]

CEE accession countries that plan to join the EU must align many aspects of its society—social, economic, and political—with those of other western EU member states. According to the European Commission, the purpose of this alignment is to ensure that an accession country can operate successfully within the EU's single market for goods, services, capital, and labor—accession is a process of integration.

In this structure, adopting the euro and joining the euro area takes integration a step further, "it is a process of much closer economic

---

[35] Roaf et al. (2014, 15).
[36] European Commission (2015a).

integration with the other euro-area Member States."[37] Adopting the euro is an exhaustive process that requires even greater economic and legal convergence.

The euro's architecture was built on the premise that market forces, combined with minimal coordination of policies, would sufficiently align economies, discipline fiscal policies, and allow countries to withstand idiosyncratic shocks. According to Susan Schadler and other scholars,

> relinquishing monetary policy could lead to greater economic volatility unless adjustment to shocks that are asymmetric with respect to the euro area occurs efficiently through other channels—primarily fiscal policy and wage and price flexibility—or the incidence of such shocks is reduced owing to the discipline of the euro area macroeconomic policy framework and the elimination of variable emerging market risk premia.[38]

At the time of Schadler's study, economists identified the Baltic states—Estonia, Latvia, and Lithuania—as having closer policy links with the euro area, while five other central European countries—the Czech Republic, Hungary, Poland, the Slovak Republic, and Slovenia—as requiring major changes in their macroeconomic policies and policy frameworks in their efforts toward adoption of the euro.[39]

In October 2004, the European Commission chose to assess the 10 countries joining the EU. Although the maximum 2-year period referred to by the Treaty had not yet elapsed for these countries in 2004, the obligatory reassessment of Sweden was taken as an opportunity to analyze also the state of convergence in the new member states. The report concluded that none of the 11 assessed countries at that stage fulfilled the necessary conditions for the adoption of the single currency.[40]

---

[37] European Commission (2015b).

[38] Schadler et al. (2005, 1).

[39] Schadler et al. (2005, 1).

[40] European Commission (2015b).

Since that time, multiple assessments of the CEE states have taken place. In 2013, the European Commission finally concluded that Latvia fulfilled all conditions for adopting the euro, and in 2014 they came to a similar conclusion regarding Lithuania. The next regular convergence assessment, covering all member states with derogation, is scheduled for June 2016.

Given the incredibly stringent rules and multiple layers of assessment, as well as the extended timetable for adoption, one might wonder what drives the CEE states (and other EU member states) to seek membership in the euro area. The European Commission sites the following benefits,

> more choice and stable prices for consumers and citizens; greater security and more opportunities for businesses and markets; improved economic stability and growth; more integrated financial markets; a stronger presence for the EU in the global economy; a tangible sign of a European identity.[41]

Less optimistically, Ott Ummelas argues, "Euro membership proved that a country had the discipline to join one of the world's most exclusive clubs."[42] On May 20, 2011, Poland's central bank governor, Marek Belka, said his country and the region would not get the benefits they had anticipated from a quick adoption of the euro. As far back as December 2010, Czech Prime Minister Petr Necas said his country could refuse to adopt the single currency as long as it deems it beneficial to keep the koruna.[43]

Yet, other CEE states have expressed a strong desire to join the euro area, or are glad they already took steps to do so. Hungarian Foreign Minister János Martonyi said on June 22 that adoption remains a primary goal. Slovenia, already a member, has profited from being a member of such a large currency zone. Estonia, Latvia's and Lithuania's

---

[41] European Commission (2015b).

[42] Ummelas (2011).

[43] Ummelas (2011).

neighbor, endured many hardships to join.[44] On balance, Harvard professor Jeffrey Frankel argues that monetary unions, such as the euro, facilitate trade. As trade patterns and cyclical correlations gradually shift toward Western Europe, the argument for euro adoption in the CEE states strengthens.[45]

---

[44] Ummelas (2011).

[45] Frankel (2008).

CHAPTER 3

Eastern Europe Regional Bloc: CEE and CIS

The future economic growth of Eastern European countries will depend largely on the European Union, which received 80 percent of Eastern Europe's exported goods in 2008.

—Alejandro Foxley

Introduction

As discussed in earlier chapters, the Central and Eastern Europe (CEE)[1] bloc is a generic term that defines the group of countries in central, southeast, northern, and eastern Europe, commonly meaning former communist states in Europe. It is in use since the collapse of the Iron Curtain[2] in 1989 to 1990, when more than 20 nations emerged from the isolation that had largely hidden them, and its citizens, from the rest of the world for more than 4 decades. As argued by Lerman, Csaki, and Feder (2004), in each of these former Soviet states, remnants of tradition and economic organization have prevented them from stepping out, beyond the curtain and onto the world stage. Nonetheless, some have been extremely successful.

The CEE bloc of countries include all the eastern bloc countries west of the post-World War II border with the former Soviet Union. The Eastern Bloc was the name used by North Atlantic Treaty Organization

---

[1] In scholarly literature, the abbreviations CEE or CEEC are often used for this concept.

[2] The notional barrier separating the former Soviet bloc and the West prior to the decline of communism that followed the political events in eastern Europe in 1989.

(NATO)-affiliated countries for the former communist states of CEE, which generally included the Soviet Union and the countries of the Warsaw Pact.[3] The terms *Communist Bloc* and *Soviet Bloc* were also used to denote groupings of states aligned with the Soviet Union, although these terms might include states outside CEE. Figure 3.1 depicts a map of countries that declared themselves to be socialist states under the Marxist–Leninist or Maoist definition, in other words communist states, between 1979 and 1983. This period marked the greatest territorial extent of communist states.[4]

In addition, the CEE bloc also includes the independent states in former Yugoslavia, which actually were not considered part of the eastern bloc, and the three Baltic States—Estonia, Latvia, and Lithuania, which chose not to join the Commonwealth of Independent States (CIS) with

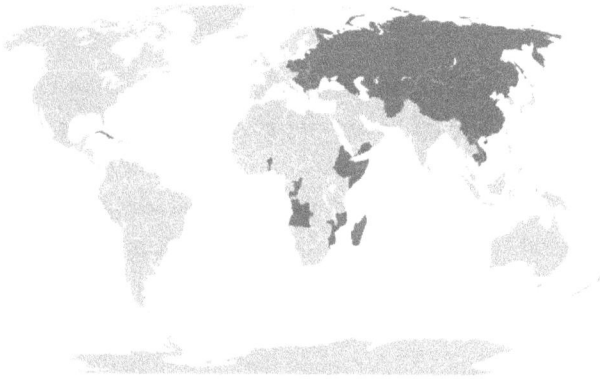

Figure 3.1 Countries that declared to be socialist or communist between 1979 and 1983

Source: Busky (2000).

---

[3] The Warsaw Pact, formally known as the Treaty of Friendship, Co-operation, and Mutual Assistance, and informally as WarPac, was a collective defense treaty among Soviet Union and seven Soviet satellite states in Central and Eastern Europe in existence during the Cold War; Hirsch, Kett, and Trefil (2002, 316). The name applied to the former communist states of eastern Europe, including Yugoslavia and Albania, as well as the countries of the Warsaw Pact; Janzen and Taraschewski (2009, 190).

[4] Busky (2000, 9). In a modern sense of the word, communism refers to the ideology of Marxism-Leninism.

the other 12 former republics of the former Union of Soviet Socialist Republics (USSR[5]).

Recently, during the summer 2015, the Russian government publicly stated to the world that the Soviet government who gave away the Baltics was illegitimate and its decisions were illegal. Russia's Prosecutor General's Office launched at the time an improbable but nonetheless serious investigation into the legality of the independence of the three Baltic countries. The Russian trial on the legal status of their independence is based on the idea that the interim Soviet government in place in 1991 was illegitimate and its decisions therefore are also illegitimate.

Since then, the three countries, whose national cultures are clearly northern European rather than Slavic have been outstanding success stories, implementing economic reforms, and gaining membership of NATO, the European Union (EU), and the United Nations. The Baltic states are located in the northeastern region of Europe, on the eastern shores of the Baltic Sea, bounded on the west and north by the Baltic Sea, which gives the region its name, on the east by Russia, on the southeast by Belarus, and on the southwest by Poland and an exclave of Russia. Figure 3.2 depicts a map of the location of the Baltic states.

Transition Countries

Both the CEE and the CIS country blocs are considered transition countries in Europe. These are transition economies that are undergoing a change from a centrally planned economy to a market economy.[6] These economies are undertaking a set of structural transformations intended to develop market-based institutions. These include economic liberalization, where prices are set by market forces rather than by a central planning organization.

In addition, a major effort is placed to remove trade barriers, while pushing to privatize state-owned enterprises and resources. State and

---

[5] A former communist country in eastern Europe and northern Asia; established in 1922; included Russia and 14 other Soviet socialist republics (Ukraine and Byelorussia and others); officially dissolved December 31, 1991.

[6] Feige (1994).

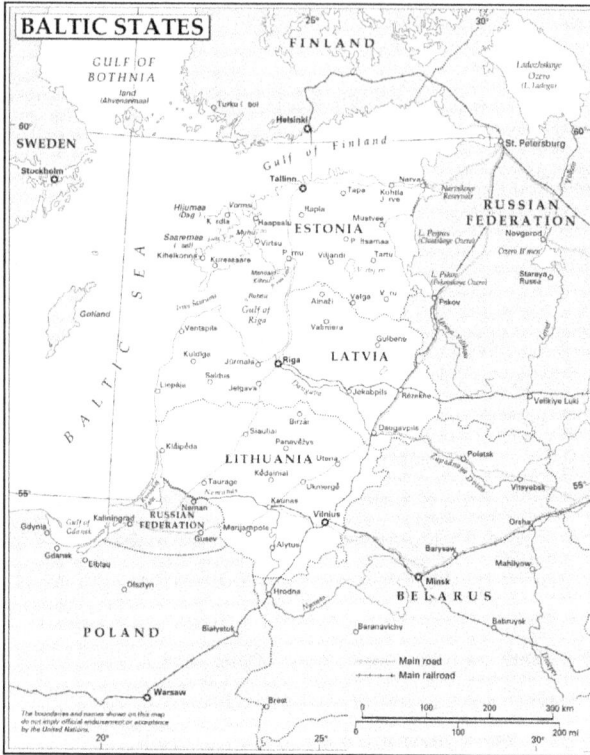

Figure 3.2 Location of the Baltic states in Europe

Source: UN (1995).

collectively run enterprises are restructured as businesses, and a financial sector is created to facilitate macroeconomic stabilization and the movement of private capital.[7] This process is not only being applied in eastern bloc countries of Europe, but has also been applied in China, the former Soviet Union, and some other emerging and frontier market countries.

The transition process is usually characterized by the change and creation of institutions, particularly private enterprises, changes in the role of the state, thereby, the creation of fundamentally different governmental institutions, and the promotion of private-owned enterprises, markets and independent financial institutions.[8] In essence, one transition

---

[7] Feige (1991).

[8] Aristovnik (2006).

mode is the functional restructuring of state institutions from being a provider of growth to an enabler, with the private sector as its engine. Due to the different initial conditions during the emerging process of the transition from planned economics to market economics, countries uses different transition model. Countries like China and Vietnam adopted a gradual transition mode; however, Russia and some other east European countries, such as the former Socialist Republic of Yugoslavia, used a more aggressive and quicker paced model of transition. These transition countries in Europe are thus classified today into two political-economic entities: CEE and CIS.

The CEE Bloc

As mentioned earlier, the CEE countries are a bloc of countries comprising Albania, Bulgaria, Croatia, the Czech Republic, Hungary, Poland, Romania, the Slovak Republic, Slovenia, and the three Baltic States: Estonia, Latvia, and Lithuania. But the CEE countries are further subdivided by their accession status to the EU.

The eight first-wave accession countries that joined the EU in May 2004 includes Estonia, Latvia, Lithuania, Czech Republic, Slovakia, Poland, Hungary, and Slovenia. The two second-wave accession countries that joined in January 2007 include Romania and Bulgaria. The third-wave accession country that joined the EU in July 2013 includes Croatia. According to the World Bank,[9] "the transition is over" for the 10 countries that joined the EU in 2004 and 2007, which can be also understood as all countries of the eastern bloc.[10]

After 15 years of economic boom in central eastern Europe, during which the countries in the region enjoyed growth levels twice as high as in western Europe, the development came to an abrupt halt as the effects of the global financial crisis that started in 2007. Several states in CEE were struck hard as many of these countries were in a state of rapid development fuelled by foreign direct investment (FDI) inflows when the crisis hit.

---

[9] Alam et al. (2008, 42).
[10] OECD (2015).

More recently, the CEE countries have been showing signs of recovery, some faster than others, reading themselves once again for the numerous opportunities for future economical development. One of the main drivers of economic growth is the regions' great location, opened to a market of over 200 million consumers. In addition, the region enjoys a large qualitative labor force at relatively low costs, which provides an inviting atmosphere for foreign investments and business development. There are still plenty of unexploited opportunities in CEE, whether in its huge surfaces of arable land, in its strong skills in technical and technological areas, numerous investment incentives, or unique touristic destinations. Figure 3.3 shows a map of the CEE country bloc.

As a whole, the CEE includes the following former socialist countries, which extend east from the border of Germany and south from the Baltic Sea to the border with Greece: Estonia, Latvia, Lithuania, Czech

Figure 3.3 The CEE country bloc

Source: Stepmap.de

Republic, Slovakia, Hungary, Poland, Romania, Bulgaria, Slovenia, Croatia, Albania, Bosnia-Herzegovina, Kosovo, Macedonia, Montenegro, and Serbia. The fundamental conditions for growth in this region are strong. This is especially so in the reform-oriented countries that had introduced business friendly politics and low tax rates in the run-up of their EU accession. In effect, several countries such as Poland and Czech Republic, the two largest economies in the region, as well as Slovakia handled the global financial crisis surprisingly well. Even the countries hit hardest like Hungary will most likely turn the crisis into an upswing in a few years time. The growth potential of these countries is also intensified by the integration of CEE countries into the eurozone and Schengen area.[11] Please refer to Appendix A for a brief scanning of the CEE countries.

The CIS Bloc

The CIS, also known as the Russian Commonwealth, is a regional bloc of countries formed during the breakup of the Soviet Union, whose participating countries are some former Soviet republics. The CIS is a loose association of countries. Although the CIS has few supranational powers, it is aimed at being more than a purely symbolic organization, nominally possessing coordinating powers in the realm of trade, finance, lawmaking, and security. It has also promoted cooperation on cross-border crime prevention.

The CIS was established on December 8, 1991, through the Belovezh Accords,[12] which also brought an end to the Soviet Union. Leaders from Russia, Ukraine, and Belarus signed these accords and then later

---

[11] Thomann (2006).

[12] The Belavezha Accords is the agreement that declared the Soviet Union effectively dissolved and established the Commonwealth of Independent States (CIS) in its place. It was signed at the state dacha near Viskuli in Belovezhskaya Pushcha on December 8, 1991, by the leaders of three of the four republics-signatories of the Treaty on the Creation of the USSR, including the Russian President Boris Yeltsin, Ukrainian president Leonid Kravchuk, and Belarusian parliament chairman Stanislav Shushkevich.

Figure 3.4 The 12 CIS bloc countries

Source: interopp.org.

that month, on the 21st, through the Alma-Ata Protocols,[13] Armenia, Azerbaijan, Kazakhstan, Kyrgyzstan, Moldova, Tajikistan, Turkmenistan, and Uzbekistan, for a total of 11 countries, also agreed to join the CIS. Georgia joined the CIS in December 1993, bringing the total membership to 12 states (the Baltic republics of Estonia, Lithuania, and Latvia never joined). Figure 3.4 illustrates the geographic location of the CIS bloc.

The organization had several goals, including coordination of members' foreign and security policies, development of a common economic space, fostering human rights and interethnic concord, maintenance of the military assets of the former USSR, creation of shared transportation and communications networks, environmental security, regulation of migration policy, and efforts to combat organized crime. The CIS had a variety of institutions through which it attempted to accomplish these goals: Council of Heads of State, Council of Heads of Government, Council of Foreign Ministers, Council of Defense Ministers, an

---

[13] The Alma-Ata Protocols are the founding declarations and principles of the CIS.

inter-parliamentary assembly, Executive Committee, Anti-Terrorism Task Force, and the Interstate Economic Committee of the Economic Union.

Although in a sense the CIS was designed to replace the Soviet Union, it was not and is not a separate state or country. Rather, the CIS is an international organization designed to promote cooperation among its members in a variety of fields. Its headquarters are in Minsk, Belarus. Over the years, its members have signed dozens of treaties and agreements, and some hoped that it would ultimately promote the dynamic development of ties among the newly independent post-Soviet states. By the late 1990s, however, the CIS lost most of its momentum and was victimized by internal rifts, becoming, according to some observers, largely irrelevant and powerless.[14]

From its beginning, the CIS had two main purposes. The first was to promote what was called a "civilized divorce" among the former Soviet states. Many feared the breakup of the Soviet Union would lead to political and economic chaos, if not the outright conflict over borders. The earliest agreements of the CIS, which provided for recognition of borders, protection of ethnic minorities, maintenance of a unified military command, economic cooperation, and periodic meetings of state leaders, arguably helped to maintain some semblance of order in the region, although one should note that the region did suffer some serious conflicts, of note, the war between Armenia and Azerbaijan, and the civil conflicts in Tajikistan, Moldova, and Georgia.

The second purpose of the CIS was to promote integration among the newly independent states. On this score, the CIS had not succeeded. The main reason is that while all parties had a common interest in peacefully dismantling the old order, there has been no consensus among these states as to what, if anything, should replace the Soviet state. Moreover, the need to develop national political and economic systems took precedence in many states, dampening enthusiasm for any project of reintegration. CIS members have also been free to sign or not sign agreements as they see fit, creating a hodgepodge of treaties and obligations among CIS states.

One of the clearest failures of the CIS has been on the economic front. Although the member states pledged cooperation, things began to

---

[14] Rettman (2015).

break down early on. By 1993, the ruble zone collapsed, with each state issuing its own currency. In 1993 and 1994, 11 CIS states ratified a Treaty on an Economic Union, in which Ukraine joined as an associate member. A free-trade zone was proposed in 1994, but by 2002 it still had not yet been fully established. In 1996 four states, including Russia, Belarus, Kyrgyzstan, and Kazakhstan, created a Customs Union,[15] but others refused to join. All these efforts were designed to increase trade, but, due to a number of factors, trade among CIS countries has lagged behind the targeted figures. More broadly speaking, economic cooperation has suffered because states had adopted economic reforms and programs with little regard for the CIS and have put more emphasis on redirecting their trade to neighboring European or Asian states.

Cooperation in military matters fared little better. The 1992 Tashkent Treaty on Collective Security[16] was ratified by merely six states. While CIS peacekeeping troops were deployed to Tajikistan and Abkhazia, a region of Georgia, critics viewed these efforts as Russia's attempts to maintain a sphere of influence in these states. As the "Monroeski Doctrine"[17] took

---

[15] A group of countries that have agreed to charge the same import duties as each other and usually to allow free trade between themselves.

[16] The Collective Security Treaty Organization, also known as the "Tashkent Pact" or "Tashkent Treaty," is an intergovernmental military alliance that was signed on May 15, 1992, by six post-Soviet states belonging to the Commonwealth of Independent States, including Russia, Armenia, Kazakhstan, Kyrgyzstan, Tajikistan, and Uzbekistan. Three other post-Soviet countries, including Azerbaijan, Belarus, and Georgia, also signed the treaty on the following year. Five years later, six of the nine, all but Azerbaijan, Georgia, and Uzbekistan, agreed to renew the treaty for five more years, and in 2002 those six agreed to create the Collective Security Treaty Organization as a military alliance.

[17] The "Monroeski Doctrine" was a colloquial description of Boris Yeltsin's foreign policy strategy in the near abroad. Adapted from the United States' 19th-century Monroe Doctrine, which prohibited European colonization of the newly independent Latin American republics, the Monroeski Doctrine affirmed the Russian Federation's position as the dominant power in the entire former Soviet Union. Moscow often invoked the doctrine when it intervened in post-Soviet conflicts in the newly independent states of Eurasia, such as the Tajik Civil War and the separatist conflicts in Nagorno-Karabakh, Transnistria, Abkhazia, and South Ossetiya.

hold in Moscow, which asserted special rights for Russia on post-Soviet territory, and Russia used its control over energy pipelines to put pressure on other states, there was a backlash by several states against Russia, which weakened the CIS. After September 11, 2001, the CIS created bodies to help combat terrorism, and some hoped that this might bring new life to the organization.

Appendix B provides a brief country scanning of the CIS member states.

Economic Challenges

According to Marek Dabrowski,[18] a scholar and professor at the Higher School of Economics in Moscow and fellow at CASE (Centre for Social and Economic Research) in Warsaw, Poland, the period of fast economic growth and relative macroeconomic stability in the CIS seems to be over. The collapse of the Russian ruble, expected recession in Russia, the stronger U.S. dollar, and lower commodity prices have negatively affected the entire region through trade, labor remittance, and financial-market channels, resulting in negative expectations and leading to either substantial depreciation of national currencies, or decline in countries' international reserves, or both. This means that the EU's entire eastern neighborhood faces serious economic, social, and political challenges coming from weaker currencies, higher inflation, decreasing export revenues and labor remittances, net capital outflows, and stagnating or declining gross domestic product (GDP).

The currency crisis started in Russia and Ukraine during 2014 as a result of the combination of global, regional, and country-specific factors. Among the latter, the ongoing conflicts between the two countries and the associated U.S. and EU sanctions against Russia have played the most prominent role. At the end of 2014 and in early 2015, the currency crisis spread to Russia and Ukraine's neighbors.

The gradual depreciation of the ruble against both the euro and U.S. dollar, as depicted in Figure 3.5, started in November 2013, before the Russian–Ukraine conflict emerged and when oil prices were high. The

---

[18] Dabrowski (2015).

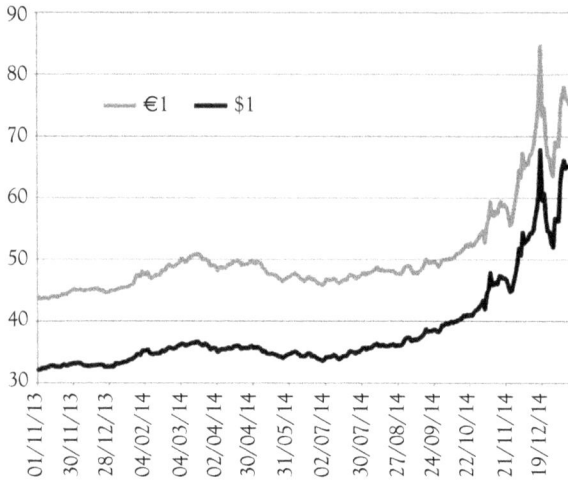

Figure 3.5 Ruble exchange rate against the euro and dollar, 2013–2015

Source: Central Bank of Russia, www.cbr.ru/eng/currency_base/dynamics.aspx

depreciation intensified in March and April 2014, after Russia's annexation of Crimea and the first round of U.S. and EU sanctions against Russia. Between May and July 2014, the ruble partly regained its previous value.

The depreciation trend, however, returned in the second half of July 2014. Its pace increased in October with a culmination in mid-December 2014, as also depicted in Figure 3.5. After a massive intervention on the foreign exchange market and the adoption by Russia of other anti-crisis measures, the situation stabilized for a while. However, depreciation started again in January 2015, boosted by Moody's and Standard & Poor's downgrading of Russia's credit rating, and the subsequent escalation of the Donbass[19] conflict in Ukraine.

---

[19] The War in Donbass, also known as the War in Ukraine or the War in Eastern Ukraine, is an armed conflict in the Donbass region of Ukraine. From the beginning of March 2014, demonstrations by pro-Russian and anti-government groups took place in the Donetsk and Luhansk oblasts of Ukraine, together commonly called the "Donbass," in the aftermath of the 2014 Ukrainian revolution and the Euromaidan movement.

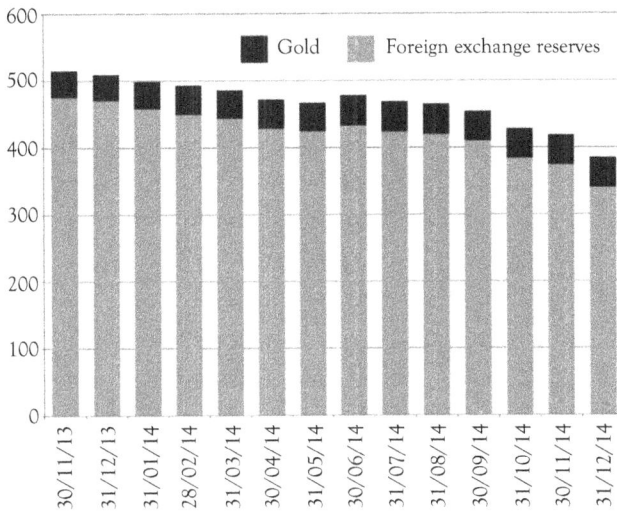

Figure 3.6 Russia's international reserves in $ billions, 2013–2014

Source: Central Bank of Russia, www.cbr.ru/eng/hd_base/default.aspx?Prtid=mrrf_m

Cumulatively, between the end of November 2013 and end of 2014, Russia lost $130 billion of its international reserves in the region, as shown in Figure 3.6, which resulted from a large-scale capital outflow estimated to exceed $150 billion in 2014. Nevertheless, Russia continues to have a sizeable current account surplus. In the first half of January 2015, the reserves decreased further by about $7 billion.

Economies at War

This currency crisis challenges in Russia and in the CIS (more on this in the next section) are in fact a result of a much bigger threat to the global economy, often dubbed by economists at large as a result of currency wars. For the past few years, at least since 2010, government officials from the G7 economies have been very concerned with the potential escalation of a global economic war. Not a conventional war, with fighter jets, bullets, and bombs, but instead, a "currency war." Finance ministers and central bankers from advanced economies worry that their peers in the G20, which also include several emerging economies, may devalue their currencies to boost exports and grow their economies at their neighbors' expense.

Brazil led the charge, being the first emerging economy to accuse the United States of instigating a currency war in 2010, when the U.S. Federal Reserve bought piles of bonds with newly created money. From a Chinese perspective, with the world's largest holdings of U.S. dollar reserves, a U.S.-lead currency war based on dollar debasement is an American act of default to its foreign creditors, no matter how you disguise it. So far, the Chinese have been more diplomatic, but their patience is wearing thin.

These two countries are not alone, as depicted in Figure 3.7, several other emerging markets, such as Saudi Arabia, Korea, Russia, Turkey, and Taiwan have also been impacted by a weak dollar. That "quantitative easing" (QE) made investors flood emerging markets with hot money in search of better returns, which consequently lifted their exchange rates. But Brazil was not alone, as Japan's Shinzo Abe, the new prime minister, has also reacted to the QEs in the United States and pledged bold stimulus to restart growth and vanquish deflation in the country.

As advanced economies, like the first three largest world economies— the United States, China, and Japan, respectively—try to kick-start their sluggish economies with ultralow interest rates and sprees of money printing, they are putting downward pressure on their currencies. The loose

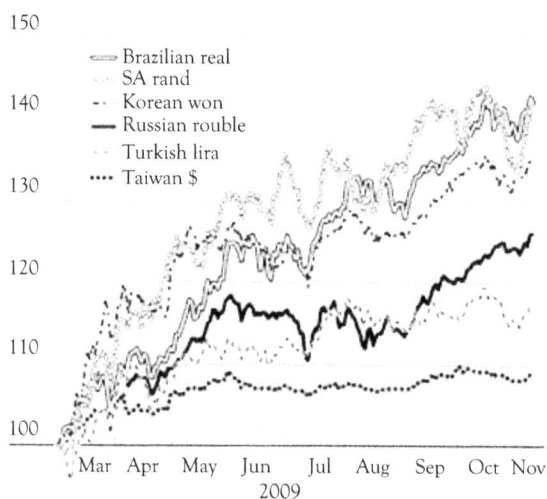

Figure 3.7 Emerging market currencies inflated by weak dollar

Source: Thompson Reuters Datastream.

monetary policies are primarily aimed at stimulating domestic demand. But their effects spill over into the currency world.

Japan is facing charges that it is trying first and foremost to lower the value of its currency, the yen, to stimulate its economy and get the edge over other countries. The new government is trying to get Japan, which has been in recession, moving again after a two-decade bout of stagnant growth and deflation. Hence, it has embarked on an economic course that it hopes will finally jump-start the economy. The government pushed the Bank of Japan to accept a higher inflation target, which has triggered speculation that the bank will create more money. The prospect of more yen in circulation has been the main reason behind the yen's recent falls to a 21-month low against the dollar and a near three-year record against the euro.

Ever since Shinzo Abe called for a weaker yen to bolster exports, the currency has fallen by 16 percent against the dollar and 19 percent against the euro. As the yen falls, its exports become cheaper, and those of Asian neighbors, South Korea, and Taiwan, as well as those countries further afield in Europe, become relatively more expensive. As depicted in Figure 3.8, central banks in the United States and Japan have flooded their economies with liquidity since mid-2012 to 2013, causing the yen and the dollar to weaken against other major currencies.

In our opinion, common sense could prevail, putting an end to the dangerous game of beggar (and blame) thy neighbor. After all, the

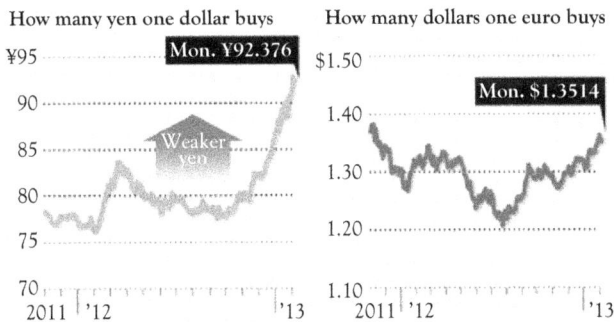

Figure 3.8 Central banks in the United States and Japan have flooded their economies with liquidity

Source: WSJ Market Data Group.

International Monetary Fund (IMF) was created to prevent such races to the bottom, and should try to broker a truce among foreign exchange competitors. The critical issues in the United States, as well as China and Japan, stem from minimally a blatantly ineffective public policy, but over-ridingly a failed and destructive economic policy. These policy errors are directly responsible for the currency war clouds, now looming overhead.[20]

So far, Europe has felt the impact of the falling yen the most. At the height of the eurozone's financial crisis in 2012, the euro was worth $1.21, which was potentially benefitting big exporters like BMW, AUDI, Mercedes, or Airbus. However, at the time of these writing, December 2013, the euro is at $1.38 even though the eurozone is still the laggard of the world economy.

Across the 17-strong euro countries, a recovery has got underway following a double-dip recession lasting 18 months, but it is a feeble one. For 2013, as the whole GDP will still continue to fall by 0.4 percent (after declining by 0.6 percent in 2012), it is expected to rise by 1.1 percent in 2014.[21] A rise in the value of euro, which is also partly to do with the diminishing threat of a collapse of the currency, will do little to help companies in the eurozone—and will hardly help getting it growing again.

Chinese policymakers reject the conventional thinking proposed by advanced economies. How about the yen's extraordinary rise over the last 40 years, from yen 360 against the dollar at the beginning of the 1970s to about yen 102 today?[22] Not to mention that despite this huge appreciation, Japan's current account surplus has only got bigger, not smaller. They could also argue that the United States' prescription for China's economic rebalancing, a stronger currency, and a boost to domestic demand, was precisely the policy followed by the Japanese in the

---

[20] Our opinion expressed here is from the point of international trade and currency exchange as far as it affects international trade, and not from the geopolitical and economic aspects of the issue. We approach the issue of currency wars not from the theoretical, or even simulation models undertaken from behind a desk in an office, but from the point of view of practitioners engaged in international business and foreign trade, on the ground, in four different countries.

[21] The Economist's Writers (2013).

[22] As of December 2013.

late-1980s, leading to the biggest financial bubble in living memory and the 20-year hangover that followed.

Furthermore, the demand by the United States, which is backed by the G7 for a renminbi revaluation, is, in our view, a policy of the United States' default. During the Asian crisis in 1997 to 1998, advanced economies, under the auspices of the IMF, insisted that Asian nations, having borrowed so much, should now tighten their belts. Shouldn't advance economies be doing the same? In addition, Chinese manufacturing margins are so slim that significant change in exchange rates could wipe them out and force layoffs of millions of Chinese. As it is, labor rates are already climbing in China, further squeezing margins. Lastly, a revaluation of the yuan would only push manufacturing to other cheaper emerging markets, such as Vietnam, Cambodia, Thailand, Bangladesh, and other lower paying nations, without improving the advanced economies trade deficits.

Notwithstanding, some G7 policymakers believe these grumbles are overdone, arguing that the rest of the world should praise the United States and Japan for such monetary policies, suggesting the eurozone should do the same. The war rhetoric implies that the United States and Japan are directly suppressing their currencies to boost exports and suppress imports, which in our view is a zero-sum game, which could degenerate into protectionism and a collapse in trade.

These countries, however, do not believe such currency devaluation strategy will threaten trade. Instead, they believe that as central banks continue to lower their short-term interest rate to near zero, exhausting their conventional monetary methods, they must employ unconventional methods, such as QE, or trying to convince consumers that inflation will rise. Their goal with these actions is to lower real (inflation-adjusted) interest rates. If so, inflation should be rising in Japan and in the United States, as shown in Figure 3.9.

As Figure 3.9 also shows, over the past decade, Japan has seen the consumer price index for most periods hover just below the zero-percent inflation line. The notable exceptions were in 2008, when inflation rose to as high as 2 percent, and in late 2009, when prices fell at close to a 2 percent rate. The rise in inflation coincided with a crash in capital spending. The worst period of deflation preceded an upturn. Of course,

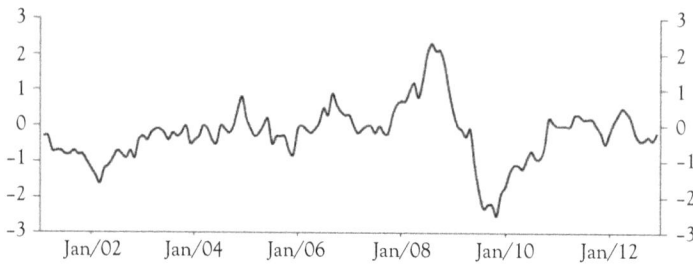

Figure 3.9 *Japan's inflation rate has been climbing since 2010 as a result of economic stimulus*

Source: Trading Economics,[23] Japan's Ministry of Internal Affairs and Communications.

the figure above does not provide enough data to infer causal effects, but it seems, however, that the relationship between growth and Japan's mild deflation may be more complicated than the Great Depression-inspired deflationary spiral narrative suggests. The principal goal of this policy was to stimulate domestic spending and investment, but lower real rates usually weaken the currency as well, and that in turn tends to depress imports. Nevertheless if the policy is successful in reviving domestic demand, it will eventually lead to higher imports.

At least that's how the argument goes. The IMF actually concluded that the United States' first rounds of QE boosted its trading partners' output by as much as 0.3 percent. The dollar did weaken, but that became a motivation for Japan's stepped-up assault on deflation. The combined monetary boost on opposite sides of the Pacific has been a powerful elixir for global investor confidence, if anything, to move hot money onto emerging markets where the interests were much higher than those in advanced economies.

The reality is that most advanced economies have been over-consumed in recent years. It has too many debts. But rather than dealing with those debts—living a life of austerity, accepting a period of relative stagnation—these economies want to shift the burden of adjustment on to its creditors, even when those creditors are relatively poor nations with low per capita incomes. This is true not only for Chinese but also for many

---

[23] www.tradingeconomics.com (accessed December 09, 2013).

other countries in Asia and in other parts of the emerging world. During the Asian crisis in 1997 to 1998, Western nations, under the auspices of the IMF, insisted that Asian nations, having borrowed too much, should now tighten their belts. But the United States doesn't seem to think it should abide by the same rules. Far better is to use the exchange rate to pass the burden on to someone else than to swallow the bitter pill of austerity.

Meanwhile, European policymakers, fearful that their countries' exports are caught in this currency war crossfire, have entertained unwise ideas such as directly managing the value of the euro. While the option of generating money out of thin air may not be available to emerging markets, where inflation tends to remain a problem, limited capital controls may be a sensible short-term defense against destabilizing inflows of hot money. Figure 3.10 illustrates how the inflows of hot-money leaving advanced economies in search of better returns on investments in emerging markets have caused these markets to significantly outperform advanced (developed) markets.

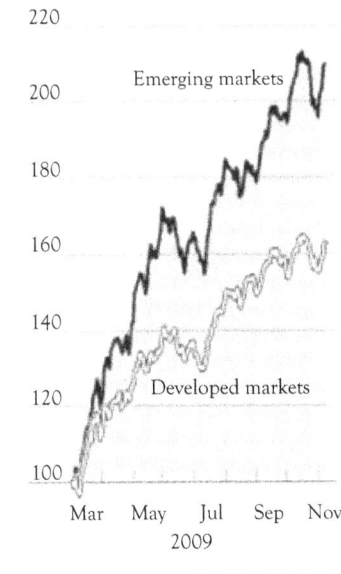

Figure 3.10 In 2009, emerging markets significantly outperformed advanced (developed) economies

Source: FTSE All-World Indices.

Currency War May Cause Damage to Global Economy

As more countries try to weaken their currencies for economic gain, there may come a point where the fragile global economic recovery could be derailed and the international financial system is thrown into chaos. That's why financial representatives from the world's leading 20 industrial and developing nations spent most of their time during the G20 summit in Moscow in September 2013.

In September 2011, Switzerland took action to arrest the rise of its currency, the Swiss franc, when investors, looking for somewhere safe to store their cash from the debt crisis afflicting the 17-country eurozone, saw in the Swiss franc the traditional instrument to fulfill that role. The Swiss intervention was viewed as an attempt to protect the country's exporters.

In our view, policymakers are focusing on the wrong issue. Rather than focus on currency manipulation, all sides would be better served to zero in on structural reforms. The effects of such strategy would be far more beneficial in the long run than unilateral U.S., China, or Japan currency action; it would also be much more sustainable. The G-20 should focus on a comprehensive package centered on structural reforms in all countries, both advanced economies and emerging markets. Exchange rates should be an important part of that package, no doubt. For instance, to reduce their current-account deficits, Americans must save more. To continue to simply devalue the dollar will not be sufficient for that purpose. Likewise, China's current-account surpluses were caused by a broad set of domestic economic distortions, from state-allocated credit to artificially low interest rates. Correcting China's external imbalances requires eliminating all of these distortions as well.

As long as policymakers continue to focus on currency exchange issues, the volatility in the currency markets will continue to escalate. It actually has become so worrisome that the G7 advanced economies have warned that volatile movements in exchange rates could adversely hit the global economy. Figure 3.11 provides a broad view (rebased at 100 percent on August 1, 2008) of main exchange rates against the dollar.

When it became clear that Shinzo Abe and his agenda of growth-at-all-costs would win Japan's elections, the yen lost more than 10 percent against the dollar and some 15 percent against the euro. In turn,

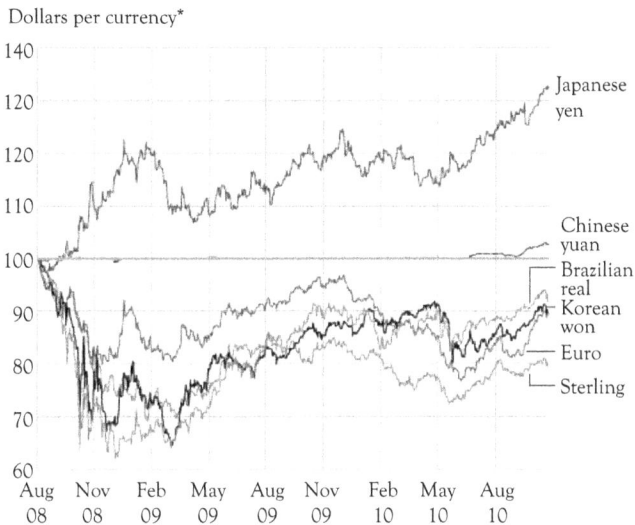

Figure 3.11 Exchange rates against the dollar

Source: Bloomberg.

the dollar has also plumbed to its lowest level against the euro in nearly 15 months. These monetary debasement strategies are adversely impacting and angering export-driven countries, such as Brazil, and many of the Brazil, Russia, India, China, and South Africa (BRICS), Association of South-East Asian Nations (ASEAN), Colombia, Indonesia, Vietnam, Turkey, and South Africa (CIVETS), and the Middle East and North Africa (MENA) blocs. But they also are stirring the pot in Europe. The eurozone has largely sat out this round of monetary stimulus and now finds itself in the invidious position of having a contracting economy and a rising currency.

These currency moves have shocked BRICS countries as well as other emerging-market economies, including Thailand. The G-20 is clearly divided between the advanced economies—the United Kingdom, the United States, Japan, France, Canada, Italy, Germany—and emerging countries such as Russia, China, South Korea, India, Brazil, Argentina, Indonesia, and the like. Top leaders of Russia, South Korea, Germany, Brazil, and China have all expressed their concern over the currency moves, which drive up the value of their currencies and undermine the competitiveness of their exports. If they decide to enter the game, like Venezuela, which has devalued its currency by 32 percent, the world would be plunged into competitive devaluations. At the end of the day, competitive devaluations would lead to run-away inflation or hyperinflation. Nobody will win with these currency wars.

James Rickards, author of *Currency Wars: The Making of the Next Global Crisis*, expects the international monetary system to destabilize and collapse. In his views, "there will be so much money-printing by so many central banks that people's confidence in paper money will wane, and inflation will rise sharply."[24]

If policymakers truly want to stage off this currency war, then it is a matter of doing what was done in 1985 with the Plaza Accord.[25] This time, however, there will be need for an upgraded version, as this time it will not be only about the United States and the G5, as it was in 1985. It will have to be an Asian Plaza Accord under the support and auspices of the G20. It will have to be about the Asia export led and mercantilist leadership agreeing amongst them. The chances of this happening, of advanced economies seeing the requirement for it, or these economies relinquishing its powers in any measurable fashion, are not at all possible under the current political gamesmanship presently being played.

Currency War Also Means Currency Suicide

Special contribution by Patrick Barron.[26]

What the media calls a "currency war," whereby nations engage in competitive currency devaluations in order to increase exports, is really "currency suicide." National governments persist in the fallacious belief

---

[24] Guerrera (2013).

[25] The Plaza Accord was an agreement between the governments of France, West Germany, Japan, the United States, and the United Kingdom, to depreciate the U.S. dollar in relation to the Japanese yen and German Deutsche Mark by intervening in currency markets. The five governments signed the accord on September 22, 1985, at the Plaza Hotel in New York City.

[26] Patrick Barron is a private consultant in the banking industry. He teaches in the Graduate School of Banking at the University of Wisconsin, Madison, and teaches Austrian economics at the University of Iowa, in Iowa City, where he lives with his wife of 40 years. We recommend you to visit his blog at http://patrickbarron.blogspot.com/ or contact him at PatrickBarron@msn.com.

that weakening one's own currency will improve domestically produced products' competitiveness in world markets and lead to an export-driven recovery. As it intervenes to give more of its own currency in exchange for the currency of foreign buyers, a country expects that its export industries will benefit with increased sales, which will stimulate the rest of the economy. So we often read that a country is trying to "export its way to prosperity."

Mainstream economists everywhere believe that this tactic also exports unemployment to its trading partners by showering them with cheap goods and destroying domestic production and jobs. Therefore, they call for their own countries to engage in reciprocal measures. Recently Martin Wolfe in *The Financial Times* of London and Paul Krugman of *The New York Times* both accuse their countries' trading partners of engaging in this "beggar-thy-neighbor" policy and recommend that England and the United States respectively enter this so-called "currency war" with full monetary ammunition to further weaken the pound and the dollar.

I, Patrick, am struck by the similarity of this currency-war argument in favor of monetary inflation to that of the need for reciprocal trade agreements. This argument supposes that trade barriers against foreign goods are a boon to a country's domestic manufacturers at the expense of foreign manufacturers.

Therefore, reciprocal trade barrier reductions need to be negotiated, otherwise the country that refuses to lower them will benefit. It will increase exports to countries that do lower their trade barriers without accepting an increase in imports that could threaten domestic industries and jobs. This fallacious mercantilist theory never dies because there are always industries and workers who seek special favors from government at the expense of the rest of society. Economists call this "rent seeking."

Contagion Effect: The Spreading of the Crisis to CIS Member Countries

Since November 2014, the crisis has spread to a number of former Soviet Union countries, especially Belarus, Armenia, Kyrgyzstan, and Moldova. It also affected, to a lesser extent, some countries in CEE. The crisis-contagion mechanisms worked through several channels: decreasing trade and deteriorating terms of trade with Russia, decreasing remittances from migrants working in Russia and, most importantly, the devaluation expectations of households and financial market players. Those former Soviet Union countries, for which Russia is an important trade partner, could not sustain continuation of the nominal appreciation of their currencies in relation to the ruble.

In addition, during the December 2014 phase of the CIS currency crisis, a degree of contagion effect was visible on foreign exchange markets in central Europe, where currencies with flexible exchange rates depreciated against both the dollar and the euro. This affected the Hungarian forint, Serbian dinar, Polish zloty, Romanian leu, and Turkish lira. However, because of the limited trade and financial links between these countries and Russia and Ukraine, investors' negative reactions to these currencies were rather short-lived.

As discussed in the previous section, among the global factors that contributed to the CIS currency crisis, U.S. monetary policy seems to have played an important role. Since mid-2013, the expectation of the phasing down of QE3, which eventually happened in October 2014, and more recently, expectations of an increase in the U.S. Federal Fund Rate in 2015,[27] has led to tighter global liquidity conditions. This could not be fully compensated for by simultaneous monetary policy easing in the euro area and Japan because of the much smaller size of financial markets in euro and yen. As result, net capital inflows into emerging-market economies decreased, growth in the latter decelerated and commodity prices started to fall[28] (see Feldstein, 2014, and Frankel, 2014, on the effects of U.S. monetary tightening on oil and commodity prices). During 2014, as depicted in Figure 3.12, especially in the fourth quarter, the dollar appreciated against most currencies with flexible exchange rates.

---

[27] Darvas (2014).
[28] Feldstein (2014).

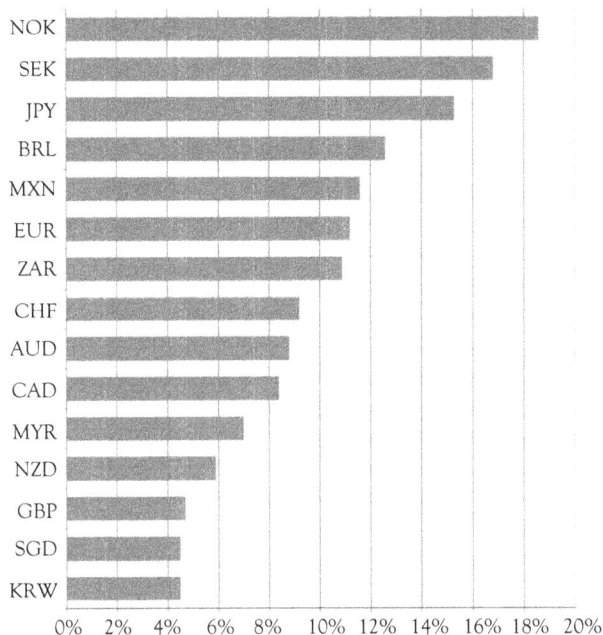

Figure 3.12 Depreciation against the dollar, in percent, December 2013 to December 2014, selected currencies

Source: U.S. Federal Reserve Board,[29] www.federalreserve.gov/releases/g5/current/default.htm

---

[29] NOK = Norwegian krone; SEK = Swedish krona; JPY = Japanese yen; BRL = Brazilian real; MXN = Mexican peso; EUR = euro; ZAR = South African rand; CHF = Swiss franc; AUD = Australian dollar; CAD = Canadian dollar; MYR = Malaysian ringgit; NZD = New Zealand dollar; GBP = British pound; SGD = Singapore dollar; KRW = South Korean won.

CHAPTER 4

The Economic Impact of Integration

Eastern enlargement is one of the biggest events in Europe in our time. However, it will take decades before a full insight into overall consequences will be possible.

—Višnja Samardžija

Overview

The integration of Central and Eastern Europe (CEE) countries with the West, in particularly the European Union (EU), is expected to produce significant benefits to all these economies in transition. In addition to positive economic changes resulting from altering tariffs, accession to the EU internal market, and free-labor movement on gross domestic product (GDP), consumption, positive terms of trade, and the absorption of EU funds could help the process of convergence and catching up.

This chapter is a discussion, from our point of view, of the economic impact and challenges being promoted by the EU enlargement into CEE economies, and how it has contributed to the economic growth of these countries. We took in consideration the macroeconomic variables such as rate of economic growth, the progress of market or structural reforms, economic freedom, foreign aid, and the foreign direct investment (FDI) inflow.

Economic integration may also be interpreted and measured by comparing GDP per capita in current international dollars, in purchasing power parity (PPP) terms of each CEE country with that of an advanced economy in the EU, such as Germany, due to its role as the largest EU national economy and major economic and trade partner of most of CEE economies on one hand, and its largely positive but rather modest rate of growth in 2000s and 2010s.[1]

Of course, there are many other variables that need to be taken into consideration, such as leveraging diversity—natural, cultural, political, ethnic, and religious—among these countries, that were for the most part omitted, as not to detract from the macroeconomic focus of this book. We did consider, however, the possible impacts of EU structural funds on FDI inflows into the region, under the circumstances of how diverse each country in CEE is, not only on the stage of transition of their economies but also on the different absorption rates for both exports and imports, as well as the potential adverse effects that the current global financial crisis could have in this process, which may affect the prospects for all economies of that region.

Economic Growth

Since the collapse of communism in the former Soviet Union, a number of CEE countries have faced the prospect of transforming their economy from centrally planned to a market-oriented one. Various researches and reviewed literature[2] (see partial list at the footnote) seem to agree that, overall, the integration of CEE economies into the EU has significantly contributed to the economic growth of those countries that have already joined the EU.

As discussed in earlier chapters, the transformation of these economies has been aided by the privatization of state-owned enterprises (SOEs) and the development of the private business sector, in which FDI inflows have been playing a major role, not only in the privatization of SOEs but also in the restructuring process of these economies.[3] The end of communism

---

[1] For the most part, our analyses were based on based on the IMF World Economic Outlook October 2014 database statistics. But a few other sources we used and cited throughout this chapter.

[2] Kapacki and Prochniak (2009); Zaman (2008); Dabrowski (2015); Mühlberger and Körner (2014); Rozmahel et al. (2013); Grabbe and Hughes (1998); Kornecki (2010).

[3] Caseand Fair (2004).

and the advanced economic integration of Europe have forever shaped global development in the 21st century.

The CEE countries recognize the importance of FDI in the development and modernization of their economies. The FDI inflows into the CEE economies have in fact been a vital force in the first stage of the privatization process during the transition period. It has increased in the past 20 years to become the most common type of capital flow needed for stabilization and economic growth,[4] with the CEE countries actively seeking to attract and promote FDI inflows to liberalize their economies and safeguard free movement of capital and profits.

As most of the privatization and restructuring process comes to an end, however, FDI inflows remains an important factor, but for a different purpose. Attracting FDI has become a major national strategy for these countries as FDI is seen as an essential factor in, among others, stimulating economic growth and expanding capital. Hence, a higher inflow of FDI in the region is becoming ever more important for the advancement of the globalization processes in CEE, including the boosting of productivity, stimulating the job market and employment, fostering innovation and technology transfer, and the enhancement of sustained economic growth.

In the economic arena, it integrates national economies with the global economy. The global economy itself is in a state of transition, ranging from a set of strong national economies to a set of interlinking trade groups. This transition has accelerated over the past few years with the collapse of communism and the coalescing of the European trading nations into a single market. One of the most important paths driving global development into the 21st century is the advanced economic integration of Europe. It has been an essential factor contributing to the growth of FDI in the CEE countries over the past few years. Never before have so many economies been open to global trade and finance flow than now, after the liberalization of the former communist economies.[5]

Looking at the period between 2001 and 2013, from the end of the dramatic period of transition-related restructuring and related prolonged

---

[4] Kornecki (2010).
[5] De la Dehesa (2006).

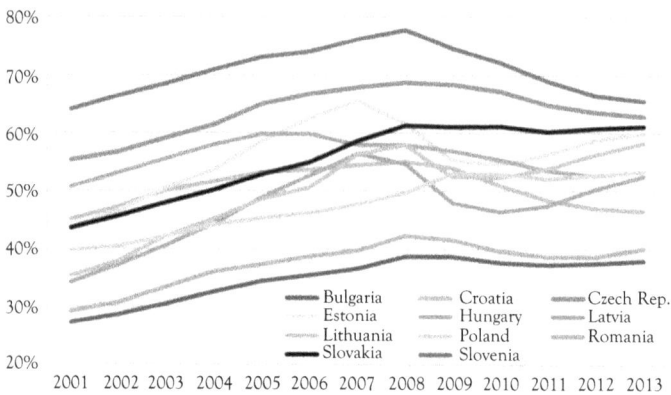

Figure 4.1 **GDP per capita in current international $, PPP adjusted, Germany = 100 percent, 2001–2013, for EU new member states**

Source: Dabrowski (2014).

output decline through mid-1990s, as well as the series of emerging-market crises on the second half of 1990s, which affected part of the region, the impact of integration is very visible, although not always positive. Based on Dabrowski's analysis,[6] Figure 4.1 provides a glimpse of such impact of integration on the current EU members, including Croatia, which joined the EU in July 2013.

Also according to Dabrowski's analysis,[7] Figure 4.2 provides an overview of GDP growth for the EU, including current and prospective country candidates in the Western Balkans region. The exception is Kosovo, for which the respective data was not available.

In both country groups depicted in Figures 4.1 and 4.2, one can clearly distinguish two subperiods, one until 2007 and 2008 with rapid catching up as a result of the convergence from a central-planned to a market-driven economy, and another after 2008 with either deconvergence or no progress in further convergence.

Some of the main factors behind this rapid convergence experienced through 2007 and 2008 include the posttransition growth recovery, the joining of the single European market, or partial access to it, in the case of

---

[6] Dabrowski (2014).

[7] Dabrowski (2014).

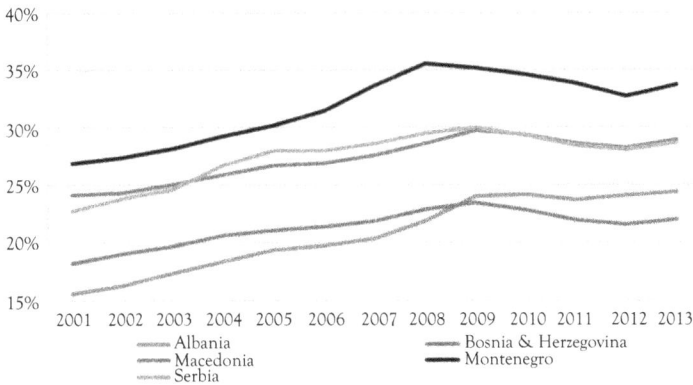

Figure 4.2 GDP per capita in current international \$, PPP adjusted, Germany = 100 percent, 2001–2013, for Western Balkan countries

Source: Dabrowski (2014).

EU candidates, and the global economic boom, which resulted in large-scale FDI inflows throughout the region. Also noticeable from Figures 4.1 and 4.2 is the fact that when the global financial crisis struck the region in 2008 and 2009, and even earlier in the Baltic countries (2007), the convergence trajectory turned negative pretty much everywhere.[8]

However, we can distinguish substantial differences across each country subgroup. The four new member states of the EU with the highest income per capita level in early 2000s, including Slovenia, Czech Republic, Hungary, and Croatia, had recorded a continuous decline in their relative GDP per capita levels, as compared to Germany after 2008. The three Baltic countries experienced an even sharper decline from 2008 to 2010 but then returned to rapid reconvergence, even though only Lithuania has managed to exceed its precrisis convergence level so far. The somewhat similar growth pattern, where there is a decline in GDP than a recovery, can be observed in most Western Balkan EU candidate countries, except for Albania. The same was true for Romania and Bulgaria although with smaller scales of changes in their convergence trajectories, particularly for Bulgaria. Lastly, Poland, Slovakia, and Albania managed to continue their convergence vis-à-vis Germany after 2008, although at a very slow pace.

---

[8] In Hungary, conversion stopped in 2005.

Growth Challenges

Looking ahead, one must ask what kind of challenges will be faced by CEE countries in their future development, and whether they will have the chance to return to their pre-2007 or 2008 convergence trajectory. Clearly the preglobal financial crisis growth bonanza based on large-scale capital inflow is unlikely to return anytime soon. We now live in a much different world. There are still many risks and challenges threatening the CEE countries growth and path to prosperity. The following are only a few main ones we find important.

The demographic trends of the region will continue to be progressively unfavorable, as a result of the declining cohorts of working-age populations. Although this is a common European problem even for Germany, the Eastern part of the region may very well experience sharper decline in this respect than their higher-income Western European neighbors.

However, the region will likely face even more dramatic challenges with respect to capital inflows and investments as a whole. The short-term investment boom of 2003 to 2007 was largely based on imported savings, which caused large current account imbalances. Unfortunately, the gross saving rate in the CEE countries is very low, in the range of 16 to 17 percent of the GDP, the lowest among emerging-market regions and much lower as compared with the eurozone,[9] as depicted in Figure 4.3, which has not improved after the global financial crisis as one would have expected. Without an increase in the gross saving rate, the CEE countries will continue to have to rely on ever larger-scale import of saving, in the range of 8 to 10 percent of GDP annually. Such massive net capital inflow seems very unlikely in the postcrisis environment of financial deleveraging. The size of net FDI has been much smaller and declining in recent years. Needless to say, excessive reliance on short-term capital inflows may increase external macroeconomic vulnerability in the case of adverse shocks, as several countries learned from 2008 to 2009. When capital inflows came to a halt in 2008, the investment rate also turned downward, especially in the Baltics, Bulgaria, and part of the Western Balkans.

---

[9] Dabrowski (2014).

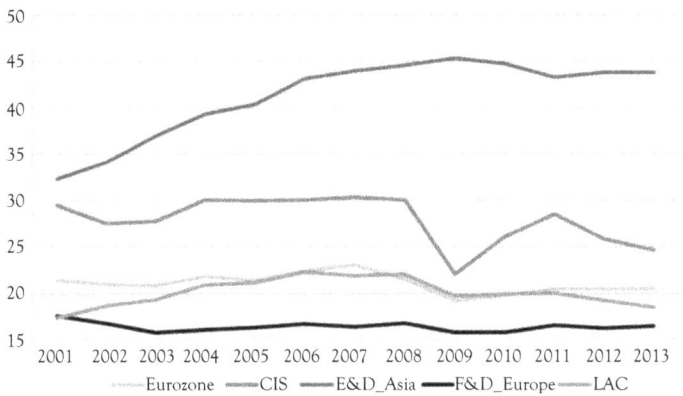

Figure 4.3 Gross national savings, percent of GDP, interregional comparison, 2001–2013

Source: Dabrowski (2014).

Overall there has been significant recovery since 2009, but it may not be sustainable due to other challenges that may lie ahead, including among many of the geopolitical and macroeconomic factors, the indebtedness of the advanced economies, currency wars, control of capital flows and currency rate, and the control of inflation. These challenges are discussed next.

Indebtedness of the Advanced Economies

Canadian Prime Minister Stephen Harper, in September of 2013, was vehemently urging G-20 leaders not to lose sight of the vital importance of reining in debt across the group after several years of deficit-fuelled stimulus spending, sticking to a common refrain in the face of weak recoveries among member countries including Canada. Harper expressed concern regarding the risks of accumulating public debt points, and he acknowledged that recoveries from the financial crisis have been disappointing because many of the advanced economies continue to grapple with high unemployment, weak growth, and rising income inequality.

In the United States, since the economic crisis of 2008, financial analysts and politicians have vocalized concerns about the economic impact of *fiscal cliffs*, debt ceiling, and defaults. Similar concerns have also resounded across Europe and the CEE region. Many fear that high debt-to-GDP ratios and deficit figures are signs of financial failure; public debt has been heralded as the harbinger of economic apocalypse. Despite these very relevant fears, an analysis of historical trends shows that many countries around the world, especially in the emerging markets during the 70s and 80s, experienced large amounts of debt. Often, this debt was in excess of 100 percent of GDP, which is very similar to what many advanced economies are experiencing right now. What makes this period unique is that while the CEE had most of their debt in external markets, denominated in foreign currencies, they also, as transition economies, have differing structures and institutions than the advanced economies.

When we look at the last quarter of the 19th century, it was a period of large accumulation of debt due to widespread infrastructure building at advanced economies around the globe, mainly due to the new innovation at the time, such as the railroads. As these economies expanded and continued to invest in infrastructure, much debt was also created. The same was true during World War I (WWI), reflecting the military spending taken on during the wartime period, and immediately after that during the reconstruction period. Then came another period of large creation of debt, during and after World War II (WWII). In this case, some of these debt levels started to build a bit earlier, as a result of the great recession, but most were the result of WWII. Lastly, we have the period where most governments and policymakers of advanced economies struggled to move from the old economic systems to the current one. During these four different periods, most advanced economies experienced 100 percent or more debt-to-GDP ratios at least once or more. The dynamics of debt-to-GDP ratios are in fact very diverse; their effects are widely varied, and based on a variety of factors. Take for example the case of the United Kingdom in 1918, the United States in 1946, Belgium in 1983, Italy in 1992, Canada in 1995, and Japan in 1997. All these countries went through a process of indebtedness, each with a full range of outcomes.

In the case of England, policymakers tried to return to the gold standard at pre-WWI levels to restore trade, prosperity, and prestige, and to also pay off as much debt as quickly as possible, to preserve the country's good credit image. They sought to achieve these goals through policies that included austerity. Their efforts did not have the intended effects. The dual pursuit of going back to a strengthened currency from a devalued one and the pursuit of fiscal austerity seemed to be a deciding factor in the failure. Trying to go back to the gold standard that had not depreciated made British exports less attractive than those of surrounding countries who had not chosen this path. Consequently, exports were low, and to combat this, British banks kept interest rates high. Those high interest rates meant that the debt the country was trying to pay off increased in value and the country's slow growth and austerity did not give them the economic power to pay the debts off as they wanted to. In trying to maintain integrity and the image of "Old Faithful Britain," the policymakers ruined their chances for swift recovery.

In the United States, policymakers chose to not control inflation, and kept a floor on government bonds. Over time, these ideas changed and bond protection measures were lifted while the government's ability to intervene in inflation situations was changed. The United States experienced rapid growth during this time, partially due to high levels of monetary inflation; but that inflation, even though it "burst" at the start of the Korean War, allowed the United States to pay off much of its debt. This, coupled with the floor on the U.S. bonds, created a favorable postwar, high debt level scenario.

Japan's initial response to its situation was the cutting of inflation rates and the introduction of fiscal stimulus programs. This did not have the intended effect, as the currency value appreciated. The underlying issues that caused high debt-to-GDP ratios were still present, and continued until 2001, when the government committed to changing policy and structure in focused ways in order to boost the country's economy. Japan still has a very high debt-to-GDP ratio, but the weaknesses in the banking sector have been fixed, and the country seems to be on a recovery path.

Italy's attempts at fiscal reform included changes in many social programs, including large cuts on pension expenditures. The reforms, though, were not implemented quickly enough and did not address adequate demographic issues to make a large impact. It wasn't until later that further fiscal consolidation was achieved. Importantly, Italy's weak GDP growth did not help to reduce debt in this period.

Similarly, Belgium used fiscal consolidation plans, but they were more widespread and implemented at a more rapid pace. The relative success of these initial fiscal consolidations helped to further growth and reduction of the Belgian debt-to-GDP ratio, and fueled another round of successful consolidation when the country needed it to enter the EU.

Canada's initial reaction included fiscal changes such as tax hikes and spending cuts, a plan of austerity. The plan failed and deepened the country's debt. The second wave of fiscal consolidation was aimed at fixing some of the structural imbalances that had caused the debt levels in the first place. It worked, helped along by the strengthening of economic conditions in the surrounding countries, mainly the United States. The Canada example shows that the external conditions are just as important in success as the policies or missions taken within the country experiencing high debt-to-GDP ratios.

From these examples, we can have an idea of the impact that advanced economies have on each other and on the CEE economies as well. In an intertwined global economy, imbalances in one country's economy virtually impacts every other country in the world; although the impact and mitigation of such impacts will always vary depending on internal and external market conditions, as well as policy development. Similar solutions, like the allowing of inflation in the United States, may not work today, or in another country. For instance, if we take the global financial crisis that started in 2008, allowing inflation to rise to higher levels could pose risks to the financial institutions, and could lead to a less globally integrated financial system.

The most pertinent choice of example would appear to be the kinds of fiscal policy used in Canada, Belgium, and Italy. All three countries attempted to achieve low inflation, but the other policy reforms of the countries varied in success. More permanent fiscal changes tend to create more prominent and lasting reductions to debt levels, and even then the country must be exposed to increased external demand for the recovery to be similar to the successful cases cited earlier. Consolidation needs to be implemented alongside measures to support growth and changes that address structural issues. The final factor to note is that even with a successful plan, the effects of that plan take time. No reduction in debt levels will be quick in today's global and interweaved economies.

The Crisis Isn't Over Yet

Advanced economies, especially EU countries and the United States, are still dealing with the global financial crisis that started sometime in 2008. Despite the positive rhetoric of policy makers and government on both sides of the Atlantic, according to Harvard economist Carmen Reinhart, the crisis is not yet over. She alleges that both the U.S. Federal Reserve and the European Central Bank (ECB) are keeping interest rates low to help governments keep out of their debt crises. Historically, we find many examples of central banks going above and beyond normal expectations to help governments of advanced economies to finance their deficits.

Nowadays, however, monetary policy is doing the job, but unlike many policy makers would like us to believe, these economies seldom are able to just grow themselves out of debt. Money to pay for these debts must come from somewhere. Reinhart[10] believes those advanced economies in debt today must adopt a combination of austerity to restrain the trend of adding to the stack of debt and higher inflation, which is effectively a subtle form of taxation, which consequently will depreciate the value of the currency, eroding people's savings.

We neither advocate nor favor the current central bank policies in these economies, and this is not the scope of this book on the first place. Advanced economies, however, need to deal with their debt one way or another, as these high debt levels prevent growth and freeze the financial system and the credit process. This too impacts CEE economies in a very negative way, at least as long as these markets continue to heavily depend on the exports to these advanced economies and FDI inflows. We do believe, however, that the indebtedness of the United States and the EU, in particular, affects the CEE economies in a major way, and that current central bank policies are not effective, as money is being transferred from responsible savers to borrowers via negative interest rates.

In other words, when the inflation rate is higher than the interest rates paid in the markets, the debts magically shrink. As dubbed by Ronald

---

[10] Dabrowski (2014).

McKinnon,[11] the term *financial repression* describes various policies that allow governments to *capture* and *under-pay* domestic savers. Such policies include forced lending to governments by pension funds and other domestic financial institutions, interest-rate caps, capital controls, and many more. Typically, governments use a mixture of these policies to bring down debt levels, but inflation and financial repression usually only work for domestically held debt—although the Eurozone is a special hybrid case. This financial repression, which is being used by advanced economies and designed to avoid an explicit default on the debt, is not only ineffective in the long run but also not fair to responsible taxpayers, and eventually may entice public revolts such as the ones already witnessed in Greece and Spain. Governments could write off part of the debt, but evidently no politician will be willing to spearhead such write-offs. After all, most citizens do not realize their savings are being eroded and that there is a major transfer of wealth taking place. Undeniably, advanced economies around the world have a problem with debt. In the past, several tactics, including financial repression, have dealt with such problems, and now it seems, it is resurging again in the wake of the global and Eurozone crises.

Financial repression, coupled with a steady dose of inflation, cuts debt burdens from two directions: first by introducing low nominal interest rates, which reduce debt-servicing costs, and then through negative real interest rates, which erodes the debt-to-GDP ratio; in other words, this is a tax on savers. Financial repression also has some noteworthy political-economic properties. Unlike other taxes, the "repression" tax rate is determined by financial regulations and inflation performance that are obscure to the highly politicized realm of fiscal measures. Given that deficit reduction usually involves highly unpopular expenditure reductions and tax increases of one form or another, the relatively *stealthier* financial repression tax may be a more politically palatable alternative for authorities faced with the need to reduce outstanding debts. In such environment, inflation, by historic standards, does not need to take market participants entirely by surprise, as it doesn't need to be very high.

---

[11] McKinnon (1973).

Unlike the United States, which is resorting to financial repression, Europe is focusing more on austerity measures, despite the fact inflation is still at a low level. Notwithstanding, debt restructuring, inflation, and financial repression are not a substitute for austerity. All these measures reduce a country's existing stock of debt, and as argued by Reinhart,[12] policy makers need a combination of both to bring down debt to a sustainable level. Although the United States is highly indebted, an advantage it has against all other advanced economies is that foreign central banks are then the ones holding most of its debts.

It is obvious that the currently very uncertain situation in the Eurozone, for which the leading indicators are pointing to a period of recession, while the sovereign debt crisis continues to escalate from one episode to the next, also has negative ramifications on CEE. In fact, back in 2012, the Austrian Raiffeisen Bank International AG[13] significantly lowered its 2012 growth forecasts for most of the countries in the CEE region, resulting in a GDP growth estimate of 2.3 percent for the region as a whole, anticipating a slowdown of GDP growth for the region. The good news is that, as mentioned earlier, even though growth in CEE is slowing down, the rate remains significantly higher than that expected for the Eurozone and advanced economies as a whole. It is also expected that the CEE region will continue its catch-up process toward the Eurozone with a positive growth through 2015.

We believe that the combination of high public and private debts in the advanced economies and the perceived dangers of currency mis-alignments and overvaluation in CEE countries facing surges in capital inflows, which in turn are causing pressures toward currency intervention and capital controls, interact to produce a home-bias in finance and a resurgence of financial repression. At present, we find that CEE economies are being forced to adopt similar policies as the advanced economies—hence the *currency wars*—but not as a financial repression, but more in the context of *macro-prudential* regulations.

---

[12] Reinhart and Kirkegaard (2012).

[13] www.rbinternational.com/eBusiness/01_template1/829189266947841370-829189148030934104_829602608694921416-829188181663843300-NA-2-EN.html

Advanced economies are developing financial regulatory measures to keep international capital out of CEE, and emerging markets as a whole, and in advanced economies. Such economic controls are intended to counter loose monetary policy in the advanced economies and discourage the so-called *hot money*,[14] while regulatory changes in advanced economies are meant to create a captive audience for domestic debt. This offers advanced and emerging market economies, including CEE economies, common ground on tighter restrictions on international financial flows, which borderlines protectionism policies. More broadly, the world is witnessing a return to more tightly regulated domestic financial environment, in other words, financial repression.

Therefore, we believe advanced economies are imposing a major strain on global financial markets, particularly on CEE economies by way of exporting inflation to those countries, because governments are incapable of reducing their debts, pressuring central banks to get involved in an attempt to resolve the crisis. Reinhart argues that such policy does not come cheap, and those responsible citizens, those everyday savers, will be the ones feeling the consequences of such policies the most; they will pay the price. While no central bank will admit it is keeping interest rates low to help governments keep out of their debt crises, they are doing whatever they can to help these economies finance their deficits.

The major danger of such a central bank policy, which can be at first very detrimental to CEE economies who are still largely dependent on consumer exports demands from advanced economies, is that it can lead to high inflation. As inflation rises among advanced economies, it is also exported to CEE economies and other emerging markets. In other words, as the U.S. dollar and the euro debases and loses buying power, CEE markets experience an artificial strengthening of their currency, courtesy of the U.S. Federal Reserve and the ECB, causing the prices of their goods and services to also increase, hurting exports in the process.

No doubt, a critical factor explaining the high incidence of negative real interest rates in the wake of the crisis is the aggressively expansive stance of monetary policy, particularly the official central bank

[14] Capital that is frequently transferred between financial institutions in an attempt to maximize interest or capital gain.

interventions in many advanced and emerging economies during this period. At the time of these writings, winter 2016, the levels of public debt in many advanced economies is at their highest levels, with some of these economies even face the prospect of debt restructuring. Moreover, public and private external debts, which we should not ignore are typically a volatile source of funding, are at historic highs, while the high and persistent levels of unemployment in many advanced economies persist. These negative trends offer further motivation for central banks and policy makers to keep interest rates low, posing renewed taste for financial repression. Hence, we believe the final crisis isn't over yet. The impact such advanced economies are imposing on emerging markets, and its own economies, is only the tip of a very large iceberg.

Currency Wars

Currency war, also known as competitive devaluation of currency, is a term raised as the alarm by Brazil's former Finance Minister Guido Mantega to describe the 2010 effort by the United States and China to have the lowest value of their currencies.[15] The rationale behind a currency war is really quite simple. The process of devaluing one's currency makes exports more competitive, assists the individual country to capture a greater share of global trade, and boosts its economy. Greater exports mean employing more workers and therefore helping improve economic growth rates, even at the eventual cost of inflation and unrest.

In currency wars, exchange rate manipulation can be accomplished in several ways.

- Direct intervention—Adopted by the People's Bank of China (PBOC) and Bank of Japan (BOJ), in which a country can sell its own currency in order to buy foreign currencies, resulting in a direct devaluation of its currency on a relative basis.
- Quantitative easing (QE)—Taken by U.S. Federal Reserve, in which a country can use its own currency to buy its own

---

[15] Amadeo (2013).

sovereign debt, or effectively foreign debt, and ultimately depreciate its currency.

- Interest rates—Exercised by BOJ, Federal Reserve, and ECB, in which a country can lower its interest rates and thereby create downward pressure on its currency, since it becomes cheaper to borrow against others.
- Threats of devaluation—Used by the United States toward China, in which a country can threaten to take any of the above actions along with other measures and occasionally achieve the desired devaluation in the open market.

The United States allows its currency, the dollar, to devalue by expansionary fiscal and monetary policies. It's doing this through increasing spending, thereby increasing the debt, and by keeping the Fed funds rate at virtually zero, increasing credit and the money supply. More importantly, through QE, it has been printing money to buy bonds, currently at $85 billion a month.

China tries to keep its currency low by pegging it to the dollar, along with a basket of other currencies. It pegs its currency by buying U.S. Treasuries, which limits the supply of dollars, thereby strengthening it. This keeps Chinese Yuan low by comparison. Obviously, both the Unites States and China were able to benefit from currency rate manipulation to secure their leading positions in the international trade.

According to the World Trade Organization (WTO) International Trade Statistics 2013, and as depicted in Figure 4.4, the United States is still the world's biggest trader in merchandise, with imports and exports totaling $3,881 billion in 2012. Its trade deficit amounts to $790 billion, 4.9 percent of its GDP. China follows closely behind the U.S., with merchandise trade totaling $3,867 billion in 2012. China's trade surplus was $230 billion, or 2.8 percent of its GDP.

Through manipulation of currency rate, devaluation is also used to cut real debt levels by reducing the purchasing power of a nation's debt held by foreign investors, which works especially well for the United States. But such currency rate manipulation has invited destructive retaliation in the form of tit-for-tat currency war among the world's largest economies. A joint statement issued by the Japanese government and the BOJ in

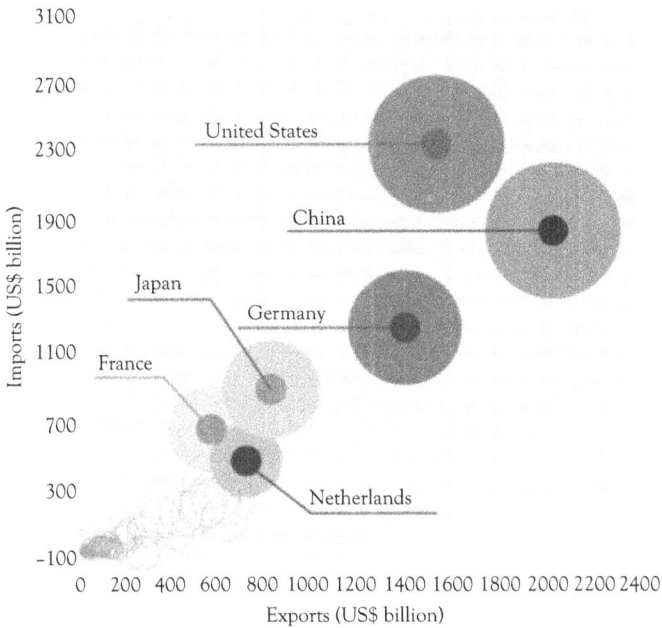

Figure 4.4 Leading export and import traders of 2012

Sources: International Trade Statistics 2013 (WTO).

January 2013 stated that the central bank would adopt a 2 percent infla-tion target. Later on, Haruhiko Kuroda, the BOJ's governor announced the BOJ's boldest attempt so far to stimulate Japan's economy and end years of deflation. The bank intends to double the amount of money in circulation by buying about ¥13 trillion in financial assets, including some ¥2 trillion in government bonds, every month as long as necessary. BOJ's effort together with the months of anticipation that preceded it has knocked the yen down sharply against the dollar and other major curren-cies, as shown in Figure 4.5, and sparked a rally in Japanese shares. But it has also further reignited fears of currency tensions around.

The EU made its move in 2013, to boost its export and fight defla-tion. The ECB, after cutting its policy rate to 0.5 percent in May, lowered such rate further to 0.25 percent on November 7, 2013. This immediately drove down the euro to dollar conversion rate to $1.3366.

Such strategy should be of concern to CEE countries because the cur-rency wars are driving their currencies higher, by comparison. This raises the prices of commodities, which fuels their manufacturing industry,

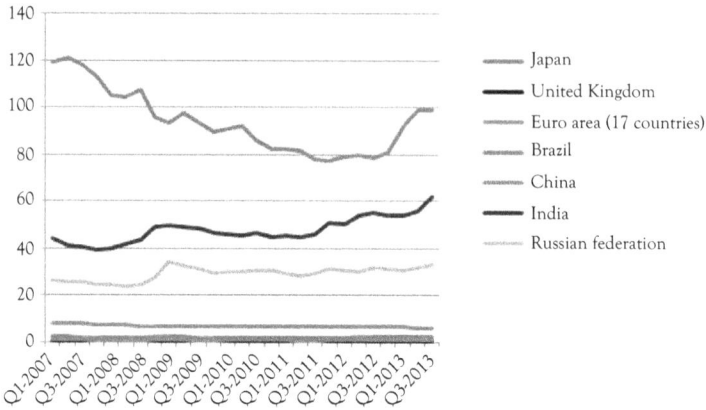

Figure 4.5 Currency exchange rates, National units per $ (quarterly average)

Source: Organization for Economic Cooperation and Development (OECD) Main Economic Indicators (MEI) database.

their primary exports. This makes CEE countries less competitive, and slows their economic growth. In fact, according to Brezinschek, Raiffeisen Research's[16] chief analyst, the impacts on CEE stem both from the region's lopsided export orientation where up to 85 percent of CEE total exports go to the EU, as well as the tensions within the European banking sector. However, Brezinschek expects the effects in the Commonwealth of Independent States (CIS) region to be less pronounced than in the CEE, due to the more robust domestic demand in the CIS countries. Raiffeisen Research also expects the CIS region's GDP to grow at higher levels than CEE region through 2015.[17]

Control of Capital Flows and Currency Rate

To avoid the repeat of such painful history and damage to international trade caused by ongoing currency war, Pascal Lamy, former

---

[16] www.rbinternational.com/eBusiness/01_template1/829189266947841370-829189148030934104_829602608694921416-829188181663843300-NA-2-EN.html

[17] www.rbinternational.com/eBusiness/01_template1/829189266947841370-829189148030934104_829602608694921416-829188181663843300-NA-2-EN.html

Director-General of WTO, in his inaugural address to the WTO Seminar on Exchange Rates and Trade on March 27, 2012, pointed out that "the international community needs to make headway on the issue of reform of the international monetary system. Unilateral attempts to change or retain the status quo will not work."

The key challenge to the rest of the world is the U.S. policy of renewed QE, which gives both potential benefits and increasing pressure to other countries. Among the benefits would be to help push back the risk of deflation that has been observed in much of the advanced world. Avoiding stagnation or renewed recession in advanced economies, such as the EU and the United States, in turn, would be a major benefit for CEE countries, whose economic cycles remain closely correlated with those in the developed world.[18] Another major plus would be to greatly reduce the threat of protectionism, particularly in the United States itself. The most plausible scenario for advanced economies protectionism would be precisely a long period of deflation and economic stagnation, as seen in the 1930s.[19]

Based on our observation, the adjustment issue has been relatively easier in other advanced economies, especially countries within the EU, which are also experiencing high unemployment and are threatened by deflation. In this situation, there could be a rationale not so much for a currency war as for a coordinated monetary easing across developed countries to help fend off deflation while also reducing the risk of big exchange rate realignments among the major developed economies.[20]

In contrast, it is more complicated for most CEE economies, as the EU enlargement brings more benefits to new entry member states and only a modest improvement for the old EU member states.[21] On the other hand, we cannot overlook that, into an integrated economic group of countries with different levels of economic and social development such as in the CEE, those more advanced benefit to a greater extent of the integration effects compared with the less developed ones. This latter view

---

[18]   Canuto (2010).

[19]   Canuto and Giugale (2010).

[20]   Portes (2010).

[21]   Lejourand Nahuis (2004).

takes into consideration the positive effects of repatriated profits generated by the large volume of FDI in CEE countries, by the earnings in the developed countries on the account of the foreign labor who are less paid compared to local workers, by the opportunities for increased production in these countries as a result of new markets opening in the new member states, and so on. Some countries, such as Poland and Lithuania, may experience relatively stronger growth and higher inflation rather than deflationary pressures. In this situation, the U.S. monetary easing policy poses more challenging policy choices by creating added stimulus for capital inflows to CEE economies, flows that have already been surging since 2008 through 2010, when the global financial crisis ensued, which was caused by both high short-term interest rate spreads and the stronger long-term growth prospects of CEE economies. To put currency rate and capital flow under reasonable control with the increasing pressure from U.S. monetary easing policy, there are three approaches suggested by the World Bank experts.[22]

First approach is to maintain a fixed exchange rate peg and an open capital account while giving up control of monetary policy as an independent policy instrument. This approach tends to suit economies, such as Latvia, Lithuania, Bulgaria, and Bosnia Herzegovina, highly integrated both economically and institutionally with the larger economies of the EU to whose exchange rates are pegged. It is less appropriate, however, for larger economies such as Poland, whose domestic cycles may not be at the same pace compared to that of the even much larger economies of the EU or the United States, in which the zloty was pegged.

In Poland's situation, in May 1991, the government sharply devalued the zloty and switched the peg from the U.S. dollar to a five-currency basket. Poland quickly realized that importing loose U.S. monetary policy tended to stimulate excessive domestic money growth, inflation in the goods market, and speculative bubbles in asset markets. By October, the end had come for a fixed exchange rate that everyone had to admit was not working. Starting in that month, the Polish authorities replaced the fixed exchange rate with a crawling peg. Under that system, the exchange

---

[22] Brahmbhatt, Canuto, and Ghosh (2010).

rate of the zloty was fixed in relation to the five-currency basket on a day-to-day basis, but at a rate that steadily depreciated. The rate of depreciation, initially 1.8 percent per month, was kept below the prevailing rate of inflation and gradually slowed as the economy stabilized. After 2000, Poland followed a policy that combined a floating exchange rate with inflation target. From 2001 to 2011, inflation was respectably moderate, averaging just lower than 3 percent per year. The floating exchange rate largely absorbed external shocks and changes in financial flows without undue damage to the real economy.[23]

Second approach is to pursue independent monetary policies that target the CEE economies' own inflation and activity levels, combined with relatively flexible exchange rates and open capital accounts, as Poland actually did, and which a growing number of CEE economies have been moving toward. Given rising inflation pressures, the appropriate monetary policy in many CEE markets at present would likely be to tighten, which will however attract even more capital inflows and further appreciate exchange rates. In fact, the Organization for Economic Cooperation and Development (OECD)[24] expects the CIS and the CEE economies to advance in 2015 and 2016 after a mixed picture in the past few years as the region tries to overcome the impact of a slump in the eurozone.

We believe Russia has very little leeway to cut interest rates while Hungary will likely keep interests on hold, even though Poland may start removing its monetary policy stimulus. We also believe Slovenia will continue to work on repairing its bank balance sheets and shoring up the sector, since, in our views, this is the most pressing task the country has to undertake to stabilize its economy. Sustained appreciation raises concerns about loss of export competitiveness and sometimes may lead to contentious structural adjustments in the real economy. So countries may also fear that large appreciations will undercut their long-term growth potential.[25] A standard recommendation for CEE and CIS countries in this position is to tighten fiscal policy, by either increasing the rate of taxation

[23] Dolan (2012).

[24] Reuters (2013).

[25] Rodrik (2009).

or cutting government spending or both, as a way of reducing upward pressure on local interest and exchange rates.

Third approach is to combine an independent monetary policy with a fixed exchange rate by closing the capital account through capital controls. Such controls may sometimes be a useful temporary expedient, but they are not unproblematic, especially in the longer term.

Figure 4.6 lists some of the main types of capital controls and some evidence on their varying effectiveness. Foreign exchange taxes can be, to some extent, effective in reducing the volume of flows in the short term, and can alter the composition of flows toward longer-term maturities. Unremunerated reserve requirements can also be effective in lengthening the maturity structure of inflows, but their effectiveness diminishes over time. There is some evidence that prudential measures that include some form of capital control, such as a limit on bank external borrowing, may be effective in reducing the volume of capital inflows.

Inflation Controls

Inflation is defined as a rise in the overall level of prices, which erodes savings, lowers purchasing power, discourages investment, inhibits growth, fuels capital outflow, and, in extreme cases, provokes social and political unrest. People view it negatively and governments consequently have tried to battle inflation by adopting conservative and sustainable fiscal and monetary policies.

All economies that made the transition from the Soviet-style centralized-administrative model to a market economy in the early 1990s experienced significant inflation. The peak inflation rate for countries in the short-lived ruble area exceeded 1,000 percent. Poland's inflation, which peaked at over 500 percent in 1990, was the highest among transition economies outside the ruble area.[26] To bring inflation under control, Poland, like several other transition economies in the CEE, turned to a fixed exchange rate. Unlike the neighboring Baltic states, however, Poland did not institutionalize the fixed rate through a currency board or similar arrangement. With neither a strong institutional framework nor

---

[26] Dolan (2012).

Types of capital controls	Volume of inflows	Composition of inflows
Foreign exchange tax	Can somewhat reduce the volume in the short-term.	Can alter the composition of inflows toward longer-term maturities.
Unremunerated reserve requirements (URRs): Typically accompanied by other measures		Have been effectively applied in reducing short-term inflows in overall inflows, but their effect diminishes over time.
Prudential measures with an element of capital control	Some evidence that prudential type controls can be effective in reducing capital inflows.	
Administrative controls: These are sometimes used in conjunction with URRs	Effectiveness depends largely on existence of other controls in the country.	

Figure 4.6 Effectiveness of capital control measures[27]

---

27 IMF (2010a, 2010b).

large foreign currency reserves, its fixed-rate disinflation strategy lacked credibility.

Macroeconomic trends have increasingly diverged across Central, Eastern and Southeastern Europe (CESEE). While domestic demand is starting to recover in most countries helped by rising consumption and still accommodative global financial conditions, overall growth continues to disappoint and is slowing everywhere except the CEE region. Inflation paths have also diverged. Declining world food and energy prices and disinflationary spillovers from the euro area have put inflation on a downtrend across most of the region except Turkey, Russia, and the rest of the CIS, where high domestic food prices and exchange rate depreciation have kept inflation high.[28]

Growth has become increasingly divergent across CESEE countries from 2014 to 2015, slowing everywhere except in the CEE and the Baltics, as shown in Figures 4.7 and 4.8.

Russia and other CIS economies, for instance, have been affected by deepening geopolitical tensions surrounding eastern Ukraine and related sanctions and counter-sanctions. Russia's growth weakened in 2014, as shown in Figure 4.4, on account of contracting investment, declining real household income, and an increase in capital outflows. The same has been true for growth in Southeastern Europe (SEE) and Turkey, which

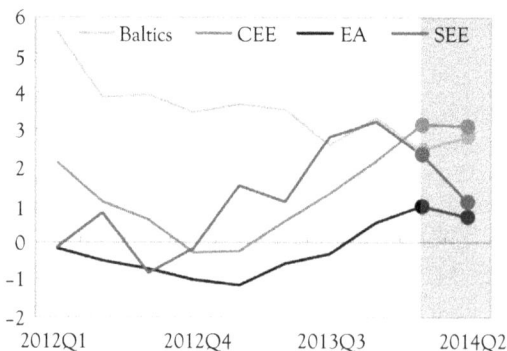

Figure 4.7 Quarterly GDP growth, 2012:Q1–2014:Q2, the Baltics, CEE, euro area, and Southeastern Europe (percent, year-over-year)

Source: Haver Analytics and International Monetary Fund (IMF) staff calculations.

---

[28] IMF (2014).

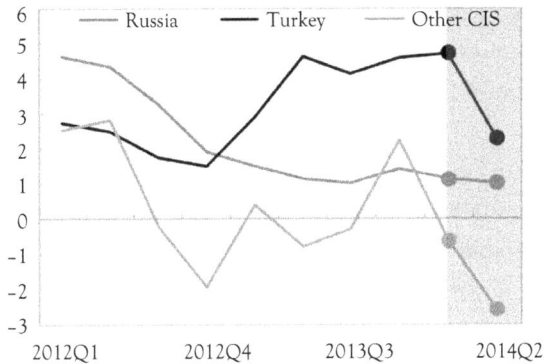

Figure 4.8 Quarterly GDP growth, 2012:Q1–2014:Q2, other CIS, Russia, and Turkey (percent, year-over-year)

Source: Haver Analytics and International Monetary Fund (IMF) staff calculations.

has decelerated due to country-specific factors. Also, floods hit the SEE countries, contributing to the slowdown in growth. In Turkey, despite stronger net exports, faltering private investments following previous policy tightening have caused growth to slow in 2014 as well, as shown in Figures 4.7 and 4.8. In contrast, however, activities accelerated further in the CEE region, which has benefited from the rise in FDI inflows, falling unemployment, and higher public spending in Hungary. In the Baltic region, growth was supported by favorable labor market conditions.

Inflation paths have, concurrently, continued to diverge as well, with inflation falling across most of the region, while picking up in Turkey, Russia, and other CIS countries. Declining world food and energy prices and low imported inflation from the euro area have continued to pull down prices in the CEE, SEE, and Baltic regions. In contrast, however, high domestic food prices, inflation expectations, and exchange rate depreciations have kept inflation persistently high in Russia and other CIS countries, as well as Turkey. The recent ban on food imports in 2014 added to the upward pressure on prices in Russia while in Turkey, lax monetary policy had a direct impact.[29]

Of major concern, however, is the fact non-euro area EU countries are importing low inflation from the euro area, causing countries pegged to

---

[29] IMF (2014).

the euro to be more exposed than those countries adopting inflation targeting. Still, however, we believe the major deflation drivers in the region
are the falling world food and energy prices as well as related administered
prices.

As illustrated in Figure 4.9, inflation has actually been falling sharply
across Europe since 2012, with current inflation being well below the
ECB's price stability objective in the euro area and in the CESEE and
EU inflation targets, while a number of CESEE and EU euro peggers
are experiencing outright deflation.[30] Across the CEE, inflation expectations have also drifted down, especially among those countries who
peg their currencies to the euro, such as Bulgaria, Croatia, and Lithuania, which has since adopted the euro on January 1, 2015, but also in
those countries that target their inflation rates, such as Czech Republic,
Hungary, Poland, and Romania. At the same time, according to the
International Monetary Fund (IMF), core inflation in the euro area
and CESEE and EU countries, euro peggers, and inflation targeters

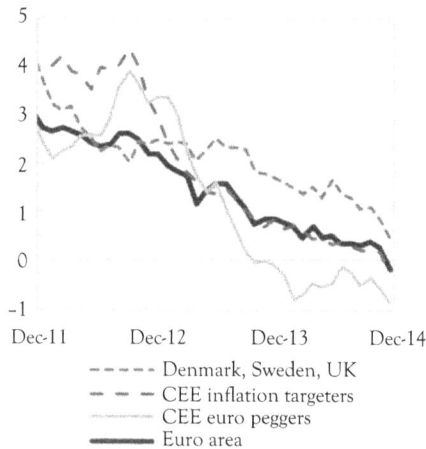

Figure 4.9 Headline inflation in the CESEE, EU, and CEE countries (12-month growth rate in %)

Source: Eurostat.

---

[30] Inflation-targeting CESEE/EU countries are the Czech Republic, Hungary,
Poland, and Romania, while euro peggers includes Bulgaria, Croatia and
Lithuania; Iossifov and Podpiera (2014).

have decoupled from developments in the rest of the world since the end of 2012.[31]

Inflation Targeting

As discussed in the previous section, the ongoing, synchronized disinflation across Europe raises the question of whether non-Eurozone EU countries are affected by the undershooting of the Eurozone inflation target, by other global factors, or by synchronized domestic, real sector developments. As argued by PlamenIossifov,[32] Senior Economist in the European Department of IMF, the falling world food and energy prices have been the main disinflationary driver. However, countries, with either more rigid exchange-rate regimes or higher shares of foreign value added in domestic demand or both, have also been affected by disinflationary spillovers from the Eurozone.

The recent drop in world food and oil prices, and relevant cuts in administered prices of energy, has reignited the debate about good versus bad disinflation due to the fact these events, as depicted in Figure 4.10, have been an important driver of disinflation across EU countries outside the Eurozone.[33]

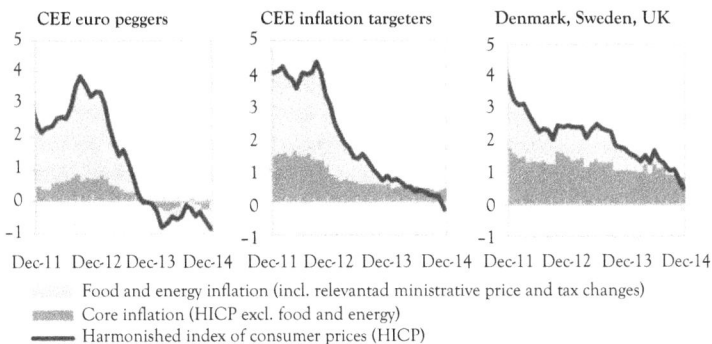

CEE euro peggers   CEE inflation targeters   Denmark, Sweden, UK

Dec-11 Dec-12 Dec-13 Dec-14   Dec-11 Dec-12 Dec-13 Dec-14   Dec-11 Dec-12 Dec-13 Dec-14

Food and energy inflation (incl. relevantad ministrative price and tax changes)
Core inflation (HICP excl. food and energy)
Harmonished index of consumer prices (HICP)

Figure 4.10 Contributions to headline inflation, 2012–2014 (percentage points contributions to 12-month growth rates of HICP)

Source: Eurostat and IMF staff estimates.

---

[31] Iossifov and Podpiera (2014).

[32] Iossifov (2015).

[33] Moghadam, Teja, and Berkmen (2014).

Furthermore, as argued by Iossifov,[34] core inflation, the overall inflation excluding volatile food and energy prices (see Figure 4.11), has also drifted down, tracing price trends in the Eurozone, and increasingly diverging from developments in the rest of the world. This suggests possible disinflationary spillovers from the Eurozone to other EU countries, in light of their close trade links.

Overall, as argued by Iossifov,[35] the fall in oil prices will likely boost growth in the short run. But, it poses challenges to monetary policymaking, which focuses on medium-term risks. A prolonged undershooting of the inflation objective could damage central banks' credibility, which would make it much harder to escape the deflation trap.

Countries that peg to the euro do not have independent monetary policies and would have to rely on the ECB's QE policy response to persistently low inflation in the Eurozone. Where fiscal space allows, countries could also use discretionary, expansionary fiscal policies. Meanwhile, inflation-targeting central banks strive to keep inflation close to target over the medium term. Consequently, when faced with renewed disinflationary pressures, Iossifov[36] recommends they aim at targeting inflation

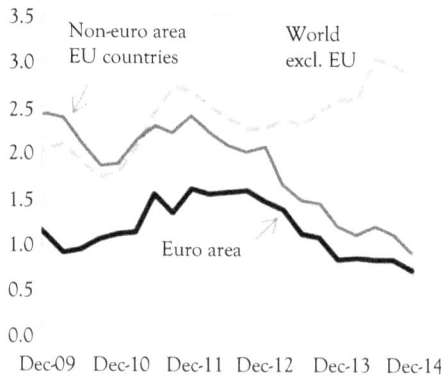

Figure 4.11 Core inflation in the non-euro area EU countries, the euro area and the world, excluding the United States, 12-month growth rate in %

Source: Haver, Eurostat, and IMF staff calculations.

---

[34] Iossifov (2015).

[35] Iossifov (2015).

[36] Iossifov (2015).

closer to its goal, by stamping out "second-round" disinflationary effects of falling energy prices.

However, this could be challenging. With policy instruments at historical lows or at the zero lower bound, further easing by inflation-targeting central banks would need to weigh the benefits of normalizing price pressures with potential concerns about the impact on financial stability and capital flows and hence exchange rates. Easing monetary policy too much may prompt capital outflows, and while this may help depreciate exchange rates and raise inflation, there is always a risk that the process may go too far. This is of particular concern for countries with a high share of debt in foreign currencies, which are more exposed to changes in investors' risk appetite, geopolitical concerns, and global financing conditions.

Because interest rates and inflation rates tend to move in opposite directions, central bankers have adopted "inflation targeting" to control the general rise in the price level based on such understanding of the links from the monetary policy instruments of interest rates to inflation. By applying inflation targeting, a central bank estimates and makes public a projected, or "target," inflation rate and then attempts to use interest rate changes to steer actual inflation toward that target. Through such "transmission mechanism," the activities of central banks more transparent, particularly the likelihood that they will raise or lower interest rates and encourage economic stability.

Inflation targeting, as a monetary-policy strategy, was introduced in New Zealand in 1990. It has been very successful in stabilizing both inflation and the real economy. As of 2010, as shown in Figure 4.12, it has been adopted by almost 30 advanced and emerging economies, including some in the CEE region (highlighted).

Inflation targeting is characterized by (1) an announced numerical inflation target, (2) an implementation of monetary policy that gives a major role to an inflation forecast and has been called forecast targeting, and (3) a high degree of transparency and accountability.[37] A major advantage of inflation targeting is that it combines elements of both "rules" and "discretion" in monetary policy. This "constrained discretion" framework

---

[37] Svensson (2008).

Targeting Inflation				
Country	Inflation targeting adoption date	Inflation rate at adoption date (%)	2010 end-of-year inflation (%)	Target inflation rate (%)
New Zealand	1990	3.30	4.03	1–3
Canada	1991	6.90	2.23	2 + or − 1
United Kingdom	1992	4.00	3.39	2
Australia	1993	2.00	2.65	2–3
Sweden	1993	1.80	2.10	2
Czech Republic	1997	6.80	2.00	3 + or − 1
Israel	1997	8.10	2.62	2 + or − 1
Poland	1998	10.60	3.10	2.5 + or − 1
Brazil	1999	3.30	5.91	4.5 + or − 1
Chile	1999	3.20	2.97	3 + or − 1
Colombia	1999	9.30	3.17	2–4
S. Africa	2000	2.60	3.50	3–6
Thailand	2000	0.80	3.05	0.5–3
Hungary	2001	10.80	4.20	3 + or − 1
Mexico	2001	9.00	4.40	3 + or − 1
Iceland	2001	4.10	2.37	2.5 + or − 1.5
S. Korea	2001	2.90	3.51	3 + or − 1
Norway	2001	3.60	2.76	2.5 + or − 1
Peru	2002	−0.10	2.08	2 + or − 1
Philippines	2002	4.50	3.00	4 + or − 1
Guatemala	2005	9.20	5.39	5 + or − 1
Indonesia	2005	7.40	6.96	5 + or − 1
Romania	2005	9.30	8.00	3 + or − 1
Serbia	2006	10.80	10.29	4–8
Turkey	2006	7.70	6.40	5.5 + or − 2
Armenia	2006	5.20	9.35	4.5 + or − 1.5
Ghana	2007	10.50	8.58	8.5 + or − 2
Albania	2009	3.70	3.40	3 + or − 1

Figure 4.12 Summary of central banks using inflation targeting to control inflation

Sources: Hammond (2011), Roger (2010), and IMF staff calculations.

combines two distinct elements: a precise numerical target for inflation in the medium term and a response to economic shocks in the short term.[38]

In emerging markets, particularly transition economies, the inflation picture can be quite different than those found in advanced economies. With unemployment rates hovering around long-term averages, these economies tend to be operating near their full potential. The concern for CEE and CIS economies is about high inflation together with potential slower growth. Inflation has started to pick up in emerging markets during 2013, even as growth has fallen short of expectations, and looks particularly disappointing when compared with figures from before the 2008 financial crisis. A poorer growth-inflation trade-off suggests that economic potential in emerging markets has slowed considerably. This observation is a particular worry in the largest emerging markets, including China, India, and Brazil. All have been growing at poor rates compared with previous years, but in none has inflation fallen significantly during the past year.

Inflation targeting has been successfully practiced in a growing number of countries over the past 20 years, and many more countries are moving toward this framework. Although inflation targeting has proven to be a flexible framework that has been resilient in changing circumstances including during the recent global financial crisis, emerging markets, however, must assess their economies to determine whether inflation targeting is appropriate for them or if it can be tailored to suit their needs. Facing the unique challenge of high inflation with slow growth, emerging economies may resort to manipulation of currency rates and other monetary and fiscal alternatives, along with interest rates adjustments, to play a more pivotal role in stabilizing inflation.

---

[38] Jahan (2012).

CHAPTER 5

Challenges for Entering Eastern European Markets

Given that countries in the CEE region are all moving at their own pace in developing new markets, trading across the region is a complex activity and requires a deep knowledge of the local markets.

—Claudio Capozzi

Overview

As the developed Western economies still try to recover fully from the global financial crisis, Eastern Europe, a part of the world often neglected by investors and business leaders, has been showing impressive growth and maturity, both economically and politically. Stock markets in Bulgaria and Romania, for example, have appreciated significantly over the past year, and improving infrastructure coupled with still relatively cheap labor provide an attractive environment for investments in the manufacturing and service sectors.

Recent political unrest in some countries of the region, however, threatens to stymie the economic progress and has reminded investors of the inherent risk that such high-return opportunities tend to carry, along with other factors discussed in this chapter, which should be seriously considered.

Even when bound by the ideology and strong embrace of the Soviet Union, eastern European countries differ widely, both economically and culturally. Additionally, as discussed throughout this book, the former USSR's varying levels of economic commitment to each country, mostly born out of different strategic priorities, led to uneven infrastructure investments and industrial development. Even today, this developmental disparity is still evident.

Another important factor is the historical and cultural perspective that each country and its people possess. An investor would be well advised to seek trusted, and if possible local, advisers with a keen understanding of each country's culture and history. Failure to grasp local customs can be a pitfall when investing in any part of the world, but one would be hard pressed to find a place where such knowledge is more important than Eastern Europe.

On the political side, newly elevated activists supported by democracy-hungry populations, along with some freshly repainted old-regime politicians, dominated the initial scrambles for power in these countries. After the early victories by the new but inexperienced leaders, however, the former communist figures, well groomed for political survival through the decades, have emerged as major players in many of these countries.

In addition, despite their relative stability and impressive growth, the global financial crisis that started in 2007 continues to ripple through these countries, and their ongoing struggle to adapt to new ways of doing business still bears watching, as does the potential for renewed political turmoil. In our experience teaching this topic, consulting for several multinational corporations (MNCs) around the world, and being a practitioner ourselves, we find that eastern European markets are not easy to enter, despite the many government incentives already discussed throughout this book. Hence, entering these markets can be a complex endeavor, but the rewards can be immense as well.

In some countries, government interference, backward infrastructure, political instability, work-skill mismatch, and even lack of skilled workers, require a lot of patience, perseverance, and specialized assistance. Opportunities in eastern European markets, therefore, come with their own set of challenges.

Emerging economies, in particular these eastern European transition economies, have also experienced large-scale structural change, in their case from the agricultural to the industrial sector. They are also often characterized by strong growth of the public sector, leading to a high share of employment in public activities often under the *clientelistic* control of ruling parties; a strong growth of informal sector; and a rapid demographic transition leading to a rapidly expanding and youthful population.

The modern urban sector employs relatively skilled labor, which attracts rural migrants with inadequate skills in search of higher wages, which leads to an oversupply of unskilled workers. The demographic transition leads to large numbers of young educated people in the labor market and high youth unemployment and consequently results in an oversupply of people with secondary education and skills. In addition, emigration of skilled workers (also known as *brain drain*) reduces the supply of skilled workers in the domestic economy, which typically also leads to shortages of highly skilled people.

The role of the state in these economies can be an important determinant of appropriate matching of skills supply and demand. Take South Korea, Singapore, and Taiwan, for example, which joined up policy making enabled developmental states to anticipate future skills needs since the state was also involved in the very industrial policies, which generated the demand for skilled labor.[1]

Yet, although the integration of economic and skill formation policies in South Korea and Taiwan through modified forms of state planning was initially relatively successful, the power of the state to compel employers to train their workers gradually waned.[2] The state-directed policy eventually came under pressure to reform although the state retains a role in steering these economies. Kuruvilla et al.[3] argued that Singapore's successful national skills development model has the potential to move constantly toward higher skills equilibrium, but they question the long-term sustainability of the model and whether it is transferable to other developing countries. Recent research by Özsagir et al.[4] has shown a positive relationship between the extent of vocational training and the index of industrial production.

Skill Mismatches

Skill mismatches and skill shortages have become a priority concern for policymakers in many countries, especially since the onset of the global

---

[1] Green et al. (1999a).
[2] Green et al. (1999b).
[3] Kuruvilla, Erickson, and Hwang (2002).
[4] Özsagir and Bayraktutan (2010).

economic crisis and its intensification through the crisis in the euro-zone. Endogenous growth models emphasize that human capital is a key resource for growth.[5] In fact, skill mismatch has an adverse effect on the efficiency of labor markets, particularly in transition economies, raising unemployment above the levels that could potentially be achieved given the level of aggregate demand. Efficient matching would reduce frictional and structural unemployment and ensure that vacancies are matched to workers with appropriate qualifications and skills.[6]

For instance, often the lack of specialized education of the work-force tends to translate into thwarted growth being curbed by the lack of a skilled workforce. According to models of endogenous growth,[7] the skill levels of the workforce, particularly in transition economies, are an important driver of economic development. This is partly due to different patterns of structural change and partly associated with demographic factors. Countries with high population growth rates may experience oversupply of educated school-leavers; countries with falling populations may experience undersupply of both skilled and unskilled workers. There is also evidence of gender-bias mismatch in these mar-kets. Among the main challenges to the development of effective skill-matching systems and its corresponding policy design in transition countries are the weak capabilities of government institutions including the employment services, underfunding of state-provided training ser-vices, slow reforms of the education systems, and low level of in-house training by employers.[8]

Most eastern European countries have experienced volatile labor mar-kets for many years. Although unemployment rates were on a falling trend till 2008, long-term unemployment has been persistently high in many countries, as shown in Table 5.1, leading to a corresponding obsolescence of skills among a large section of the workforce. After almost a decade of

---

[5] Romer (1994).

[6] Petrolongo and Pissarides (2001).

[7] Endogenous growth is long-run economic growth at a rate determined by forces that are internal to the economic system, particularly those forces govern-ing the opportunities and incentives to create technological knowledge.

[8] Bartlett (2013).

Table 5.1 Unemployment rates for eastern European countries

Country	Unemployment rate	Last updated	Previous %	Highest %	Lowest %
Albania	17.5	Sep, 2015	17.3	22.3	12.1
Bosnia and Herzegovina	42.81	Oct, 2015	42.97	46.1	39.03
Bulgaria	9.9	Nov, 2015	9.5	19.27	4.68
Croatia	17.7	Nov, 2015	17.2	23.6	12.2
Czech Republic	5.9	Nov, 2015	5.9	9.69	0.09
Estonia	5.2	Sep, 2015	6.5	20.1	0.5
Hungary	6.2	Nov, 2015	6.4	11.8	5.5
Kosovo	35.3	Dec, 2014	30	57	30
Latvia	9.7	Sep, 2015	9.8	20.7	5.4
Lithuania	8.4	Nov, 2015	8.3	15.3	2.7
Macedonia	25.48	Sep, 2015	26.84	37.3	25.48
Montenegro	16.35	Nov, 2015	15.67	31	10.2
Poland	9.6	Nov, 2015	9.6	20.7	0.3
Romania	6.7	Nov, 2015	6.8	8.1	5.4
Serbia	17.3	Sep, 2015	17.9	25.5	13.3
Slovakia	10.8	Nov, 2015	11	19.79	7.36
Slovenia	11.7	Oct, 2015	11.5	15.5	6.3

Source: tradingeconomics.com

sustained economic growth, the global economic crisis brought about an abrupt reversal of fortunes and began to increase in most countries of the region.[9] Long-term unemployment in the region is a serious problem, especially affecting older workers with obsolete skills. Youth unemployment is generally high,[10] particularly in countries with a rapidly growing population. On the demand side of the labor market, many old large-scale industries declined or closed down, while most new jobs emerged in the service industries among which a range of new skills are needed.[11]

---

[9] ETF (2011, 27).
[10] Kolevand Saget (2005).
[11] Bartlett (2007).

Regional mismatch also emerged as a specific problem due to the collapse of industries in peripheral areas and mono-industrial towns.[12]

Education System

Education systems in many transition countries are still character-ized by poor quality and irrelevance of much education provision in the region.[13] It is increasingly been recognized that curricula inherited from the previous communist system were unsuited to the development of a service-oriented post-Fordist[14] market economy and have not been upgraded sufficiently to reflect the new occupations that have emerged in the service sectors and in high technology industries. Skills that are taught in vocational education institutions tend to be too specialized in obsolete occupations. Education methods often outdated and dependent on rote learning, based on memorization techniques and repetition rather than problem solving. There is generally a deficit of education in transferable skills (so-called "soft skills").

Skills produced by the education system are often no longer demanded in the labor market. A recent study of the development of skills mis-matches in Eastern Europe found that

> even when people hold the correct qualification for an occupation they may not necessarily have the skills needed to effectively per-form the job and satisfy employer expectations. Rapid technolog-ical and economic change makes difficult to predict what types of skills will be needed in the near and more distant future and what kinds of new jobs will appear.[15]

---

[12] Bornhorstand Commander (2006); Newell and Pastore (2006).

[13] Sondergaard and Murthi (2012).

[14] Post-Fordism is the name given by some scholars to what they describe as the dominant system of economic production, consumption and associated socio-economic phenomena, in most industrialized countries since the late 20th century.

[15] ETF (2011, 229).

Moreover, because of structural change, it seems that skill mismatch is a more permanent phenomenon in eastern European markets than in the advanced economies resulting in high levels of long-term unemployment, and that skills mismatch increases with the age of workers, rather than falling as it does in the developed economies.

Economic Restructuring

Skill shortages and surpluses of various types are challenges for eastern European countries as a consequence of economic restructuring. The process of economic transition involved a simultaneous process of job destruction and job creation in which unskilled workers lost employment disproportionately as the skill content of blue-collar work increased due to technological change.[16] Newly created jobs typically require different types of skills to those that have been destroyed. This process of restructuring and the expansion of demand for new skills have often taken place more rapidly than the education and the training system has been adept at leading these skill shortages.[17] Figure 5.1 provides a sample of a handful of

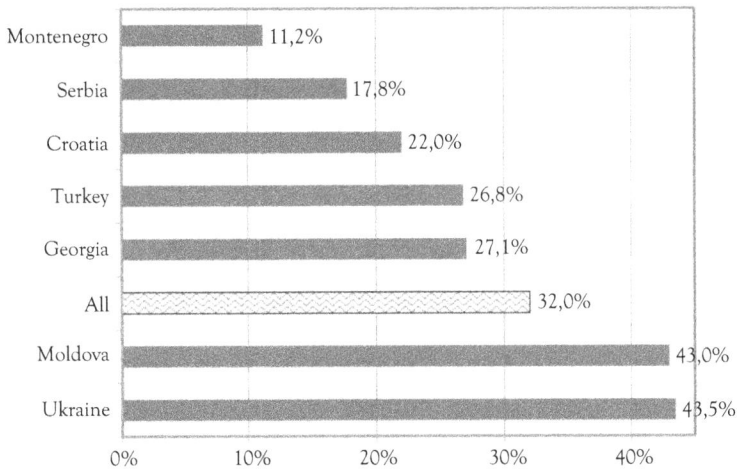

Figure 5.1 Proportion of firms reporting that an inadequately educated workforce is a "major or very severe" obstacle to the firm (%)

Source: BEEPS Survey 2010, European Bank for Reconstruction and Development (EBRD).

---

[16] Bilsen and Konings (1998).

[17] ETF (2011, 186).

eastern Europeans countries, depicting the proportion of business organizations reporting that an inadequately educated workforce is *a major or
very severe* obstacle to the firm, in percentage points.

Legal Framework and Trading Policies

Other challenges that arise are legal frameworks with regard to trade policies, which may be absent or underdeveloped, or tendencies for political paternalism or blatant interferences, especially in those countries that
have not yet joined the European Union (EU), such as Albania, Armenia,
Belarus, Bosnia and Herzegovina, Kosovo, and Macedonia, to name a few.

All EU countries, for example, do not recognize Kosovo's independence, although a surprise Serbia-Kosovo deal, brokered by EU High
Representative Catherine Ashton in 2013, paves the way for its eventual
EU membership. The other Western Balkan countries have all been told
that they can one day follow Croatia into the EU, as long as they make
progress on democratic and economic reforms. Moving closer toward
the EU implies meeting the criteria and conditions for each stage. These
relate to the Copenhagen membership criteria[18] and the stabilization and
association process,[19] including on regional cooperation, good neighborly
relations, and full cooperation with the International Criminal Tribunal
for the former Yugoslavia (ICTY).[20] The Western Balkan countries need

---

[18] The Copenhagen criteria are the rules that define whether a country is eligible
to join the European Union. The criteria require that a state has the institutions
to preserve democratic governance and human rights, has a functioning market
economy, and accepts the obligations and intent of the EU.

[19] In talks with countries that have expressed a wish to join the European Union,
the EU typically concludes Association Agreements in exchange for commitments to political, economic, trade, or human rights reform in that country. In
exchange, the country may be offered tariff-free access to some or all EU markets
(industrial goods, agricultural products, etc.), and financial or technical assistance.

[20] The International Tribunal for the Prosecution of Persons Responsible for Serious Violations of International Humanitarian Law Committed in the Territory
of the Former Yugoslavia since 1991, more commonly referred to as the International Criminal Tribunal for the former Yugoslavia (ICTY), is a body of the UN
established to prosecute serious crimes committed during the Yugoslav Wars, and
to try their perpetrators. The tribunal is an ad hoc court, which is located in The
Hague, Netherlands; Debating Europe (2014).

to effectively address the priorities set out in their accession or European partnerships. The pace of each country's progress is determined by its own achievements in this respect.

As for most industrialized countries, trade volumes increased significantly in the period after World War II, trade has been identified as one potential culprit for the worsened position of low-skilled workers.[21] Trade is thought to have affected the demand for low-skilled workers in two ways. It is thought to have reduced the relative demand for low-skilled labor and to have made the demand more responsive to changes in the price of low-skilled labor. Both effects would reduce the relative wages of low-skilled workers in economies with flexible labor markets. In economies where labor market rigidities prevent wages from falling, an increased relative unemployment rate of low-skilled labor may result. Country-specific labor-market characteristics would thus have an important effect on whether and to which extent relative wages or trade or both affect the relative unemployment rates.

With strong increases in skill inequalities over the 80s and part of the 90s and continuing integration of economies around the world, trading in emerging markets, particularly in eastern Europe, where some markets are very well developed and worker's skills are high, versus other markets in the region lacking both. We'd argue that there is potentially negative effect of trade with developing countries in Eastern Europe on low-skilled workers in industrialized countries.[22]

Public administration in eastern European economies has much to be desired, although overall it ranks much better than Brazil, Russia, India, China, and South Africa (BRICS) and other leading emerging market blocs. The *Doing Business 2015*[23] study by the World Bank, which ranks economies on their ease of doing business on a scale of 1 to 189, where a high ease of doing business ranking means the regulatory environment is more conducive to the starting and operation of a

---

[21] Other factors that affect wage and/or employment inequalities are migration, technological change and changes in the skill distribution of the labor force.

[22] WTO staff working (2000).

[23] The World Bank (2015).

local firm.[24] As depicted in Table 5.2, the study ranks Macedonia 12th, Lithuania 20th, and Latvia 22nd as the easiest countries of doing business

Table 5.2 Ascending list of most ease of doing business countries in Europe and central Asia

Economy	Ease of doing business rank
Macedonia, FYR	12
Lithuania	20
Latvia	22
Georgia	24
Armenia	35
Romania	37
Bulgaria	38
Croatia	40
Kazakhstan	41
Belarus	44
Montenegro	46
Cyprus	47
Russian Federation	51
Moldova	52
Turkey	55
Serbia	59
Azerbaijan	63
Kosovo	66
Kyrgyz Republic	67
Bosnia and Herzegovina	79
Ukraine	83
Uzbekistan	87
Albania	97
Tajikistan	132

Source: World Bank (2015).

---

[24] The rankings are determined by sorting the aggregate distance to frontier scores on 10 topics, each consisting of several indicators, giving equal weight to each topic. The rankings for all economies are benchmarked to June 2015.

in Europe and central Asia, out of 189 countries, while ranking Kosovo 66th, Bosnia and Herzegovina 79th, and Albania 97th. The discrepancy between the first three and the last ones are remarkable. By comparison, the study ranks Brazil 116th, Russia 51st, India 130th, China 84th, and South Africa 73rd, respectively, out of 189 countries.

Does all this mean that foreign investors should avoid trading with or investing in eastern European markets? On the contrary, however, any organized program of opening up to eastern European markets must include specialized expertise, on-the-ground knowledge, local partnerships, and, most of all, patience.

Why Multinationals Fail in Eastern European Markets

Pacek and Thorniley[25] identified an exhaustive range of factors contributing to the failure of companies from advanced economies into eastern European markets. These factors may be divided into external and internal factors and almost all are related to strategic and leadership issues.

- Leaders fail to consider eastern European markets as an integral part of strategy and acknowledge that such markets need to be approached with a distinct set of criteria for judging progress and success.
- Top leaders fail to commit sufficient resources to get businesses established and growing in eastern European markets, or acknowledge that it is never a short-term affair.
- MNCs fail to appoint a head manager for eastern European markets and often assign this responsibility to an international manager who is responsible for markets in both advanced and emerging markets. The problem with this is that operational approaches are distinct in each of these markets, as evidenced in Table 5.3.
- MNCs fail to understand that business is driven by heads of regions and business units rather than by heads of functional areas. While the former has a focus and appreciation for the

---

[25] Pacek and Thorniley (2007).

Table 5.3 **External factors and sample questions**

Understanding the market	
Market potential	• How large and wealthy is the market? • Is there unsatisfied demand for the product or service?
Understanding local consumers or customers	• Who are the consumers or customers? What are their characteristics? • How do consumers make their decisions?
Reaching the consumer or customer	• How difficult or easy is it to reach potential consumers or customers? • How do competitors and noncompetitors reach their customers?
Competition	• Which competitors are already operating in the market? • How strong are these competitors?
Lessons learned by noncompetitors	• What do noncompetitors say about the business environment in the country? • What have been the largest obstacles to successful operations?
Local culture	• What aspects of local culture are relevant to running a successful local business?
Understanding the political and economic environment	
Economic outlook	• How sustainable is economic growth? • What is driving economic growth?
Political outlook	• What is the level of political risk and how it will or might affect the business?
Government policies	• Does the government allow a level playing field? • Is the government in the hands of local lobbies?
Understanding the business environment	
Finance	• Is it possible to finance operations locally? • What access do customers or consumers have to finance?
Labor market	• What are the wage or salary rates for the employees who will be needed? • What are the most effective ways of recruiting local employees?
Taxation	• What are the current levels of taxation? • What is the outlook for tax incentives?
Legal environment	• How effective and efficient is the local judiciary? • Is there any hope that the legal system will improve?
Bureaucratic obstacles to business	• What are the most common bureaucratic obstacles for business? • How easy or difficult it is to set up business in the country?

Crime and corruption	• Is crime a problem for business? • What is the level of corruption?
Infrastructure	• What is the quality of local transport infrastructure? • And telecommunications?
Foreign trade environment	• Is the country a World Trade Organization (WTO) member? • Does it belong to any trading blocs or regional free-trade areas?
Cost of building a business and brand	• How expensive is it to build a brand? • How much time will it take to do what is necessary to get the business off the ground?

eastern Europe economies, the latter tends also to be interested in advanced markets.

- MNCs do not acknowledge that eastern European markets operate under distinct business models and structures, and often merely transfer practices tested in advanced economies without considering adaptation.
- The board members of many MNCs have limited diversity in terms of culture and ethnic background and do not develop sufficient appreciation for the peculiarities of the eastern European markets.
- MNCs underestimate the potential and often early competition from smaller international and domestic companies, thus never accepting that they may be destined as a follower in eastern European markets.
- Economic and political crises also exist in eastern European markets, as discussed earlier, and have a significant impact on business performance. Top managers need to understand this, be prepared to adapt and introduce new tactics rather than changing strategy, which despite having short-term success, tends to be the wrong approach in long term.
- MNCs get alarmed by short-term slippages and cut costs to attain favorable temporary results, yet this is likely to have a structural impact on strategy implementation and long-term results.
- MNCs set unrealistic targets to achieve, which leave managers with limited maneuvering space and short-lived careers.

- MNCs fail to recognize that entering the market early is fundamental in establishing networks, developing brands, and learning the larger context from which it will operate.
- Senior leaders fail to recognize that developing a network of reliable contacts often requires establishing friendships with locals, which requires time and visibility in eastern European markets.
- MNCs fail to empower regional and country managers and delegate decision-making power to local managers.
- Foreign companies fail to recognize that eastern European markets are more price-sensitive and often stick to their pricing structures instead of adapting to local sensitivities.
- International firms fail to recognize that their product portfolio is not tailored to the lower and middle segments of emergent markets and do not develop innovations that are context oriented.
- Foreign companies underestimate the competition from local companies in emergent markets, which gradually move up from lower to upper segments. Local companies understand better than anyone about local markets, sometimes employ dubious practices, and often have the support of local governments.
- One of the largest obstacles that foreign companies face may be the unwillingness to change long-standing business practices.
- Another challenge is to appoint senior managers who are not familiar with the local market, culture, and language in emerging countries.
- The fact that demand is volatile and unpredictable in emerging and frontier markets may discourage multinationals, which often expect reliable market information.

The failure factors are numerous and diverse but as Pacek and Thorniley noted, it all boils down to a lack of adequate market entry preparation. Preparation requires companies to continuously research the external environment and know how to use internal resources to take

Table 5.4 Internal factors and sample questions

Resources	• How much time and money will be required? • Is the CEO committed to support business development and provide necessary resources and the senior managers? • What human resources are needed?
Products	• Is the product portfolio right for the market? • Will investment be available for developing new products?
Organization	• Could existing internal processes and operational practices help or hinder what is planned? • What existing capabilities can be drawn?
Risks	• Can the risks that have been identified be managed? • How would entry be financed?

advantage of opportunities. Hence, a preliminary audit that focuses on external and internal factors is essential. The external factors may be examined by posing questions concerning the market, the political environment, the economic environment, and the business environment, as depicted in Table 5.3.

By the same token, the internal factors must inquire about resources, products, organization, and risks, as depicted in Table 5.4.

Having done a preliminary external and internal audit, managers need to prepare a business proposal describing what to do, how to do it, by when, and resources required. Businesses must then ask themselves whether there are similar or better opportunities available in other eastern European markets. How then, can we compare the potential of different eastern European markets?

Ranking Eastern European Markets

According to the GlobalEdge[26] team at the International Business Center (IBC) at The Eli Broad Graduate School of Management, Michigan State University, in the state of Michigan, United States, there are three main reasons why eastern European markets are attractive. They are target markets, manufacturing bases, and sourcing destinations.

As manufacturing bases, they present advantages such as low wages, high-quality labor for manufacturing and assembly operations. Slovakia

---

[26] Based on GlobalEdge. http://globaledge.msu.edu/mpi

has been the world's largest producer of cars per capita[27] with currently three automobile assembly plants in the country, including Volkswagen's in Bratislava, PSA Peugeot Citroën's in Trnava, and Kia Motors' Žilina Plant, and by 2018, Jaguar Land Rover is set to open the country's fourth automobile assembly plant in Nitra.[28] The Czech Republic's long and rich scientific traditions, with research based on cooperation between universities, the Academy of Sciences of the Czech Republic and other specialized research centers often bring new inventions and contributions to market, including, but not limited to, the modern contact lens, the separation of modern blood types, and the production of Semtex plastic explosive. Several MNCs are already present in Lithuania, including PricewaterhouseCoopers, Ernst & Young, Societe Generale, UniCredit, Thermo Fisher Scientific, Phillip Morris, Kraft Foods, Mars, Marks & Spencer, GlaxoSmithKline, United Colors of Benetton, Deichmann, Statoil, Neste Oil, Lukoil, Tele2, Hesburger, and Modern Times Group.

From Indicators to Institutions

It is common wisdom that size and growth potential are the two best criteria to select an eastern European market. Not so for Khanna and Palepu[29] who argue that the lack of institutions, such as distribution systems, credit cards systems, or data research firms, is the primary factor to consider when entering into an emerging market. The eastern European markets are no different. For them, the fact that eastern European markets have poor institutions, thus, inefficient business operations, present the best business opportunities for companies operating in such dynamic markets. However, the ways businesses enter into eastern European markets is different, and are contingent upon variations presented by the institutions and the abilities of the firms.

Khanna and Palepu point out that the use of composite indexes to assess the potential of emerging markets, as executives often do, has limited use in eastern European markets because these indicators do not

---

[27] IndustryWeek (2008).
[28] Pitas (2015).
[29] Khanna and Palepu (2010).

capture the soft infrastructures and institutions. These composite indexes are useful in ranking market potential of countries when and only these countries have similar institutional environments. When soft infrastructures differ, we must then look at the institutional context in each market.

Best Opportunities Fill in Institutional Voids

From an institutional viewpoint, the market is a transactional place embedded in information and property rights, and eastern European markets are a place where one or both of these features are underdeveloped.[30] Most definitions of eastern European markets are descriptive based on poverty and growth indicators, and their *stage* as a transition economy. In contrast, a structural definition as proposed by Khanna and Palepu points to issues that are problematic, therefore allowing an immediate identification of solutions. Moreover, a structural definition allows us not only to understand commonalities among eastern European markets but also to understand what differentiates each of these markets. Finally, a structural approach provides a more precise understanding of the market dynamics that genuinely differentiates eastern European markets from advanced economies.

To illustrate, let us contrast the equity capital markets of South Korea and Chile. According to the International Finance Corporation (IFC) definition, South Korea is not an emerging market because it is an Organization for Economic Co-operation and Development (OECD) member; however, when we look at its equity capital market, we notice that until recently it was not functioning well. In other words, it has an institutional void. Chile, on the other hand, is considered an emerging market in Latin America but it has an efficient capital market; thus no institutional void appears in this sector. However Chile has institutional voids in other markets such as the products market. Similar factors exist among eastern European countries that are already members of the EU versus those that are not.

Strategy formulation in eastern European markets, therefore, must begin with a map of institutional voids. What works in the headquarters

---

[30] Khanna and Palepu (2010).

of a multinational company does not *per se* work in new locations with different institutional environments. The most common mistake companies do when entering eastern European markets is to overestimate the importance of past experience. This common error reflects a recency bias: a person assumes that recent successful experiences may be transferred to other places. A manager may incorrectly assume that the way people are motivated in one country would be the same in the new country (context). It may be assumed that everyone likes to be appreciated, but the way of expressing appreciation depends on the institutional environment. Khanna and Palepu point out that the human element is the cornerstone of operating in new contexts. Ultimately, human beings, who provide a mix of history, culture, and interactions, create institutions.

In short, based on Khanna and Palepu's institutional approach to eastern European markets, it is necessary to answer several questions, including but not limited to:

- Which institutions are working and missing?
- Which parts of our business model (in the home country) would be affected by these voids?
- How can we build competitive advantage based on our ability to navigate institutional voids?
- How can we profit from the structural reality of eastern European markets today by identifying opportunities to fill voids, serving as market intermediaries?

Strategies for Eastern European Markets

The work of Khanna and Palepu indicates that there are four generic strategic choices for companies operating in emerging markets, which also applies for eastern European markets:

- Replicate or adapt?
- Compete alone or collaborate?
- Accept or attempt to change market context?
- Enter, wait, or exit?

Eastern European markets attract two competing types of firms, the developed market-based multinationals and the emerging market-based companies. Both bring different advantages to fill institutional voids. MNCs bring brands, capital talent, and resources, such as the case of several ones based in Lithuania, whereas local companies contribute with local contacts and context knowledge. Because they have different strengths and resources, foreign and domestic firms will compete differently and must develop strategies accordingly. Table 5.5 summarizes the strategies and options for both MNCs and local companies.

Table 5.5 Responding to institutional voids

Strategic choice	Options for MNCs from developed countries	Options for eastern European market-based companies
Replicate or adapt?	• Replicate business model, exploiting relative advantage of global brand, credibility, know-how, talent, finance, and other factor inputs. • Adapt business models, products, or organizations to institutional voids.	• Copy business model from developed countries. • Exploit local knowledge, capabilities, and ability to navigate institutional voids to build tailored business models.
Compete alone or collaborate?	• Compete alone. • Acquire capabilities to navigate institutional voids through local partnerships or joint ventures (JVs).	• Compete alone. • Acquire capabilities from developed markets through partnerships or JVs with multinational companies to bypass institutional voids.
Accept or attempt to change market context?	• Take market context as given. • Fill institutional voids in service of own business.	• Take market context as given. • Fill institutional voids in service of own business.
Enter, wait, or exit?	• Enter or stay in market spite of institutional voids. • Emphasize opportunities elsewhere.	• Build business in home market in spite of institutional voids. • Exit home market early in corporate history if capabilities unrewarded at home.

Source: Khanna and Palepu (2010).

Anand P. Arkalgud[31] provides a good example of how companies fill institutional voids. Take the example of India, where road infrastructure is still underdeveloped in terms of quality and connectivity. Traditionally Tata Motors has been the dominant player in the auto industry but when it started to receive competition from Volvo in the truck segment and by Japanese automakers in the car segment, Tata responded. It created a mini-truck that not only provided more capacity and safety than the two- and three-wheeled pollutant vehicles used to access market areas but also an environmentally sound vehicle, one that could easily maneuver U-turns in such narrow streets.

Another case in India involved Coca Cola, who discovered that their beverages were being sold "warm." Coca Cola realized that it needed a solution to sell its product "chilled." The reason for the warm bottles was electricity supplies in these remote locations, which was unstable especially in summer periods. Thus the company developed a solar-powered cooler and partnered with a local refrigeration company.

Tarun Khanna and Krishna Palepu propose the following five contexts as a framework in assessing the institutional environment of any country. The five contexts include the markets needed to acquire input (product, labor, and capital), and markets needed to sell output. This is referred to as the products and services market. In addition to these three dimensions, the framework includes a broader sociopolitical context defined by political and social systems and degrees of openness. When applying the framework, managers need to ask a set of questions in each dimension. An example of these questions is indicated in Table 5.6.

Labor Markets

1. How strong is the country's education infrastructure, especially for technical and management training? Does it have a good elementary and secondary education system as well?
2. Do people study and do business in English or in another international language, or do they mainly speak a local language?
3. Are data available to help sort out the quality of the country's educational institutions?

---

[31] Arnand Prasad Arkalgud (2011).

Table 5.6 Framework to assess institutional voids

Institutional dimension	Questions
Product markets	1. Can companies easily obtain reliable data on customer tastes and purchase behaviors? Are there cultural barriers to market research? Do world-class market research firms operate in the country? 2. Can consumers easily obtain unbiased information on the quality of the goods and services they want to buy? Are there independent consumer organizations and publications that provide such information? 3. Can companies access raw materials and components of good quality? Is there a deep network of suppliers? Are there firms that assess suppliers' quality and reliability? Can companies enforce contracts with suppliers? 4. How strong are the logistics and transportation infrastructures? Have global logistics companies set up local operations? 5. Do large retail chains exist in the country? If so, do they cover the entire country or only the major cities? Do they reach all consumers or only wealthy ones? 6. Are there other types of distribution channels, such as direct-to-consumer channels and discount retail channels that deliver products to customers? 7. Is it difficult for multinationals to collect receivables from local retailers? 8. Do consumers use credit cards, or does cash dominate transactions? Can consumers get credit to make purchases? Are data on customer creditworthiness available? 9. What recourse do consumers have against false claims by companies or defective products and services? 10. How do companies deliver after-sales service to consumers? Is it possible to set up a nationwide service network? Are third-party service providers reliable? 11. Are consumers willing to try new products and services? Do they trust goods from local companies? How about from foreign companies? 12. What kind of product-related environmental and safety regulations are in place? How do the authorities enforce those regulations?

4. Can employees move easily from one company to another? Does the local culture support that movement? Do recruitment agencies facilitate executive mobility?

5. What are the major post recruitment-training needs of the people that multinationals hire locally?

6. Is pay for performance a standard practice? How much weight do executives give seniority, as opposed to merit, in making promotion decisions?

7. Would a company be able to enforce employment contracts with senior executives? Could it protect itself against executives who leave the firm and then compete against it? Could it stop employees from stealing trade secrets and intellectual property?

8. Does the local culture accept foreign managers? Do the laws allow a firm to transfer locally hired people to another country? Do managers want to stay or leave the nation?

9. How are the rights of workers protected? How strong are the country's trade unions? Do they defend workers' interests or only advance a political agenda?

10. Can companies use stock options and stock-based compensation schemes to motivate employees?

11. Do the laws and regulations limit a firm's ability to restructure, downsize, or shut down?

12. If a company were to adopt its local rivals' or suppliers' business practices, such as the use of child labor, would that tarnish its image overseas?

Capital Markets

1. How effective are the country's banks, insurance companies, and mutual funds at collecting savings and channeling them into investments?

2. Are financial institutions managed well? Is their decision making transparent? Do noneconomic considerations, such as family ties, influence their investment decisions?

3. Can companies raise large amounts of equity capital in the stock market? Is there a market for corporate debt?

4. Does a venture capital industry exist? If so, does it allow individuals with good ideas to raise funds?

5. How reliable are sources of information on company performance? Do the accounting standards and disclosure regulations permit investors and creditors to monitor company management?

6. Do independent financial analysts, rating agencies, and the media offer unbiased information on companies?

7. How effective are corporate governance norms and standards at protecting shareholder interests?

8. Are corporate boards independent and empowered, and do they have independent directors?

9. Are regulators effective at monitoring the banking industry and stock markets?

10. How well do the courts deal with fraud?

11. Do the laws permit companies to engage in hostile takeovers? Can shareholders organize themselves to remove entrenched managers through proxy fights?

12. Is there an orderly bankruptcy process that balances the interests of owners, creditors, and other stakeholders?

Political and Social System

1. To whom are the country's politicians accountable? Are there strong political groups that oppose the ruling party? Do elections take place regularly?

2. Are the roles of the legislative, executive, and judiciary clearly defined? What is the distribution of power between the central, state, and city governments?

3. Does the government go beyond regulating business to interfering in it or running companies?

4. Do the laws articulate and protect private property rights?

5. What is the quality of the country's bureaucrats? What are bureaucrats' incentives and career trajectories?

6. Is the judiciary independent? Do the courts adjudicate disputes and enforce contracts in a timely and impartial manner? How effective are the quasi-judicial regulatory institutions that set and enforce rules for business activities?

7. Do religious, linguistic, regional, and ethnic groups coexist peacefully, or are there tensions between them?

8. How vibrant and independent is the media? Are newspapers and magazines neutral, or do they represent sectarian interests?

9. Are nongovernmental organizations, civil rights groups, and environmental groups active in the country?

10. Do people tolerate corruption in business and government?

11. What role do family ties play in business?

12. Can strangers be trusted to honor a contract in the country?

Openness

1. Are the country's government, media, and people receptive to foreign investment? Do citizens trust companies and individuals from
some parts of the world more than others?

2. What restrictions does the government place on foreign investment?
Are those restrictions in place to facilitate the growth of domestic
companies, to protect state monopolies, or because people are suspicious of multinationals?

3. Can a company make greenfield investments and acquire local companies, or can it only break into the market by entering into JVs?
Will that company be free to choose partners based purely on economic considerations?

4. Does the country allow the presence of foreign intermediaries such
as market research and advertising firms, retailers, media companies,
banks, insurance companies, venture capital firms, auditing firms,
management consulting firms, and educational institutions?

5. How long does it take to start a new venture in the country? How
cumbersome are the government's procedures for permitting the
launch of a wholly foreign-owned business?

6. Are there restrictions on portfolio investments by overseas companies or on dividend repatriation by multinationals?

7. Does the market drive exchange rates, or does the government control them? If it's the latter, does the government try to maintain a
stable exchange rate, or does it try to favor domestic products over
imports by propping up the local currency?

8. What would be the impact of tariffs on a company's capital goods
and raw materials imports? How would import duties affect that
company's ability to manufacture its products locally versus exporting them from home?

9. Can a company set up its business anywhere in the country? If the government restricts the company's location choices, are its motives political, or is it inspired by a logical regional development strategy?

10. Has the country signed free-trade agreements with other nations? If so, do those agreements favor investments by companies from some parts of the world over others?

11. Does the government allow foreign executives to enter and leave the country freely? How difficult is it to get work permits for managers and engineers?

12. Does the country allow its citizens to travel abroad freely? Can ideas flow into the country unrestricted? Are people permitted to debate and accept those ideas?

Conclusion

Entry mode[32] is determined by product, market, and organizational factors. In regard to products and services, MNCs need to know whether the nature and range of the product or service, along with available marketing strategies, will require any adaptation. If so, they should consider a partner in the eastern European country they plan to enter. Usually a higher level of control and resource commitment in the foreign market is required for new or wider product offerings as well as higher levels of adaptation. When taking into account market factors, managers need to consider physical distance and experience, as well as identify appropriate marketing strategies and distribution channels, and priorities in revenues, costs, and profits.

Organizationally, major concerns are communication with foreign operations and control of overseas activities. One particular concern in foreign markets is the control of assets. Firms will prefer to internalize activities where there is a higher chance of opportunism by the partners in those markets.

For eastern Europe in particular, the region is poised for further growth, but some major obstacles remain on the road to prosperity. Chief

---

[32] http://globaledge.msu.edu/reference-desk/online-course-modules/market-research-and-entry

among them are social and economic tensions between ethnic groups, which can create problems ranging from labor markets conflicts to security risks for local businesses. Such dynamics are a special concern during periods of economic distress, high unemployment, and political unrest—known causes of nationalistic, antioutsider fervor.

The role of Russia is another concern. After the Soviet Union's fall, eastern Europe began shifting its allegiances to the West. With Russia struggling through its own economic problems at the time, it seemed likely that the realignment would endure. Today, trade with the West is up and several countries in the eastern European region are members of NATO and the EU.

But Russia should not be underestimated. It still plays an important role in the economies of eastern Europe. And Vladimir Putin has been frank about his ambition to create a Eurasian economic union, composed mainly of former Soviet states, as a counterweight to the EU. The long-term possibility of new realignments, this time toward the East, cannot be dismissed.

A case in point, most recently, the developments in Crimea have shown that despite years of change and effort toward global integration, Russian strategic goals in the region should not be overlooked. Putin's rule, reminiscent of the iron hands that governed Russia during the Soviet era, coupled with those weakened by the *Great Recession* in the West, is a recipe for a meal that's only served very cold.

Russia's annexation of Crimea, and even more importantly, the inability of the West to do much to prevent it, shows the complex political and economic relations in the region and the political, and military, power that Russia still holds. The brazen move by President Putin is a source of much anxiety in eastern Europe, particularly by neighbors of the big superpower, Poland being one of them. Several of the eastern European countries are NATO members, which eases a bit worries of invasion, but Russia remains a strong business partner to much of Europe and especially to countries from the former eastern European bloc, and economic sanctions against Russia would surely be felt and have a lasting effect across the continent.

CHAPTER 6

Political Risk in Eastern Europe

The transition of power from one regime to the next has traditionally been less than seamless. And all too often, this can lead to civil unrest in the streets to go along with the political conflict in the cabinet.

—Jared Wade

The decision of whether or not to invest in emerging markets should include an assessment of the political environment. Political discontinuities create a level of uncertainty for companies and individuals because they can lead to significant shifts in policies, regulations, governmental administration, and other potential risk factors that are not typically associated with advanced economies. Political instability can lead to restrictions on products, technology, and labor and even lead to practices of discrimination against foreign firms. This chapter will survey the impact of a series of political and economic risk assessments that include factors such as economic growth, labor unrest, social unrest, armed conflict, and how those elements interact with local investments and foreign direct investment (FDI).

Table 6.1 provides data across a series of government indicators. Table 6.2 follows these indicators with a set of rankings of political risk for Central and Eastern Europe (CEE) countries and nearby states in the region based on Freedom House indices. Countries are rated on a scale of 1 to 7, with 1 representing the highest and 7 the lowest level of democratic progress. The average rating across the categories of "Electoral Process," "Civil Society," "Independent Media," "National Democratic Governance," "Local Democratic Governance," "Judicial Framework and Independence," and "Corruption" is average to create the overall country score. Each ranking is calculated using a series of variables derived from the most recent political data available (as of December 2014).

Table 6.1 Country comparisons of select government indicators

Country	Total tax rate (% of commercial profits)	Proportion of seats held by women in national parliaments (%)	Population growth (annual %)	Public spending on education, total (% of GDP)	Literacy rate, (% of people ages 15 and above)
Bosnia and Herzegovina	23.3	21.4	-0.12	-	98.153
Bulgaria	27.0	24.6	-0.56	4.097	98.352
Croatia	18.8	23.8	-0.349	4.308	99.125
Czech Republic	48.5	19.5	0.102	4.507	-
Estonia	49.3	19.0	-0.03	5.152	99.863
Hungary	48.0	9.3	-0.233	4.712	99.374
Latvia	35.0	25.0	-1.034	4.935	99.896
Lithuania	42.6	24.1	-1.065	5.198	99.816
Montenegro	22.3	14.8	0.049	-	98.442
Poland	38.7	34.3	-0.013	5.171	99.748
Romania	43.2	13.5	-0.565	3.073	98.604
Slovakia	48.6	18.7	0.12	4.057	-
Slovenia	32.0	33.3	0.162	5.681	99.701
United States	43.8	18.3	0.716	5.42	-
China	64.6	23.4	0.494	1.907	95.124

Source: World Bank API.

Table 6.2 Country ranking by political risk

Country	Score
Slovenia	1.93
Estonia	1.96
Latvia	2.07
Poland	2.21
Czech Republic	2.21
Lithuania	2.36
Slovakia	2.64
Hungary	3.18
Bulgaria	3.29
Romania	3.46
Serbia	3.68
Croatia	3.68
Montenegro	3.89
Macedonia	4.07
Albania	4.14
Bosnia and Herzegovina	4.46
Kosovo	5.14

Note: The democracy scores and regime ratings are based on a scale of 1 to 7, with 1 representing the highest level of democratic progress and 7 the lowest. The 2015 ratings reflect the period January 1 through December 31, 2014.[1]

The reader might wonder why assess democratic governance in relation to political risk. A new field in political science has emerged, which attempts to explore greater connections between these two phenomena. There is a renewed interest in the how political risk affects multinational corporations operating in emerging markets, and much of the research has focused on the relationship between democratic institutions and the

---

[1] *Nations in Transit* is the only comprehensive, comparative, and multidimensional study of reform in the former communist states of Europe and Eurasia. *Nations in Transit* tracks the reform record of 29 countries and administrative areas and provides Freedom House's most in-depth data about this vast and important region. The 2014 edition covers events from January 1 through December 31, 2013. It is an updated edition of surveys published in 2013, 2012, 2011, 2010, 2009, 2008, 2007, 2006, 2005, 2004, 2003, 2002, 2001, 1999–2000, 1998, 1997, and 1995. For information, see www.freedomhouse.org/report-types/nations-transit#.VdSJr86lSLg

flow of FDI. Nathan Jensen finds, for example, the democratic regimes reduce risks for multinational investors, specifically through increasing constraints on the executive.[2]

These relationships, and the variables noted in the Freedom House rankings, will be explored in more detail in country-specific case studies in this chapter. Finally, the chapter will conclude with a discussion on the merits and challenges of attempting to quantify and index political risk.

The next section of this chapter will provide broader analysis and context for the results assigned to each state, including an update on consequential political events from 2015.

Bosnia and Herzegovina

In 1995, the presidents of Bosnia, Croatia, and Serbia signed a General Framework Agreement for Peace to end the war in Bosnia. Also known as the "Dayton Accords," the treaty preserved Bosnia as a single state made up of two parts, the Bosniak-Croat federation and the Bosnian Serb Republic, with Sarajevo remaining as the undivided capital city. The Bosnian administration split into two distinct entities: the Bosnia-Herzegovina federation, composed of 10 cantons, and the Bosnian-Serb Republic. The complexity of this structure weakens the central executive power, led by the Prime Minister Vjekoslav Bevanda, a Bosnian Croat. The rotating presidency chaired between the three representatives of the Bosnian Muslim, Croatian catholic, and Serbian orthodox communities maintains political inertia and struggles to transcend the ethnic divisions.[3]

In this context, widespread frustration has increased, culminating in February 2014, in an unprecedented outbreak of violence since peace was restored in 1995.[4] Exasperated by the negligent attitudes of privatized companies and unpaid for several months, workers initiated protests and demonstrations. Although most social classes and ethnic groups joined the protest, the movement was strongest within the Bosnia-Herzegovina federation, where nearly half of the prime ministers resigned. This situation highlights the deep unease caused by widespread corruption in a country

---

[2] Jensen (2008).

[3] For more information on the impact of the Dayton Accords, see Gelazis (2005).

[4] Dzidic (2014); Bilefsky (2014).

that had demonstrated the struggle of undertaking reforms. Compounded by widespread flooding that directly affected around one-quarter of the country's population, the lack of coordination and a late response increased frustration against the ruling political class as a whole.[5]

The country held legislative and presidential elections in October 2014, which focused mainly on economic and social issues: allegedly corrupt politics, stagnation, and high unemployment. At the time of the elections, the unemployment rate in Bosnia was roughly 27.5 percent, consistently among the highest in the Balkans. Two in three young people reported being jobless. Meanwhile, the salary of lawmakers was six times the country's average wage, making Bosnia's members of parliament among the richest in Europe.[6]

Voter turnout, however, suggests that citizens did not view the elections as an opportunity to change the country's fortunes. The National Democratic Institute reported that more than 90 percent of citizens surveyed believed the country was moving in the wrong direction and 75 percent were dissatisfied with the performance of governing institutions. Those who did vote supported traditionally "national" parties—SDA (The Party of Democratic Action, Bosnika), HDZ BiH (The Croatian Democratic Union of Bosnia and Herzegovina, Croat), and SNSD (Alliance of Independent Social Democrats, Serb). Thus, ethnic identity continued to be the main driver of politics.[7]

Meanwhile, in February 2014 the European Commission announced the end of negotiations regarding European Union (EU) membership, after 7 years of discussions, given the lack of reforms undertaken by the authorities. All levels of government are going to be faced with a dire economic situation. Following the census in spring 2015, the first since the Dayton Accords, political analysts expect to see ethnicity continue to frame political negotiations and the work of government. Finally, the business environment is hampered by corruption, inefficiency in the administrative, and judicial systems, as well as the size of the informal sector.

Table 6.3 displays a series of ratings across various government indicators for Bosnia and Herzegovina.

---

[5] Thomas (2014); *The Guardian* (2014).
[6] Nardelli, Dzidic, and Jukic (2014).
[7] National Democratic Institute for International Affairs (2014).

Table 6.3 Bosnia and Herzegovina—Nations in Transition Scores (2014)

	2005	2006	2007	2008	2009	2010	2011	2012	2013	2014
Electoral Process	3.25	3.00	3.00	3.00	3.00	3.25	3.25	3.25	3.25	3.25
Civil Society	3.75	3.75	3.50	3.50	3.50	3.50	3.50	3.50	3.50	3.50
Independent Media	4.00	4.00	4.00	4.25	4.50	4.75	4.75	4.75	4.75	4.76
National Democratic Governance	4.75	4.75	4.75	5.00	5.00	5.25	5.25	5.50	5.50	5.75
Local Democratic Governance	4.75	4.75	4.75	4.75	4.75	4.75	4.75	4.75	4.75	4.75
Judicial Framework and Independence	4.25	4.00	4.00	4.00	4.00	4.00	4.25	4.25	4.25	4.25
Corruption	4.50	4.25	4.25	4.25	4.50	4.50	4.50	4.50	4.75	4.75
Democracy Score	4.18	4.07	4.04	4.11	4.18	4.25	4.32	4.36	4.39	4.43

Note: The ratings are based on a scale of 1 to 7, with 1 representing the highest level of democratic progress and 7 the lowest. The democracy score is an average of ratings for the categories tracked in a given year.
Source: The data above are drawn from The World Bank, *World Development Indicators 2014*.

Bulgaria

As a post-communist state, Bulgaria has developed a system of democratic governance, joined North Atlantic Treaty Organization (NATO) in 2004 and the EU in 2007. The government has held a number of free and fair general, presidential, and local elections.

Over the last few years, however, the country has showed signs of increasing political instability in key democratic institutions. Since 2012, Bulgaria has had three governments, and inefficiency and graft within the political system, including the judiciary, are considered major obstacles to fighting high-level corruption and organized crime.[8] In 2014, an alleged personal conflict between Deylan Peevski, media mogul and politician, and Tsvetan Vassilev, the owner of Corporate Commercial Bank (KTB), led to a banking crisis, a government bailout, and numerous arrests.[9]

Further, the most recent parliament, elected in October 2014, became the most fragmented in Bulgaria's democratic history. With eight parties and alliances winning seats, the number of parties doubled compared to the previous parliament.[10] The Citizens for European Development of Bulgaria (GERB) emerged as the strongest party, returning to power after being ousted in February 2013.

The next challenge to Bulgaria's political system, as depicted in Table 6.4, will come in 2015, when the coalition government will work to preserve its majority in the parliament and simultaneously implement unpopular reforms. Local elections will be held in October and the coalition government will certainly be watching the returns.

Croatia

Croatia has been unable to gain momentum in implementing reforms as part of membership in the EU. Economic indicators show that the economy contracted for 12 successive quarters as the Social Democratic Party of Croatia (SDP) and its opposition, Croatian Democratic Union

---

[8] G.K. (2014); Novinite.com (2015); R.P. (2015).

[9] Brunwasser (2013); V.V.B. (2013); Novinite.com (2013).

[10] "Bulgaria's 2014 parliamentary election: CEC announces final results" (2014).

Table 6.4 Bulgaria—Nations in Transition Scores (2015)

	2006	2007	2008	2009	2010	2011	2012	2013	2014	2015
Electoral Process	1.75	1.75	1.75	1.75	1.75	1.75	2.00	2.00	2.25	2.25
Civil Society	2.75	2.50	2.50	2.50	2.50	2.50	2.50	2.50	2.25	2.25
Independent Media	3.25	3.50	3.50	3.75	3.75	3.75	3.75	4.00	4.00	4.00
National Democratic Governance	3.00	3.00	3.00	3.25	3.25	3.50	3.50	3.50	3.75	3.75
Local Democratic Governance	3.00	3.00	3.00	3.00	3.00	3.00	3.00	3.00	3.00	3.00
Judicial Framework and Independence	3.00	2.75	2.75	3.00	3.00	3.00	3.25	3.25	3.25	3.50
Corruption	3.75	3.75	3.50	4.00	4.00	4.00	4.00	4.00	4.25	4.25
Democracy Score	2.93	2.89	2.86	3.04	3.04	3.07	3.14	3.18	3.25	3.29

Note: The ratings are based on a scale of 1 to 7, with 1 representing the highest level of democratic progress and 7 the lowest. The democracy score is an average of ratings for the categories tracked in a given year.

Source: The data above are drawn from The World Bank, World Development Indicators 2015.

(HDZ), continued their political battles over the legacy of Yugoslav communism and privatization efforts in the 1990s. The inability to provide effective political and economic leadership has led decreasing citizen confidence in government and the emergence of a third party, Croatian Sustainable Development (ORaH).

In the context of an open, transparent society, the relationship between business interests and government officials is unhealthy. In November 2012, former Prime Minister Ivo Sanader was convicted on charges of bribery and kickbacks involving nearly 13 million euros in the biggest corruption trial in Croatia's history. In a prebankruptcy settlement, the government also forgave taxes owed by media conglomerate Europapress Holding (EPH), leading to criticisms of lack of transparency and favorable treatment in return for positive media coverage. There is widespread concern that other interests groups are using the referendum process to circumvent the legislature, some attempting to address economic concerns and others targeted at restricting the rights of minorities.

Even with the high-profile arrest of Zagreb Mayor Milan Bandic in October 2014 on suspicion of corruption and abuse of office, public distrust in government still remains high. Thus, Croatia's governing parties are preparing for confrontational campaigns in 2015. Table 6.5 provides the country's scores.

Czech Republic

The Czech Republic has established stable, democratic institutions and a vibrant civil society (see Table 6.6 below). In 2013, the country experienced a handful of national politics scandals, most notably the spying scandal and resignation of former Prime Minister Petr Nečas.[11] Centering on his alleged love affair with his chief of staff, the abuse of secret services, and alleged corruption, the center-right prime minister and his cabinet were forced out of office nearly a year before elections were scheduled.

While the new government formed under Prime Minister Bohuslav Sobotka places significant emphasis on fighting corruption, most analysts view the passage of the Law on Civil Service and other reforms as

---

[11] K.S. (2013).

Table 6.5 Croatia—Nations in Transition Scores (2015)

	2006	2007	2008	2009	2010	2011	2012	2013	2014	2015
Electoral Process	3.25	3.25	3.25	3.25	3.25	3.25	3.25	3.25	3.25	3.25
Civil Society	2.75	2.75	2.75	2.75	2.75	2.50	2.50	2.50	2.75	2.75
Independent Media	3.75	4.00	3.75	4.00	4.00	4.00	4.00	4.00	4.00	4.00
National Democratic Governance	3.50	3.50	3.50	3.50	3.50	3.50	3.50	3.50	3.50	3.50
Local Democratic Governance	3.75	3.75	3.75	3.75	3.75	3.75	3.75	3.75	3.75	3.75
Judicial Framework and Independence	4.25	4.25	4.25	4.25	4.25	4.25	4.25	4.25	4.50	4.50
Corruption	4.75	4.75	4.50	4.50	4.50	4.25	4.00	4.00	4.00	4.00
Democracy Score	3.71	3.75	3.64	3.71	3.71	3.64	3.61	3.61	3.68	3.68

Note: The ratings are based on a scale of 1 to 7, with 1 representing the highest level of democratic progress and 7 the lowest. The democracy score is an average of ratings for the categories tracked in a given year.
Source: The data above are drawn from The World Bank, *World Development Indicators 2015.*

Table 6.6 Czech Republic—Nations in Transition Scores (2015)

	2006	2007	2008	2009	2010	2011	2012	2013	2014	2015
Electoral Process	2.00	1.75	1.75	1.50	1.50	1.25	1.25	1.25	1.25	1.25
Civil Society	1.50	1.50	1.25	1.50	1.75	1.75	1.75	1.75	1.75	1.75
Independent Media	2.00	2.25	2.25	2.50	2.50	2.50	2.50	2.50	2.75	2.75
National Democratic Governance	2.50	3.00	2.75	2.75	2.75	2.75	2.75	2.75	3.00	2.75
Local Democratic Governance	2.00	1.75	1.75	1.75	1.75	1.75	1.75	1.75	1.75	1.75
Judicial Framework and Independence	2.25	2.00	2.00	2.25	2.00	2.00	2.00	1.75	1.75	1.75
Corruption	3.50	3.50	3.25	3.25	3.25	3.25	3.25	3.25	3.50	3.50
Democracy Score	2.25	2.25	2.14	2.18	2.21	2.18	2.18	2.14	2.15	2.21

Note: The ratings are based on a scale of 1 to 7, with 1 representing the highest level of democratic progress and 7 the lowest. The democracy score is an average of ratings for the categories tracked in a given year.

Source: The data above are drawn from The World Bank, *World Development Indicators 2015*.

modest.[12] The government maintained high approval ratings throughout the year, with around 40 to50 percent of respondents expressing trust in the coalition.[13]

Former Prime Minister Milos Zeman won the first direct Czech presidential election in January 2013, beating conservative Foreign Minister Karel Schwarzenberg by a margin of 55 percent to 45 percent. Unlike his predecessor, the notoriously euro-sceptic Vaclav Klaus, President Zeman describes himself as a euro-federalist and has advocated closer European integration, though he believes that the Czech Republic should take its time over joining the euro.[14] Other statements from the president defending authoritarian regimes around the world, including China, questioning Western involvement in Ukraine, and xenophobic anti-Islamic speeches have drawn severe criticism from the population. By the end of 2014, the president's approval ratings had significantly dropped.[15]

The government has been eager to support exports, including signing a joint declaration with China in April 2014. Economic cooperation will also be supported by new direct flight connections, operational in October 2015, from Prague to Beijing with Hainan Airlines (and planned route from Prague to Shanghai). These projects are strongly supported by the Czech government, in addition to a plan to create economic and technological zones for Chinese investors in the Moravia-Silesia region. The agreement did draw criticism from the Czech public because of a clause noting that Tibet is Chinese territory, but the biggest challenge facing the government is the Czech deficit in the bilateral trade. The imports from China to the Czech Republic reached 359 billion Kč and Czech exports to China remained at 42 billion Kč in 2014, creating a deficit of 317 billion Kč.[16]

The coalition government will need to continue to work together to maintain stability and achieve successful legislative reform, and with no elections scheduled for 2015, there is reason to be optimistic. The

---

[12] Mráz (2015).

[13] Kunštát (2015).

[14] Czech Republic Profile—Leaders (2015).

[15] Czech Republic Profile—Leaders (2015).

[16] Gatien Du Bois and Michael Davidova (2015); Czech News Agency (2015).

government should also benefit from continuing improvement in the economy, without much danger of slipping back into recession.

Estonia

In early 2014, the Estonian government formed a new cabinet following the resignation of veteran Prime Minister Andrus Ansip after 9 years, who accepted a new position in the European Commission. The country held elections in 2015 and re-elected the governing Reform Party, led by Prime Minister Taavi Roivas. The youngest prime minister in Europe, Roivas called for an "Estonian-minded government" in the weeks leading up the election.

Perhaps reflecting the most significant issue facing Estonia today is public-political debate on economic issues and fears over defense due to Russia's actions in Ukraine. Estonia has seen a number of airspace violations by Russia, and last year a security official was detained on accusations of spying by Russian security agencies. Prime Minister Roivas voiced concerns that Russia could seek to destabilize other former Soviet states following the conflict in Ukraine, while the Centre Party leader, Edgar Saavisar, favors a friendlier approach to Moscow, and has previously suggested that Russia's annexation of Crimea could be legitimate. Saavisar's position reflects nearly one-quarter of Estonia's 1.3 million population who identify themselves as ethnic Russians, and many of who are Centre Party supporters.[17] Saavisar lost some political momentum for his case, however, when he was arrested on charges of bribery in September 2015.

Estonia is consistently acknowledged as one of the least corrupt countries in the EU, according to most recent 2014 and 2015 indices. Key anticorruption measures adopted in 2013 established a framework for enhancing accountability in the civil sector. Although some scandals involving bribery and political influence led to public discussions about lobbying practices, the country remains highly rated in terms of transparency.[18]

---

[17] Mardiste (2015).

[18] Hinsburg, Matt, and Vinni (2015).

Table 6.7 Estonia—Nations in Transition Scores (2015)

	2006	2007	2008	2009	2010	2011	2012	2013	2014	2015
Electoral Process	1.50	1.50	1.50	1.50	1.75	1.75	1.75	1.75	1.75	1.75
Civil Society	2.00	2.00	1.75	1.75	1.75	1.75	1.75	1.75	1.75	1.75
Independent Media	1.50	1.50	1.50	1.50	1.50	1.50	1.50	1.50	1.50	1.50
National Democratic Governance	2.25	2.25	2.25	2.25	2.25	2.25	2.25	2.25	2.25	2.25
Local Democratic Governance	2.50	2.50	2.50	2.50	2.50	2.50	2.50	2.50	2.50	2.50
Judicial Framework and Independence	1.50	1.50	1.50	1.50	1.50	1.50	1.50	1.50	1.50	1.50
Corruption	2.50	2.50	2.50	2.50	2.50	2.25	2.25	2.50	2.50	2.50
Democracy Score	1.96	1.96	1.93	1.93	1.96	1.93	1.93	1.96	1.96	1.96

Note: The ratings are based on a scale of 1 to 7, with 1 representing the highest level of democratic progress and 7 the lowest. The democracy score is an average of ratings for the categories tracked in a given year.
Source: The data above are drawn from The World Bank, World Development Indicators 2015.

Hungary

The government of Prime Minister Viktor Orbán consisting of the right-wing Young Democrats' Alliance-Hungary Civic Union (Fidesz) and the Christian Democratic People's Party (KDNP) was elected to a second four year term in 2014, winning a two-third majority in the parliament. Those assessing democratic governance, transparency, and judicial independence in Hungary have good reasons to be concerned (see Table 6.8 below). In a July 2014 speech, Orbán openly discussed his plans to construct an "illiberal democracy."

The Fidesz-controlled legislature passed a law in 2010 that established a body, appointed by the parliament—and thus by Fidesz—to regulate the media. The law made it a crime, punishable by fines of up to $900,000, to publish "imbalanced news coverage" or material deemed "insulting" to a group or "the majority" or that insulted "public morality."

In 2011, parliament passed a law on the "Right of Freedom of Conscience and Religion," which bore the same relation to freedom of conscience that the media law did to freedom of speech. The law required religious organizations to gain official approval through a two-third vote of parliament, thus creating separate classes of favored and nonfavored faiths.

Peter Kreko, Director of the Political Capital Institute, a think tank in Budapest, admits that he is alarmed by the racial rhetoric Orbán has employed since the refugee crisis began because he is worried that it is effective in engendering support for Orbán's misguided policies. "At bottom," he says, "the real source of Orbán's power is the popularity of his ideas." In that sense, the problem lies with the Hungarian people. As James Staub and other political analysts note, not long ago Hungary was widely considered the most progressive of the ex-Soviet states. Growing disillusionment with democracy and the free market over the last decade might make Hungarians receptive to ideas they once would have rejected.

These circumstances are further complicated by close ties between political and economic elites, which remain a major source of corruption for the state. Despite several corruption scandals surfacing in Hungarian media, whistleblowers and the U.S. State Department allege that

Table 6.8 Hungary—Nations in Transit Scores (2015)

	2006	2007	2008	2009	2010	2011	2012	2013	2014	2015
Electoral Process	1.25	1.75	1.75	1.75	1.75	1.75	2.25	2.25	2.25	2.75
Civil Society	1.25	1.50	1.50	1.75	1.75	2.00	2.00	2.25	2.25	2.50
Independent Media	2.50	2.50	2.50	2.50	2.75	3.25	3.50	3.50	3.50	3.75
National Democratic Governance	2.00	2.25	2.25	2.50	2.50	3.00	3.50	3.50	3.75	3.75
Local Democratic Governance	2.25	2.25	2.25	2.50	2.50	2.50	2.50	2.75	2.75	3.00
Judicial Framework and Independence	1.75	1.75	1.75	1.75	1.75	2.00	2.25	2.75	2.50	2.75
Corruption	3.00	3.00	3.00	3.25	3.50	3.50	3.50	3.50	3.75	3.75
Democracy Score	2.00	2.14	2.14	2.29	2.39	2.61	2.86	2.89	2.96	3.18

Note: The ratings are based on a scale of 1 to 7, with 1 representing the highest level of democratic progress and 7 the lowest. The democracy score is an average of ratings for the categories tracked in a given year.
Source: The data above are drawn from The World Bank, *World Development Indicators 2015*.

numerous cases have gone uninvestigated by the government.[19] Hungary's corruption rating remains unchanged for the current year, despite ratings declining in nearly every other category for the Nations in Transit scores.

Latvia

In January 2014, Laimdota Straujuma, an economist and member of the center-right Unity Party, was sworn in as Latvia's first female prime minister. Her term was short-lived, however, as she resigned in December 2015 amid political infighting within her three-way ruling coalition, leaving the small Baltic nation bereft of a government at a time of growing tension with neighboring Russia.[20]

Despite these setbacks in national democratic governance (see Table 6.9 below), Latvia continues to craft a new national vision for the state. It successfully administered European Parliament and Saeima elections in 2014 and assumed the presidency of the Council of the EU in 2015.

The security crisis in eastern Ukraine remains a significant concern for Latvian domestic and foreign policy, as in Estonia and other border states. Russian warships and military planes operated very closely to Latvian waters and airspace throughout 2014, prompting widespread fears that Latvia's Russian minority might be the next to be "liberated" by Moscow.[21] According to Freedom House and other reports, the Latvian government leadership "maintained a united position on the need to protect Latvia from potential Russian military aggression and lobbied hard to increase the presence of NATO troops in Latvia."[22]

Public opinion polls from March 2014 indicate that an increased NATO presence was supported by 50 percent of respondents.[23] By year's

---

[19] Human Rights First (2014); Gulyas (2014); Szakacs (2014).

[20] "Apstiprināta jaunā valdība Laimdotas Straujumas vadībā" (2014); Kaza (2015).

[21] "Šogad Krievijas bruņoto spēku lidmašīnas un kuģi Latvijai pietuvojušies vairāk nekā 250 reizes" (2014).

[22] Bukovskis and Sprūds (2015).

[23] Aprinķis.lv (2014).

Table 6.9 Latvia—Nations in Transition Scores (2015)

	2006	2007	2008	2009	2010	2011	2012	2013	2014	2015
Electoral Process	1.75	2.00	2.00	2.00	2.00	1.75	1.75	1.75	1.75	1.75
Civil Society	1.75	1.75	1.75	1.75	1.75	1.75	1.75	1.75	1.75	1.75
Independent Media	1.50	1.50	1.75	1.75	1.75	1.75	1.75	1.75	2.00	2.00
National Democratic Governance	2.00	2.00	2.00	2.50	2.50	2.25	2.25	2.25	2.00	2.00
Local Democratic Governance	2.50	2.50	2.25	2.25	2.25	2.25	2.25	2.25	2.25	2.25
Judicial Framework and Independence	1.75	1.75	1.75	1.75	1.75	1.75	1.75	1.75	1.75	1.75
Corruption	3.25	3.00	3.00	3.25	3.25	3.50	3.25	3.00	3.00	3.00
Democracy Score	2.07	2.07	2.07	2.18	2.18	2.14	2.11	2.07	2.07	2.07

Note: The ratings are based on a scale of 1 to 7, with 1 representing the highest level of democratic progress and 7 the lowest. The democracy score is an average of ratings for the categories tracked in a given year.
Source: The data above are drawn from The World Bank, *World Development Indicators 2015*.

end, Latvia—together with its Baltic neighbors, Estonia and Lithuania—had received commitments of military solidarity from NATO as a whole and several individual member states, including the United Kingdom, the United States, Germany, and Norway. Latvia also pledged to increase military spending to 2 percent of gross domestic product (GDP) by the year 2020, with special emphasis on improved weaponry and airspace defense.[24]

Lithuania

In May 2014, incumbent President Dalia Grybauskaitė won the presidential run-off against Zigmantas Balčytis, a member of the LSDP (Social Democratic Party of Lithuania). Popular among Lithuanians, Grybauskaitė became the first Lithuanian president elected to two consecutive terms. Lithuanian politics are composed of shifting coalitions among several different parties. The two largest minority groups, Polish (6.6 percent of the population) and Russian (5.8 percent), are represented by the LLRA (Electoral Action of Poles in Lithuania) and the Russian Alliance parties who plan to form a coalition for local elections in 2015.[25]

While corruption remains an issue in Lithuania, Freedom House and other sources note that progress has been achieved (see Table 6.10 below). Lithuania ranked 39 out of 175 countries and territories in Transparency International's 2014 Corruption Perceptions Index.[26] The EU has noted Lithuania's strong commitment to fighting corruption and venerable anticorruption legal framework. However, the EU also noted room for improvement; Lithuania has the highest percentage in the EU of people who have been asked or were expected to pay a bribe: 29 percent.[27]

In 2014, Grybauskaitė declared that she would not approve ministers whose deputies were included on a so-called "blacklist" created by the Secret Investigation Service (STT). The blacklist contained eight vice-ministers who were allegedly involved in corruption cases. All eight

---

[24] Lsm.lv (2014).
[25] "Stirring the Pot" (2015).
[26] www.transparency.org/cpi2014/results
[27] European Commission (2015e).

Table 6.10 Lithuania—Nations in Transition Scores (2015)

	2006	2007	2008	2009	2010	2011	2012	2013	2014	2015
Electoral Process	1.75	1.75	1.75	1.75	1.75	1.75	1.75	2.00	2.00	2.00
Civil Society	1.50	1.75	1.75	1.75	1.75	1.75	1.75	1.75	1.75	1.75
Independent Media	1.75	1.75	1.75	1.75	1.75	1.75	2.00	2.00	2.25	2.25
National Democratic Governance	2.50	2.50	2.50	2.75	2.75	2.75	2.75	2.75	2.75	2.75
Local Democratic Governance	2.50	2.50	2.50	2.50	2.50	2.50	2.50	2.50	2.50	2.50
Judicial Framework and Independence	1.50	1.75	1.75	1.75	1.75	1.75	1.75	1.75	1.75	1.75
Corruption	4.00	4.00	3.75	3.75	3.50	3.50	3.50	3.50	3.50	3.50
Democracy Score	2.21	2.29	2.25	2.29	2.25	2.25	2.29	2.32	2.36	2.36

Note: The ratings are based on a scale of 1 to 7, with 1 representing the highest level of democratic progress and 7 the lowest. The democracy score is an average of ratings for the categories tracked in a given year.
Source: The data above are drawn from The World Bank, *World Development Indicators 2015.*

vice-ministers rapidly resigned, including one from the ministry of justice, one from the ministry of agriculture, three from the ministry of environment, and three from the ministry of transport and communications.[28]

After completing its 6-month presidency at the council of the EU, Lithuania prepared for the introduction of the euro despite public ambivalence.[29] In January of 2015, the council recognized Lithuania's accession to the eurozone and the country became its 19th member. Lithuania actively pushed for membership in the Organization for Economic Cooperation and Development (OECD), and in October 2015, the OECD outlined a plan for Lithuanian accession.[30] The Heritage Foundation increased the economic freedom score for Lithuania in 2015, raising to the 15th freest in the world.[31] Lithuania also improved on the World Economic Forum's Global Competitiveness Report in 2015, moving up to 5 spots to 36th place. This is the 2nd year in a row that Lithuania has seen a significant rankings increase in both sets of reports.[32]

Poland

Although recent articles have praised central and eastern Europe as a "tranquil port in emerging market storm," there are still reasons to be cautious.[33] Poland, central Europe's biggest economy and "anchor" of stability, will hold parliamentary elections in October that may bring a change of government. In Poland, central and eastern Europe's biggest economy, the prime minister has the most powers, but the president wields clout as head of the armed forces, has a say in foreign policy and the power to veto legislation.

In this context, *Reuters* reports that the presidential election has become a dress rehearsal for the parliamentary vote, when Prime Minister

---

[28] "Lithuanian Minister of Interior Resigns" (2015); Jurkynas (2015).

[29] "Vyriausybės naujienlaiškis" (2014).

[30] "OECD Established Roadmap for Membership with Lithuania" (2015).

[31] www.heritage.org/index/ranking

[32] http://reports.weforum.org/global-competitiveness-report-2015-2016/competitiveness-rankings/

[33] Jones (2015).

Ewa Kopacz's center-right Civic Platform party will face a strong challenge from the euro-sceptic Law and Justice Party (PiS), a significant
front-runner in the polls.[34]

Although the government has a strong record on the economy and
Poland was the only EU country to avoid recession after the 2008 financial crash (see Chapter 6), it is still struggling to counter a sense among
voters that they want to see some fresh faces in power (see Table 6.11
below). The government also lost its strongest political asset last year
when Donald Tusk left his position as prime minister to take a senior EU
post in Brussels. In an interview in 2014, Rafal Pankowski, an expert on
Poland's political rights, expressed concerns about the impact of Tusks's
departure: "Without him it is difficult to imagine how the party will sur-
vive and maintain the same level of support," he commented. "There is
no successor who has the same track record as he does. He holds the party
together."[35]

In May 2015, Polish President Bronsilaw Komorowski campaigned
on a platform that he is a "safe pair of hands" on national security. That
message appealed to voters worried that after Russia's intervention in
Ukraine, Poland could become the next target. Andrzej Duda, the conservative challenger, campaigned on a promise to lower the retirement age
and warned that if Poland adopts the euro currency, which Komorowski
has said he wants eventually to happen, the prices of goods will go up. On
May 24, 2015, *Global Press* reported that Komorowski conceded defeat
to conservative challenger Duda, a result that set off alarms across the
government, which faces its own election race later this year. The victory for 43-year-old Duda marks the first major electoral wins in almost
a decade for his party, the opposition Law and Justice Party. It is close
to the Catholic Church, socially conservative, and markets see it as less
business-friendly than the governing Civic Platform. These concerns were
further indicated when Poland's zloty currency fell 1 percent against the
euro after the election exit poll was released, a sign that some investors are
already expecting a change in government.[36]

---

[34] Goclowski and Florkiewicz (2015).
[35] Day and Waterfeld (2014).
[36] Sobczak and Barteczko (2015).

Table 6.11 Poland—Nations in Transition Scores (2015)

	2006	2007	2008	2009	2010	2011	2012	2013	2014	2015
Electoral Process	1.75	2.00	2.00	2.00	1.75	1.50	1.25	1.25	1.25	1.50
Civil Society	1.25	1.50	1.25	1.50	1.50	1.50	1.50	1.50	1.50	1.50
Independent Media	1.75	2.25	2.25	2.00	2.25	2.25	2.25	2.50	2.50	2.50
National Democratic Governance	2.75	3.25	3.50	3.25	3.25	2.75	32.50	2.50	2.50	2.50
Local Democratic Governance	2.00	2.25	2.25	2.00	1.75	1.75	1.75	1.75	1.50	1.50
Judicial Framework and Independence	2.25	2.25	2.50	2.25	2.50	2.50	2.50	2.50	2.50	2.50
Corruption	3.25	3.00	3.00	2.75	3.25	3.25	3.25	3.25	3.50	3.50
Democracy Score	2.14	2.36	2.39	2.25	2.32	2.21	2.14	2.18	2.18	2.21

Note: The ratings are based on a scale of 1 to 7, with 1 representing the highest level of democratic progress and 7 the lowest. The democracy score is an average of ratings for the categories tracked in a given year.

Source: The data above are drawn from The World Bank, *World Development Indicators 2015*.

Romania

Many political analysts were surprised by the 2014 election of Klaus Iohannis, former mayor of Sibiu and an ethnic German, as the next president of Romania. He achieved a record number of votes from nearly 400,000 Romanians living abroad, and with nearly 1.5 million Facebook followers, he has more digital "fans" than most European politicians. His victory over the political machine of Victor Ponta, the Prime Minister, is regarded as a strong commitment among Romanians for cleaner, more transparent politics (see Table 6.12 below).

In a recent survey, over 90 percent of Romanians expressed beliefs that graft is endemic among their political and economic elites. Freedom House and other corruption indices noted that 2014 was the most successful year so far for the National Anticorruption Directorate (DNA). Prosecutors working with the organization secured important convictions in both the public and private sector, including exposing a serious corruption scandal that operated under four successive government administrations. All told, DNA prosecutors won more than 1,000 convictions and indicted more than 1,100 suspects in 2014; more than 90 percent of those indicted were convicted.

Additionally, President Iohannis faces the difficult balance in foreign policy between positive relations with Russia and the EU. In the fall of 2015, he affirmed Romania's commitment to EU sanctions imposed on Russia for its actions in Ukraine and welcomed NATO's increasing presence in an increasingly insecure border region.[37]

Serbia

On the promise of economic revitalization and a commitment to anti-corruption, the Serbian Progressive Party (SNS) won nearly two-third of the seats in parliament in the 2014 elections. This mandate allowed the party to adopt new legislation enabling future EU membership and

---

[37] "Romania Supports Sanctions Against Russia until Full Implementation of Minsk Agreements" (2015).

Table 6.12 Romania—Nations in Transition Scores (2015)

	2006	2007	2008	2009	2010	2011	2012	2013	2014	2015
Electoral Process	2.75	2.75	2.75	2.50	2.75	2.75	3.00	3.00	3.00	3.25
Civil Society	2.25	2.25	2.25	2.50	2.50	2.50	2.50	2.50	2.50	2.50
Independent Media	4.00	3.75	3.75	3.75	4.00	4.00	4.00	4.25	4.25	4.25
National Democratic Governance	3.50	3.50	3.75	3.75	4.00	3.75	3.75	4.00	3.75	3.75
Local Democratic Governance	3.00	3.00	3.00	3.00	3.00	3.00	3.00	3.00	3.00	3.00
Judicial Framework and Independence	4.00	3.75	4.00	4.00	4.00	4.00	3.75	3.75	3.75	3.75
Corruption	4.25	4.00	4.00	4.00	4.00	4.00	4.00	4.00	4.00	3.75
Democracy Score	3.39	3.29	3.36	3.36	3.46	3.43	3.43	3.50	3.46	3.46

Note: The ratings are based on a scale of 1 to 7, with 1 representing the highest level of democratic progress and 7 the lowest. The democracy score is an average of ratings for the categories tracked in a given year.
Source: The data above are drawn from The World Bank, *World Development Indicators 2015*.

efforts to normalize relations with Kosovo, which marks a sharp departure from the ultra-nationalism espoused by the state for decades following the break-up of Yugoslavia.[38]

The government, under the leadership of Prime Minister Aleksandar Vucic, is attempting to attract foreign investors and improve the environment for doing business in Serbia. Traditionally a strong ally of the Russian government, Vucic has signaled a strong desire to align Serbia with the United States and EU.[39] Jose Manuel Barroso, then European Commission president, hailed accession negotiations as "an entirely new chapter in our relations and a major success."[40] EU officials, however, recently emphasized that no new members would be taken before 2020. For Serbia, the key will be the implementation of the 2013 Kosovo agreement, improvement in the efficiency of its judicial processes, and the SNS Party's ability to make good on its anticorruption promises (see Table 6.13 below).

Slovakia

The 2014 elections marked a historic shift in Slovak electoral politics. In a surprise upset, Robert Fico, Slovakia's prime minister, lost the presidential run-off election to Andrej Kiska, a businessman and philanthropist. Prior to the March election, Fico dominated domestic politics in Slovakia for most of the last decade.[41] This was followed by the equally surprising resignation of Pavol Paška, then fellow Smer Party speaker of parliament, following a corruption scandal.[42] These political shifts highlight the unfortunate lack of transparency, as well as continuing clientelism and corrupt practices that persist across the country. No prosecutions moved forward against prominent officials, including Paška in 2014.

Slovakia does have a progressive institutional framework for fighting graft and improving transparency in the public sphere, but corruption

---

[38] "Serbian Prime Minister Vucic Pledges Millions to Srebrenica" (2015).

[39] Skrpec (2015).

[40] European Commission (2014).

[41] "Fico's Suprising Defeat" (2014).

[42] Cuprik (2014).

Table 6.13 Serbia—Nations in Transition Scores (2015)

	2005	2006	2007	2008	2009	2010	2011	2012	2013	2014
Electoral Process	3.25	3.25	3.25	3.25	3.25	3.25	3.25	3.25	3.25	3.25
Civil Society	2.75	2.75	2.75	2.75	2.50	2.25	2.25	2.25	2.25	2.25
Independent Media	3.25	3.50	3.75	3.75	4.00	4.00	4.00	4.00	4.00	4.25
National Democratic Governance	4.00	3.75	4.00	4.00	3.75	3.75	3.75	3.75	3.75	3.75
Local Democratic Governance	3.75	3.75	3.75	3.75	3.50	3.50	3.50	3.50	3.50	3.50
Judicial Framework and Independence	4.25	4.25	4.50	4.50	4.50	4.50	4.50	4.50	4.50	4.50
Corruption	4.75	4.50	4.50	4.50	4.50	4.25	4.25	4.25	4.25	4.25
Democracy Score	3.71	3.68	3.79	3.79	3.71	3.64	3.64	3.64	3.64	3.68

Note: The ratings are based on a scale of 1 to 7, with 1 representing the highest level of democratic progress and 7 the lowest. The democracy score is an average of ratings for the categories tracked in a given year.
Source: The data above are drawn from The World Bank, *World Development Indicators 2015*.

remains a serious problem, most notably in public procurement and the health sector (see Table 6.14).[43] The Slovak constitution does include a provision on conflict of interest, barring the president, cabinet members, constitutional court justices, and other top officials from pursuing any business activities, receiving pay for brokering deals between the government and private entities or corporations, or receiving income in excess of the minimum wage generated by a side job.[44] However, public officials are not required to give a full public accounting of the sources of their income and there are no laws regulating the private gifts they accept.[45]

According to Transparency International's 2014 Corruption Perceptions Index, one in five households in Slovakia reported paying a bribe for health care every year, and health care was perceived as the sector most affected by corruption. Slovakia's ranking in the Transparency International study improved in 2014, primarily because of the new law protecting whistleblowers, new legislation for the formation of political parties, and the proposed e-marketplace for public procurement bids (although the report expressed reservations about implementation of new laws).[46]

As in many of the other CEE states, President Kiska also faces the diplomatic and foreign policy challenges of balancing relations with Russia and the West. In a statement to the NATO 2020 conference, he remarked:

> This new situation is not a challenge only for military strategic planners. It is a profound political and psychological challenge. Because the single most important and historically verified purpose of NATO is not only its capacity to defend sovereignty of members states by military force. But it's also our ability to deter anyone who would like to think about testing their own capacity.[47]

In a follow-up tweet to the conference, he reinforced his belief that "NATO is not a winter coat" to be put on when cold, but that the alliance

---

[43] Cunningham (2015).

[44] Dumbrovsky (2014).

[45] Terenzani-Stankova (2014).

[46] Transparency International (2014); Radka Minecherová (2014).

[47] Andrej Kiska (2015).

Table 6.14 Slovakia—Nations in Transition Scores (2015)

	2006	2007	2008	2009	2010	2011	2012	2013	2014	2015
Electoral Process	1.25	1.50	1.50	1.50	1.75	1.50	1.50	1.50	1.50	1.50
Civil Society	1.25	1.50	1.50	1.75	1.75	1.75	1.75	1.75	1.75	1.75
Independent Media	2.25	2.25	2.50	2.75	3.00	3.00	2.75	2.75	2.75	3.00
National Democratic Governance	2.00	2.25	2.50	2.75	3.00	2.75	2.75	2.75	3.00	3.00
Local Democratic Governance	2.00	2.00	2.25	2.50	2.50	2.50	2.50	2.50	2.50	2.50
Judicial Framework and Independence	2.00	2.25	2.50	2.75	3.00	2.75	2.75	3.00	3.00	3.00
Corruption	3.00	3.25	3.25	3.25	3.75	3.50	3.50	3.75	3.75	3.75
Democracy Score	1.96	2.14	2.29	2.46	2.68	2.54	2.50	2.57	2.61	2.64

Note: The ratings are based on a scale of 1 to 7, with 1 representing the highest level of democratic progress and 7 the lowest. The democracy score is an average of ratings for the categories tracked in a given year.
Source: The data above are drawn from The World Bank, World Development Indicators 2015.

requires a more enduring commitment from all parties to be an effective deterrent.

Slovenia

Slovenia is one of the most politically and economically integrated countries in the region, joining the United Nations in 1992, the Council of Europe in 1993, and the EU and NATO in 2004 (see scores in Table 6.15 below). The state adopted the euro currency and entered the Schengen Area in 2007, followed by achieving full membership in the OECD in 2010.

As Slovenia's economy showed strong signs of recovery in 2014, political conflict and instability set in. Prime Minister Alenka Bratusek resigned from her post after serving only 13 months, leaving no clear leadership or mandate for the government. This prompted concerns among political analysts who viewed the instability as a risk to the structural reform agenda for 2014 to 2015, including the privatization of key state-owned enterprises.[48] Since that time, Bratusek has been under investigation by Slovenian antigraft authorities on suspicion of abuse of power.[49]

In August 2014, Dr. Miro Cerar assumed the position of prime minister and emphasized long-term sustainable economic growth as the first priority of his administration. In an initial step, the state adopted the asset management strategy for state-owned enterprises, and this commitment was echoed in his statements at the FDI Summit of 2014. When interviewed by the *Slovenia Times*, Cerar reiterated that the government has been

> preparing and implementing measures to lower the administrative burden, amend labor legislation, and lower labor costs. On the other hand, we are creating better business conditions by building and maintaining the infrastructure, promoting and further developing our educational system and innovation-oriented ecosystems.[50]

---

[48] "Slovenia Prime Minister Alenka Bratusek Resigns" (2014).

[49] "Police Search Home of Former Slovenian Premier" (2015).

[50] Drolc (2015).

Table 6.15 Slovenia—Nations in Transition Scores (2015)

	2006	2007	2008	2009	2010	2011	2012	2013	2014	2015
Electoral Process	1.50	1.50	1.50	1.50	1.50	1.50	1.50	1.50	1.50	1.50
Civil Society	1.75	2.00	2.00	2.00	2.00	2.00	2.00	2.00	2.00	2.00
Independent Media	1.75	2.00	2.25	2.25	2.25	2.25	2.25	2.25	2.25	2.25
National Democratic Governance	2.00	2.00	2.00	2.00	2.00	2.00	2.00	2.00	2.00	2.00
Local Democratic Governance	1.50	1.50	1.50	1.50	1.50	1.50	1.50	1.50	1.50	1.50
Judicial Framework and Independence	1.50	1.50	1.50	1.75	1.75	1.75	1.75	1.75	1.75	1.75
Corruption	2.25	2.25	2.25	2.50	2.50	2.50	2.25	2.25	2.50	2.50
Democracy Score	1.75	1.82	1.86	1.93	1.93	1.93	1.89	1.89	1.93	1.93

Note: The ratings are based on a scale of 1 to 7, with 1 representing the highest level of democratic progress and 7 the lowest. The democracy score is an average of ratings for the categories tracked in a given year.
Source: The data above are drawn from The World Bank, *World Development Indicators* 2015.

Cerar may be able to achieve many of these goals, given the consistent and stable support he receives from the National Assembly.

An ongoing issue that may distract from Cerar's economic reforms is an open border dispute with Croatia. In 2009, the two former Yugoslav states agreed to a deal wherein the five-member tribunal would reach a binding decision on 5 square miles (13 square kilometers) of mostly uninhabited land and coastline. Both Slovenia and Croatia were asked to propose one member for the panel and a key element of impartiality was that no member discusses the tribunal's work with their government. Slovenia has only 29 miles (46 kilometers) of coastline and argues that its access to international waters hangs in the balance as Croatia, with its 1,050 miles of coastline, seeks to draw the border right through the middle of the disputed bay.[51] Croatia recently withdrew from negotiations, calling them "dead" and accusing Slovenia of compromising the integrity of the panel, and Slovenia continues to have issues finding a satisfactory appointment to represent their interests at arbitration. The panel was scheduled to set an agreement by the end of 2015, but no information has been released to date.

Assessing Political Risk

As barriers to regional and international trade are lowered, investors continue to seek new opportunities in emerging markets around the world. As we have seen in the individual case studies, these markets are vulnerable to a wide range of forces, known as political risk, which are beyond the control of potential investors. These risks might include corruption, unstable government institutions, reforming financial systems, uncertain legal systems or regulatory regimes, and even currency instability.

Techniques for assessing these risks are wide ranging, from traditional methods employing comparative ratings and mapping systems (as illustrated in the case studies of this chapter), to special reports, expert systems, modeling, and logit analysis. No assessment method is perfect, and correlating the individual variables does not often yield accurate measurements of potential loss generated by political risk.

---

[51] "Croatia to Pull Out of Border Dispute Arbitration with Slovenia" (2015).

Yet, companies acknowledge that no matter their size, they must consider the political environment when planning to conduct business abroad. As noted in previous publications within this series, "one of the most undeniable and crucial realities of international business is that both host and home government are integral partners."[52]

Further, it is important to recognize that political risk is taking new and different forms in both advanced and emerging economies. This includes dealing with real or perceived income inequality, sovereign debt, state actions to promote state-owned companies, erecting of trade barriers—all of which have the potential to pose serious threats to companies.

Businesses increasingly focus their attention on financial, market, and operational forms of risk, particularly in the wake of the 2008 economic crisis. According to a recent Global Risk Management study, most companies neither measure nor manage political risk. Instead, they tend to accept (or ignore) them, or avoid entering situations that post significant risk, even when they might lead to a significant opportunity for growth.[53]

Conclusion

The level of political risk in CEE states reflects the mixture of economic, political, and social progress in reform across the region. On the one hand, political analysts express concern about the growing authoritarian tendencies of regimes in central Europe and central Asia. Since 2000, Freedom House reports that the number of "consolidated authoritarian regimes" across both regions has more than doubled. While opponents of democracy are far less powerful in central and southeastern Europe, there are notable cases where parties and personalities have emerged with strong antidemocratic rhetoric. This is most evident in Hungary, where media freedom, national democratic governance, and the openness of the electoral process have declined dramatically in the years since Viktor Orbán's and the Fidesz party came to power, more than in any other country in the same period.

---

[52] Goncalves et al. (2014).
[53] Deloitte (2012).

On the other hand, nearly all EU member states in central and eastern Europe have reformed their governing institutions and created significant protection for civil society organizations and media outlets. Analysts rank Slovenia, Estonia, Latvia, Poland, Czech Republic, Lithuania, and Slovakia as "consolidated democracies," with Hungary, Bulgaria, Romania, Serbia, and Croatia, and Bosnia and Herzegovina making strides toward consolidation. Despite concerns about partisan friction and influence over media, the Czech Republic continued to see stability and improvement in its new government. Romania escalated a high number of corruption cases, while Slovakia took steps to improve transparency in its judiciary.

CHAPTER 7

Future Considerations and Challenges

Even if CEE economies manage to return on the convergence path its speed will be much slower than it used to be before 2008.

—Marek Dabrowski

Overview

In the preceding chapters, we have provided an introduction to historical context for eastern Europe's integration into the European Union (EU), a survey of convergence and divergence among the individual Central and Eastern Europe (CEE) states, a careful examination of the challenges to entering CEE markets, and an assessment of political risk in the democratic transition states. Drawing on these analyses, this chapter will conclude our discussion with future considerations and challenges for the economies and politics of the CEE states.

"The Emerging Europe and Central Asia region is facing some daunting challenges amid a cloudy outlook for growth," said Laura Tuck, Vice-President for the World Bank's Emerging Europe and Central Asia region. "The tensions in Ukraine have clearly had an impact on the country's growth and have disrupted economic activity. But many of the structural problems that confront countries in the region existed before the crisis and still need to be urgently addressed."[1]

Although reports in late 2014 and early 2015 warned of a cloudy economic outlook in the CEE states, they showed solid growth in 2015. Strong domestic demand, particularly private consumption, was strengthened by falling unemployment, higher real wages, improved

---

[1] "Cloudy Outlook for Growth in Emerging Europe and Central Asia" (2014).

credit growth for consumers as well as lower commodities prices, which supported households' disposable income. After a mild slowdown in the second quarter of 2015, the region's economy gained some momentum in the third quarter. CEE's gross domestic product (GDP) expanded 3.4 percent year-on-year in the third quarter of 2015, which was above the 3.2 percent increase in the second quarter. Data across the region showed that almost all economies in the CEE picked up pace in the third quarter.[2] The exceptions were Estonia—where GDP cooled notably in the third quarter[3]—as well as Hungary and Slovenia. Economic growth in the Czech Republic inched down in the third quarter relative to the second quarter, but was still robust.[4]

Volatility in the global financial markets in 2015 was driven by several factors, including concerns about the potential for a new Greek crisis (Grexit) in May 2015, the Chinese slowdown in the second half of 2015 and the fall in global commodities prices throughout the year. With respect to CEE states, the re-emergence of concerns about a "Grexit" and the corresponding correction in 10-year bonds in the eurozone (particularly German bunds) had little impact on financial markets. Economists believe this was due to high confidence among investors and the European Central Bank's (ECB) asset purchase program, known as quantitative easing (QE), the spillover effects of which had a positive effect in equity and bond markets across the CEE.[5]

Meanwhile, concerns about the Chinese slowdown also had little impact on the region as trade links between the CEE economies and China are relatively small (see e.g., Chapter 1). Some economists argue that the impact that China's rebalancing has on global commodities prices actually had a positive effect on the CEE economies' terms of trade.[6] That said, these economies are not immune to an increase in global risk aversion, which could result in sustained capital outflows, potentially impacting

---

[2] Aceves (2016).
[3] Jean-Phillippe Pourcelot (2015).
[4] "Czech Republic Economic Outlook" (2016).
[5] Aceves (2016).
[6] Aceves (2016).

the CEE states (such as Hungary and Poland) that rely on a high share of foreign direct investment in their local markets.

Outlook in 2016

Most economists expect the CEE's economy to continue expanding at a solid pace in 2016. The region will continue to benefit from the recovery in the eurozone as well as from still-low commodities prices. Forecasters surveyed by *Focus Economics* expect that the economy of the CEE will grow at a healthy 3.1 percent in 2016.[7]

However, the potential for a stronger-than-expected impact of the normalization of the U.S. monetary policy, risks to trade and capital flows stemming from a possible further slowdown in emerging economies, and the ongoing refugee crisis could all create challenges for the CEE states in 2016. The improving growth outlook for 2016 reflected that growth projections for Bulgaria,[8] Croatia,[9] and Romania[10] were raised over the previous month, while forecasts for the remaining economies surveyed were left unchanged. Latvia was the only country for which forecasts were cut.[11]

"The Emerging Europe and Central Asia region is facing some daunting challenges amid a cloudy outlook for growth," said Laura Tuck, Vice-President for the World Bank's Emerging Europe and Central Asia region.

> The tensions in Ukraine have clearly had an impact on the country's growth and have disrupted economic activity. But many of the structural problems that confront countries in the region existed before the crisis and still need to be urgently addressed.[12]

---

[7] Ricardo Aceves (2016).
[8] "Bulgaria Economic Outlook" (2016).
[9] "Croatia Economic Outlook" (2016).
[10] "Romania Economic Outlook" (2016).
[11] "Latvia Economic Outlook" (2016).
[12] "Cloudy Outlook for Growth in Emerging Europe and Central Asia" (2014).

As discussed in Chapter 6, political risk within the CEE states and in the region at large can create potential challenges for growth and stability.

The other potential regional factor to consider is stability within Russia, as emerging European states would benefit from stabilization in the state's sizeable economy. If the Russian economy is able to stabilize in 2016, this should ease the pressure on the Commonwealth of Independent States (CIS) countries that have been impacted by lower trade, investment, and remittances from their neighbor.

In the same respect, stabilization in Russia, stronger growth in the EU, low interest rates, QE in the ECB, and subdued commodity prices should contribute to the CEE growth. Regional political tensions should not detract from the excellent progress that many CEE states have made in terms of reform and growth, but analysts point that there are still political, institutional, and policy challenges that remain.

The CEE states experienced several significant periods of transition in the 20th century, marked by the events of 1918, 1945, and 1989. In both 1918 and 1945, the CEE and Balkan economies were suffering from devastating losses, destruction, and dislocation. Although they needed to focus on economic restructuring and stabilization, they did not have to profoundly reinvent their economic and political systems. The post-1989 transformations, however, were complicated by large foreign debts and debt-service payments inherited from the outgoing communist regimes. They were not in the process of recovering from a World War, but did struggle to recover from a state of economic collapse, high levels of inflation, severe infrastructure neglect and decay, environmental crises, the political anxieties of the Cold War, and, in some cases, internal ethnic conflict.

In our text, we have highlighted CEE as a region in "transition," exploring the historical, political, social, and economic transitions of the individual states and country blocs. Our work analyzed the economic impact and challenges promoted by the EU enlargement into CEE economies, and how it has contributed to the economic growth of these countries. This growth has not been without challenges, and in this respect, we discussed strategies employed by CEE states to adjust to the recent global financial crisis. In Chapter 5, for example, we noted that the CEE states, a part of the world often neglected by investors and business leaders, have shown themselves to be resilient, exhibiting impressive growth and maturity, both economically and politically. In the context of that economic and political growth, we reminded readers of the importance of political risk by providing state-by-state surveys of the impact of a series of political and economic risk assessments.

We hope that this information has provided the reader with an introduction to the economic and political structure of CEE states, as well as an overview of the principle criteria in evaluating emerging market (EME) countries, which constitute approximately 80 percent of the global population and represent about 20 percent of the world's economies. EMEs are characterized as transitional markets, meaning they are in the process of moving from a closed economy to an open market economy, while building accountability within the system. EMEs must also balance this tremendous potential for reform and growth against local political and social factors as they attempt to open up their economies to the world. Those living in transition countries may be distrustful of foreign investment, or because of national pride, may be opposed to having foreigners owning parts of the local economy. The process of emergence may be difficult, slow, and often stagnant. As many of the CEE case studies examined in our work have shown, many emerging economies through the transitioning eastern European region may be able to look forward to brighter opportunities and offer new areas of investment for foreign and developed economies, while still balancing the impact of an open economy on their citizens.

APPENDIX A

A Brief Scanning of the CEE Countries

The following is a brief scanning of the Central and Eastern Europe (CEE) countries to help in the understanding of their challenges and competitive advantages in furthering their economies and global market integrations that were discussed throughout the book.

Estonia

Estonia, with a population of only 1.3 million, is one of the least-populous member states of the European Union (EU), Eurozone, the North Atlantic Treaty Organization (NATO) and the Schengen Area.[1] Ethnic Estonians are Finns,[2] and the official language, Estonian, is a Finno-Ugric language closely related to Finnish and the Sami languages, and distantly to Hungarian.

Estonia came under Soviet occupation in the summer of 1940. As part of the Nazi-Soviet nonaggression pact, Union of Soviet Socialist Republics (USSR) and Nazi Germany divided Europe, with the Baltic states coming under Russian rule. Joseph Stalin pressured Estonia to allow 25,000 Soviet soldiers to be stationed in Estonia, as part of the defense and mutual assistance pact. The Estonian leadership agreed due

---

[1] An area comprising 26 European countries that have abolished passport and any other type of border control at their common (internal) borders. It mostly functions as a single country for international travel purposes, with a common visa policy.

[2] Finns consist of the peoples inhabiting the region around the Baltic Sea in northeastern Europe who speak Finnic languages, including the Finns proper, Karelians (including Ludes and Olonets), Veps, Izhorians, Votes, Livonians, and Estonians (including Võros and Setos).

to lack of outside support and a weak military that numbered only 15,000 troops. Within months, the country was under full occupation, with the Communist Party installed at the head of the government.

While being a part of the Soviet Union, Estonians have overwhelmingly rejected Russia, often refusing to speak the Russian language, despite fluency. When Mikhail Gorbachev came to power, liberalizing both Soviet economy and human rights, Estonians saw an opportunity to break free and declare independence on November 16, 1988. Gorbachev refused to recognize the nation's independence, but by 1991, the USSR had shattered and Estonians broke free.

After breaking up from the Soviet Union, Estonia became a democratic parliamentary republic divided into 15 counties, with its capital and largest city being Tallinn. Its political culture is stable, with political power held between two to three parties that have been in politics for a long time. This situation is similar to other countries in northern Europe. The country is now a member of the EU and NATO.

The government of Estonia, the executive branch, is formed by the prime minister, nominated by the president, and approved by the parliament. The government exercises executive power pursuant to the Constitution of Estonia and the laws of the Republic of Estonia and consists of 12 ministers, including the prime minister. Former Prime Minister Andrus Ansip, who served from 2005 through 2014, is Europe's longest-serving prime minister. The current prime minister is Taavi Rõivas, who is the former minister of social affairs and the head of the Reform Party.

Estonia has pursued the development of the e-state and e-government. Internet voting has been used on elections in Estonia since 2005 for local elections and in 2007 for the first time on a parliamentary election. Voters actually are allowed to invalidate their electronic vote in traditional elections, if they wish to.

Estonia, although a tiny country of 1.5 million population, has emerged as one of the fastest growing economies in the world, and a nation that is studied by governments around the world, as they try to copy Estonia's spectacular success that occurred despite suffering under Soviet repression for half a century.[3] The country ranks very high in the

---

[3] Storobin (2005).

United Nations (2015) Human Development Index[4] (HDI), and performs favorably in measurements of economic freedom, civil liberties, education, and press freedom, placing third in the world as of 2012 according to Reporters Without Borders.[5] The country is often described as one of the most wired countries in Europe.[6]

The new Estonian fiscal policy became a model of economic progress for developing nations. Because of the toll of moving the country from communism to capitalism, between 1988 and 1991, the people's real wages decreased by more than 50 percent, inflation skyrocketed, and several new private banks went bankrupt. Despite such economic hardships, however, few Estonians sought a return to communism.

As part of the country's reorientation toward the West, the government decided to embrace foreign trade. Europe quickly replaced Russia as Estonia's main partner, driven in part by the country's embrace of foreign trade and in part by large-scale privatization of government assets, causing a large volume of foreign direct investments (FDI) inflows into the country. The state's money became stable, with the government controlling supply and increasing dollar reserves, which allowed entrepreneurs to have greater confidence in long-term investments.

By 1993, the economy fully recovered, with the country running a budget surplus of about 5 percent. Within a few short years, wages were far above what they were under communism. In 1994, Estonia became among the first in the world to adopt the flat tax, with a uniform rate of 26 percent regardless of the income a person makes. Rejecting claims of unfairness in taxing the poor and the rich at the same percentage rate, the government decided to take on this radical experiment—and succeeded wildly, as the nation's economy boomed. Estonia is now a developed country with an advanced, high-income economy[7] and high-living standards.

---

[4] The HDI is a composite statistic of life expectancy, education, and income per capita indicators, which are used to rank countries into four tiers of human development.

[5] Borders (2012).

[6] Costiganand Perry (2012, 7).

[7] Storobin (2005).

Multiple former Soviet republics have begun adopting Estonian policies. One the most popular Estonian policies have been the flat tax, which was adopted by Russia with a flat tax rate of 13 percent, Ukraine also 13 percent, and Latvia 25 percent. Slovakia, another formerly communist nation, recently adopted a 19-percent flat income tax. Even China is now seriously considering adopting a flat tax. As a result, all countries saw increased investment, both domestic and foreign, as well as increased tax revenue due to a decrease in tax evasion.

As depicted in Figure A.1, Estonia has throughout the year's experienced a consistent increase in its gross domestic product (GDP), which has grown from €6 billion in 1996 to more than €12 billion in 2014, this despite the global financial crisis that started in 2007.

A balanced budget, almost nonexistent public debt, flat-rate income tax, free-trade regime, competitive commercial banking sector, innovative e-services, and even mobile-based services are all hallmarks of Estonia's market economy. The country is ranked 8th in the Heritage's 2015 Index of Economic Freedom, and the fourth freest economy in Europe. Because of its rapid growth, Estonia has often been described as a Baltic tiger beside Lithuania and Latvia. According to Eurostat,[8] Estonia had the lowest ratio of government debt to GDP among EU countries at 6.7 percent at the end of 2010. *The Economist* magazine has actually suggested in an article

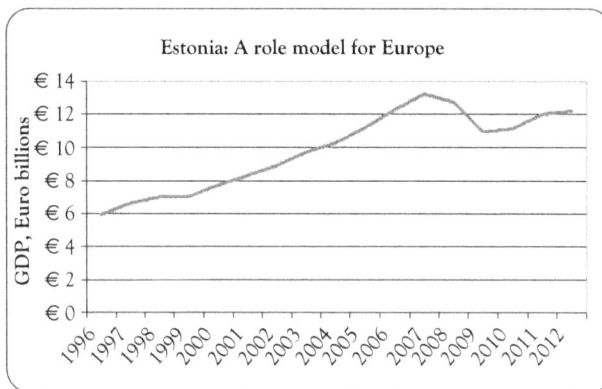

Figure A.1 Estonia's economic success post-communism

Source: IMF.

---

[8] http://ec.europa.eu/eurostat/help/new-eurostat-website

titled "The Best Balt will be Nordic," that Estonia can now be compared to a Nordic country, emphasizing the economic, political, and cultural differences between Estonia and its less successful Baltic neighbors.[9] The country's per capita GDP as of 2013, based on purchasing power parity (PPP) of €17,472 ($18,783.06) is the highest of any country that used to be part of the USSR, as shown in Figure A.2.

Estonia has a strong information technology (IT) sector, which has been mentioned as the most "wired" and advanced country in Europe in the terms of e-government of Estonia.[10] The well-known Internet application, Skype, was written by Estonia-based developers Ahti Heinla, Priit Kasesalu, and Jaan Tallinn, who had also originally developed Kazaa.[11]

Estonia has had a market economy since the end of the 1990s. Proximity to the Scandinavian markets, its location between the East and West hemisphere, competitive cost structure, and a highly skilled labor force have been the major Estonian comparative advantages in the beginning of this century. As the largest city, Tallinn has emerged as a financial center and the Tallinn Stock Exchange joined recently with the Nasdaq

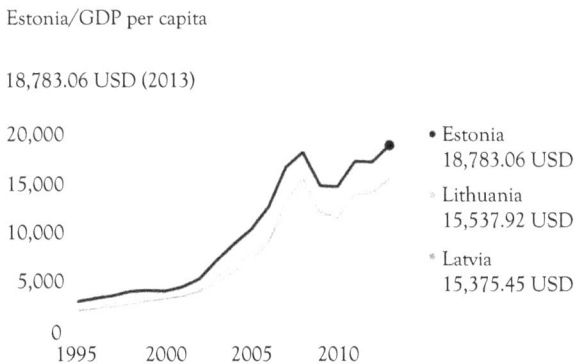

Estonia/GDP per capita

18,783.06 USD (2013)

- Estonia 18,783.06 USD
- Lithuania 15,537.92 USD
- Latvia 15,375.45 USD

Figure A.2 GDP per capita for Estonia since 1995 through 2013

Source: World Bank.

[9] www.economist.com/blogs/theworldin2011/2010/12/baltic_states_will_show_their_differences_2011

[10] Storobin (2005).

[11] Thomann (2006).

OMX[12] system. The current government has pursued tight fiscal policies, resulting in balanced budgets and low public debt.

The Estonian economic miracle also challenged the claims by the International Monetary Fund (IMF) that devaluation of money is good for developing economies. Just as importantly, it also invalidated claims that formerly occupied, small states cannot rapidly develop due to their history as a colonized people. As argued by Storobin,[13] "the model of economic progress developed by Estonians should serve as an example to all the other developing nations in the world that seek to quickly improve the well-being of their people."

Latvia

Latvia, as depicted in Figure A.3, is another one of the three countries in the Baltic region of northern Europe, is bordered by Estonia to the north, Lithuania to the south, Russia to the east, and Belarus to the southeast,

Figure A.3 Latvia is bordered by Estonia to the north, Lithuania to the south, Russia to the east, and Belarus to the southeast, as well as a maritime border to the west alongside Sweden

Source: Map data, Google.

---

[12] OMX AB (Aktiebolaget Optionsmäklarna/Helsinki Stock Exchange) is a Swedo-Finnish financial services company, formed in 2003 through a merger between OM AB and HEX plc and is a part of the NASDAQ OMX Group since February 2008.

[13] Storobin (2005).

as well as a maritime border to the west alongside Sweden. Latvia, with 2 million inhabitants, is a democratic parliamentary republic established in 1918. It is a unitary state, divided into 118 administrative divisions, of which 109 are municipalities and 9 are cities. Riga, the capital, was elected the European Capital of Culture 2014.[14]

Latvians and Livs are the indigenous people of Latvia. Latvian is an Indo-European language; Latvian and Lithuanian are the only two surviving Baltic languages. Despite foreign rule from 13th to 20th century, the Latvian nation maintained its identity throughout the generations via the language and musical traditions. Latvia and Estonia share a long common history. As a consequence of the Soviet occupation, both countries are home to a large number of ethnic Russians and Estonian, some of whom are noncitizens.

In 1940, the country was forcibly incorporated into the Soviet Union, invaded and occupied by Nazi Germany in 1941, and reoccupied by the Soviets in 1944 to form the Latvian Soviet Socialist Republic (SSR) for the next 50 years. The peaceful Singing Revolution, starting in 1987, called for the Baltic emancipation of Soviet rule. It ended with the Declaration on the Restoration of Independence of the Republic of Latvia on May 4, 1990, and restoring de facto independence on August 21, 1991.[15]

Much as Estonia, Latvia is a democratic and developed country with an advanced high-income economy, a high quality of life, and a very high standard of living. The country is a member of NATO, the EU, the UN, the Council of Europe, the IMF, and the World Trade Organization (WTO), among other international organizations. It is currently in the accession process for joining the Organization for Economic Cooperation and Development (OECD). In 2014, Latvia was listed 46th on the HDI and as a high-income country.[16] It used the Latvian lats as its

---

[14] Latvian Institute (2011).

[15] On August 21, 1991, after the Soviet coup d'état attempt, the Supreme Council adopted a Constitutional law, "On statehood of the Republic of Latvia," declaring Article 5 of the Declaration to be invalid, thus ending the transitional period and restoring de facto independence.

[16] http://hdr.undp.org/en/countries/profiles/LVA

currency until it was replaced by the euro in January 2014.[17] According to statistics in late 2013, 45 percent of Latvians supported the introduction of the euro, while 52 percent opposed it.[18] Following the introduction of the euro, Eurobarometer surveys in January 2014 showed support for the euro to be around 53 percent, close to the European average.[19]

During the post-war period, Latvia was forced to adopt Soviet-farming methods, and rural areas were forced into collectivization.[20] At the same time, much as in Estonia, an extensive program to impose bilingualism was initiated in the country, limiting the use of Latvian language in official uses in favor of using Russian as the main language. All of the minority schools (Jewish, Polish, Belorussian, Estonian, and Lithuanian) were closed down, leaving only two media of instructions in the schools: Latvian and Russian.[21] In consequence, an influx of laborers, administrators, military personnel, and their dependents from Russia and other Soviet republics started. By 1959 about 400,000 people arrived from other Soviet republics and the ethnic Latvian population had fallen to 62 percent.[22]

Since Latvia had maintained a well-developed infrastructure and educated specialists, Moscow decided to base some of the Soviet Union's most advanced manufacturing units in Latvia, promoting the development of new industries, including a major machinery factory Riga Autobus Factory (RAF) in Jelgava, electro technical factories in Riga, chemical factories in Daugavpils, Valmiera, and Olaine, in addition to some food and oil processing plants.[23] Latvia's manufacturing industry grew, producing a large array of products including trains, ships, minibuses, mopeds, telephones, radios and hi-fi systems, electrical and diesel engines, textiles, furniture, clothing, bags and luggage, shoes, musical instruments, home

---

[17] Bank of Latvia (n.d.).

[18] Apollo (n.d.).

[19] *The Economist* (2014).

[20] O'Connor (2003, 29); Lumans (2006).

[21] Bleiere (1996, 411).

[22] Bleiere (1996, 418).

[23] Bleiere (1996, 319).

appliances, watches, tools and equipments, aviation and agricultural equipments, and long list of other goods, even its own film industry and musical records factory (LPs).

In the second half of the 1980s, Soviet leader Mikhail Gorbachev started to introduce political and economic reforms in the Soviet Union. In the summer of 1987, the first large demonstrations were held in Riga at the Freedom Monument—a symbol of independence. In the summer of 1988, Latvia along with the other Baltic republics was allowed greater autonomy. In 1989, the Supreme Soviet of the USSR adopted a resolution on the occupation of the Baltic states, in which it declared the occupation "not in accordance with law," and not the "will of the Soviet people." In 1988, the old pre-war flag of Latvia flew again, replacing the Soviet Latvian flag as the official flag in 1990.[24]

Foreign investment in Latvia is still modest compared with the levels in north-central Europe. A law expanding the scope for selling land, including to foreigners, was passed in 1997. Representing 10.2 percent of Latvia's total FDI, American companies have invested $127 million in 1999, while exporting $58.2 million of goods and services to Latvia and imported $87.9 million. Eager to join Western economic institutions like the WTO, OECD, and the EU, Latvia signed a Europe Agreement with the EU in 1995—with a 4-year transition period. Latvia and the United States have signed treaties on investment, trade, and intellectual property protection and avoidance of double taxation. Since 2000, Latvia has had one of the highest GDP growth rates in Europe, as depicted in Figure A.4.[25]

The economic crisis of 2009 proved earlier assumptions that the country's fast-growing economy was heading for implosion of the economic bubble, because it was driven mainly by growth of domestic consumption, financed by a serious increase of private debt, as well as a negative foreign trade balance. This resulted in a collapse of the economy and of its GDP in late 2008, aggravated by the global economic crisis, which caused a shortage of credit and huge money resources needed for the bailout of

---

[24] O'Connor (2003, 29).

[25] Eurostat (2015).

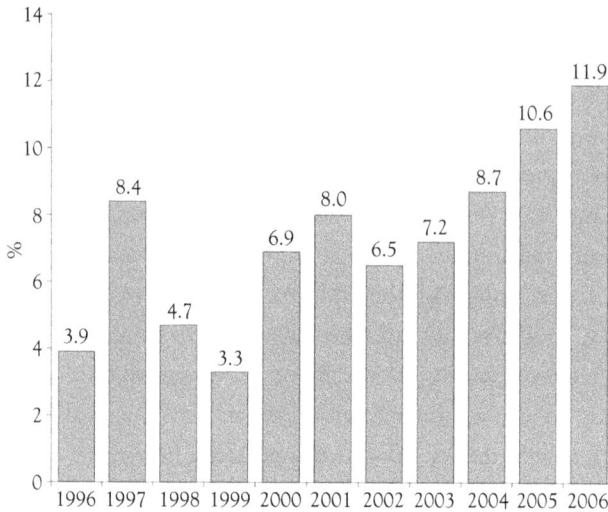

Figure A.4 Real GDP growth in Latvia 1996–2006

Source: Eurostat Database.

Parex bank.[26] The Latvian economy fell 18 percent in the first 3 months of 2009, the biggest fall in the EU.[27]

Despite the hardships, Latvia withered the crisis well. Hundreds of banks went bankrupt in Russia; the situation in the neighbor country was very tough, but Latvia managed to get away by only closing down one minor commercial bank and by recovering out another larger commercial bank Rigas Komercbanka. The IMF concluded the First Post-Program Monitoring Discussions with Latvia in July 2012 announcing that Latvia's economy has been recovering strongly since 2010, with real GDP growth of 5.5 percent in 2011 reinforced by export growth and a recovery in domestic demand. The growth momentum has continued into 2012 and 2013 despite deteriorating external conditions, and the economy was expected to expand by 4.1 percent in 2015.[28]

---

[26] Kolyako (2009).

[27] Eglitis (2009); Latvian Economy in Rapid Decline (2009).

[28] IMF (2012b).

Lithuania

Lithuania is another country in northern Europe, the third of the Baltic states after Estonia and Latvia, situated along the southeastern shore of the Baltic Sea, to the east of Sweden and Denmark. As depicted in Figure A.5, the country is bordered by Latvia to the north, Belarus to the east and south, Poland to the south, and Kaliningrad Oblast, a Russian exclave, to the southwest. Lithuania's population is estimated to be 2.9 million people as of 2015. Vilnius, its largest city and capital, is classified as a Gamma

Figure A.5 Map of Lithuania, bordered by Latvia to the north, Belarus to the east and south, Poland to the south, and Kaliningrad Oblast, a Russian exclave, to the southwest

Source: Infoplease.com

global city according to GaWC[29] studies, and is known for its old town of beautiful architecture, declared a United Nations Educational, Scientific and Cultural Organization (UNESCO) World Heritage Site in 1994. Its Jewish influence until the 20th century has led to it being described as the "Jerusalem of Lithuania" and Napoleon named it "the Jerusalem of the North" as he was passing through in 1812. In 2009, Vilnius was the European capital of culture, together with the Austrian city of Linz. Lithuanians are Baltic people. The official language, Lithuanian, along with Latvian, are the only two living languages in the Baltic branch of the Indo-European language family.

As World War II (WWII) neared its end in 1944 and the Germans retreated, the Soviet Union reoccupied Lithuania. On March 11, 1990, a year before the formal dissolution of the Soviet Union, Lithuania became the first Soviet republic to declare itself independent, resulting in the restoration of an independent state of Lithuania. Lithuania is a member of the EU, the Council of Europe, a full member of the Schengen Agreement and NATO, and other regional and international organizations.

Much as with the other two Baltic countries, Lithuania's UN's HDI is of a "very high human development." Lithuania has been among the fastest growing economies in the EU and is ranked 20th in the world in the World Bank's Ease of Doing Business Index. In January 2015, Lithuania adopted euro as the official currency and became the 19th member of the Eurozone. A curious fact about Lithuania is that after a re-estimation of the boundaries of the continent of Europe in 1989, Jean-George Affholder, a scientist at the Institut Géographique National (French National Geographic Institute) determined that the geographic centre of Europe is in Lithuania, specifically 26 kilometers (16 miles) north of its capital city, Vilnius.

As depicted in Figure A.6, Lithuania experienced very high real GDP growth rates in the decade before 2009, peaking at 11.1 percent in 2007. As a result, the country was often termed as a Baltic Tiger. However, 2009

---

[29] Considered the leading institute ranking world cities. Cities are ranked into Alpha, Beta, and Gamma cities by taking into account many factors; economic factors are deemed more important than cultural or political factors though in this ranking.

marked a dramatic decline in GDP at –14.9 percent attributed to over-heating of the economy. The economy, however, not only resumed growth in the following years but also at more sustainable pace, driven by domestic demand and exports rather than housing and financial bubbles.[30]

The government of Lithuania offers special incentives for investments into the high-technology sectors and high-value-added products. Most of the trade Lithuania conducts is within the EU and Russia. The country has a flat tax rate rather than a progressive scheme. According to Eurostat,[31] small business income tax is only 5 percent, with the personal income tax and corporate taxes set at 15 percent, which are among the lowest in the EU. The country has the lowest implicit rate of tax on capital, of 9.8 percent, in the EU. Lithuania also has the lowest overall taxation as a percentage of GDP, 27.2 percent, in the EU as well.[32] Nonetheless, the country's income levels are somewhat lower than in older EU member states but higher than in most new EU member states that have joined in the last decade. The litas was the national currency until 2015, when it was replaced by the euro at the rate of EUR 1.00 = LTL 3.45280.[33]

Structurally, there is a gradual but consistent shift toward a knowledge-based economy with special emphasis on biotechnology, for both

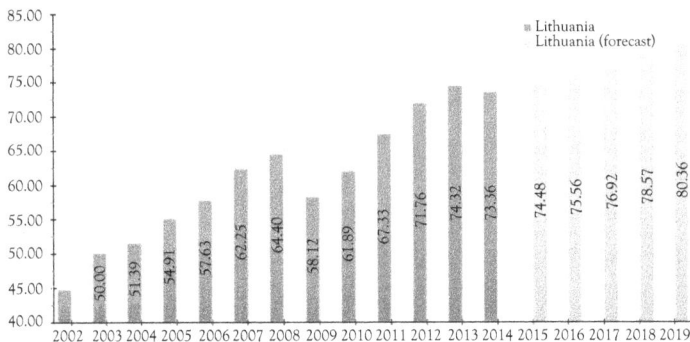

Figure A.6 Lithuania's GDP per capita PPP

Source: TheBanks.eu

---

[30] SEB Bank (2014).

[31] Eurostat (2014).

[32] Eurostat (2014).

[33] "ISO Currency—ISO 4217 Amendment Number 159" (n.d.).

industrial and diagnostic sectors. The major biotechnology companies and laser manufacturers of the Baltics, which include Ekspla and Šviesos Konversija, are concentrated in Lithuania. Also mechatronics and IT are seen as prospective knowledge-based economy directions.

In 2009, Barclays established Technology Centre Lithuania—one of four strategic engineering centers supporting the Barclays retail banking businesses across the globe. In 2011, Western Union officially opened their new European regional operating centre in Vilnius.[34] Among other international companies operating in Lithuania are: PricewaterhouseCoopers, Ernst & Young, Societe Generale, UniCredit, Thermo Fisher Scientific, Phillip Morris, Kraft Foods, Mars, Marks & Spencer, GlaxoSmithKline, United Colors of Benetton, Deichmann, Statoil, Neste Oil, Lukoil, Tele2, Hesburger, and Modern Times Group. TeliaSonera, ICA, and Carlsberg respectively own local telecommunications company Omnitel, retailer Rimi, beer breweries (Švyturys, Kalnapilis, and UtenosAlus), and the banking sector, which are dominated by the Scandinavian banks, Swedbank, Swedish banking group (officially named SEB since 1997), Nordea, Danske Bank, and DNB ASA, Norway's largest financial services group.

Czech Republic

As depicted in Figure A.7, the Czech Republic, which includes the historical territories of Bohemia, Moravia, and Czech Silesia, is a landlocked country in central Europe bordered by Germany to the west, Austria to the south, Slovakia to the east, and Poland to the northeast. The capital and largest city, Prague, has over 1.2 million residents.

The Czech state was formed in the late 9th century as the Duchy of Bohemia under the Great Moravian empire. After the fall of the empire in 907, the center of power was transferred from Moravia to Bohemia under the Přemyslids dynasty.[35] In 1004, the duchy was formally recognized as

---

[34] The Lithuania Tribune (2005).

[35] The Přemyslids were a Bohemian (Czech) royal dynasty that reigned in Bohemia and Moravia (9th century–1306), and partly also in Hungary, Silesia, Austria, and Poland.

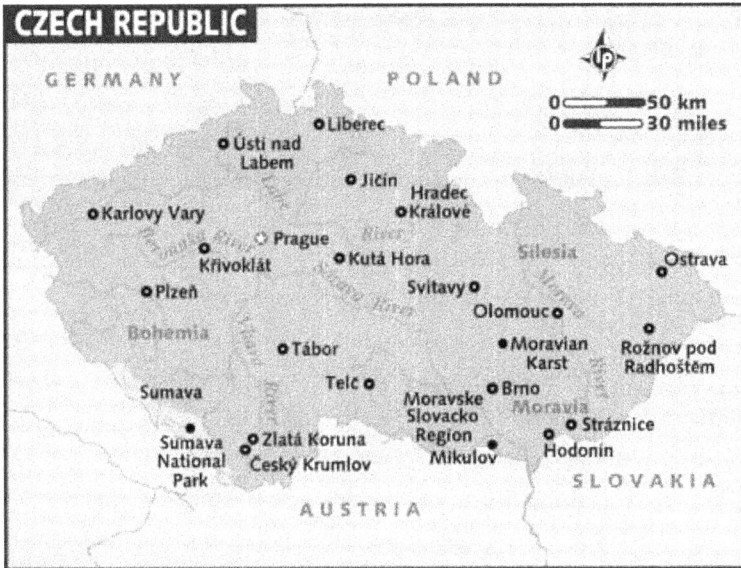

Figure A.7 The Czech Republic is a landlocked country in central Europe bordered by Germany to the west, Austria to the south, Slovakia to the east, and Poland to the northeast

Source: worldtravels.com

part of the Holy Roman Empire,[36] becoming the Kingdom of Bohemia in 1212, and reaching its greatest territorial extent in the 14th century. The King of Bohemia ruled not only Bohemia itself, but also other lands, which together formed the so-called Crown of Bohemia, and he had a vote in the election of the Holy Roman Emperor. In the Hussite wars of the 15th century, driven by the Bohemian reformation, the kingdom faced economic embargoes and defeated five crusades proclaimed by the leaders of the Roman Catholic Church and organized mainly by the emperor and princes of the Holy Roman Empire.

Czechoslovakia was occupied by Germany in WWII, and was liberated in 1945 by Soviet and American forces. Most of the German-speaking inhabitants were expelled after the war and thus the country lost its sizeable minority and its bilingual character. The Communist Party of Czechoslovakia won the 1946 elections. Following the 1948 coup

---

[36] Mlsna, Šlehofer, and Urban (2010).

d'état, Czechoslovakia became a one-party communist state under Soviet influence. In 1968, increasing dissatisfaction with the regime culminated in a reform movement known as the Prague Spring, which ended in a Soviet-led invasion. Czechoslovakia remained occupied until the 1989 Velvet Revolution, when the communist regime collapsed and a multi-party parliamentary republic was formed. On January 1, 1993, Czecho-slovakia peacefully dissolved, with its constituent states becoming the independent states of the Czech Republic and Slovakia.[37]

The Czech Republic is a developed country with an advanced, high-income economy and high living standards.[38] The UNDP ranks the country 15th in inequality-adjusted human development.[39] The Czech Republic also ranks as the 10th most peaceful country, while achieving strong performance in democratic governance. It is a member of the UN, the EU, NATO, the OECD, and few other international agencies.

The country has a long and rich scientific tradition. The research based on cooperation between universities, the Academy of Sciences of the Czech Republic, and specialized research centers often bring new inventions and contributions to market. Important inventions include the modern contact lens, the separation of modern blood types, and the production of Semtex plastic explosive.

One of the most stable and prosperous of the post-communist states, the Czech Republic has seen significant real GDP growth since 1994, with a slowdown during the financial market crises of 2000, and even more so with the global financial crisis of 2007, as depicted in Figure A.8. But the economy has recovered from its lows and is growing again since 2010, led by exports to the EU, especially Germany, and foreign invest-ment, while domestic demand continues to revive.

Most of the economy has been privatized, including the banks and telecommunications. A 2009 survey in cooperation with the Czech Eco-nomic Association found that the majority of Czech economists favor continued liberalization in most sectors of the economy.[40] The country

[37] Čumlivski (2012).

[38] Velinger (2006).

[39] UNDP (2014).

[40] Stastny (2010).

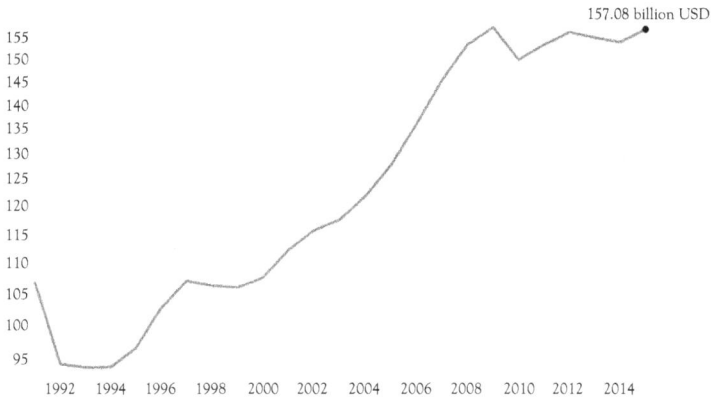

Figure A.8 Czech Republic real GDP growth 1992–2015

Source: World Bank.

has been a member of the Schengen Area since, abolished border controls, and completely opened its borders with all of its neighbors (Germany, Austria, Poland, and Slovakia) in 2007.[41] In 2012, nearly 80 percent of Czech exports went to, and more than 65 percent of Czech imports came from, other EU member states.[42]

The Czech National Bank, whose independence is guaranteed by the constitution, conducts monetary policy. The official currency is the Czech crown, and it had been floating until July 2013, when the central bank temporarily pegged the exchange rate at 27 crowns per euro in order to fight deflation.[43] When it joined EU, the Czech Republic obligated itself to adopt the euro, but the date of adoption has not been determined.

Slovakia

Slovakia is a country in central Europe. As illustrated in Figure A.9, the country is bordered by the Czech Republic and Austria to the west, Poland to the north, Ukraine to the east, and Hungary to the south. Its

---

[41] White (2006).

[42] "MIT Observatory of Economic Complexity" (n.d.).

[43] http://byznys.ihned.cz/c1-61176370-cnb-po-11-letech-zahajila-intervence-koruna-okamzite-spadla-na-ctyrlete-minimum

Figure A.9 Slovakia is bordered by the Czech Republic and Austria to the west, Poland to the north, Ukraine to the east, and Hungary to the south

Source: lonelyplanet.com

population is over 5 million, comprised mostly of ethnic Slovaks. The capital and largest city is Bratislava. The official language is Slovak, a member of the Slavic language family.

The Slavs arrived in the territory of present-day Slovakia in the 5th and 6th centuries. In the 10th century, the territory was integrated into the Kingdom of Hungary,[44] which itself became part of the Habsburg empire and the Austro-Hungarian empire. After World War I (WWI) and the dissolution of the Austro-Hungarian empire, in 1918, Slovakia and the regions of Bohemia, Moravia, Czech Silesia, and Carpathian Ruthenia formed a common state, Czechoslovakia, with the borders confirmed by the Treaty of Saint Germain and Treaty of Trianon. A separate Slovak Republic (1939 to 1945) existed, however, during the WWII, as a client state of Nazi Germany. In 1945, Czechoslovakia was re-established under communist rule as a Soviet satellite.

---

[44] Dixon-Kennedy (1998).

The end of communist rule in Czechoslovakia in 1989, during the peaceful Velvet Revolution, was followed once again by the country's dissolution, this time into two successor states. In July 1992 Slovakia, led by Prime Minister Vladimír Mečiar, declared itself a sovereign state, meaning that its laws took precedence over those of the federal government. Throughout the autumn of 1992, Mečiar and Czech Prime Minister Václav Klaus negotiated the details for disbanding the federation. In November, the federal parliament voted to dissolve the country officially on December 31, 1992. The Slovak Republic and the Czech Republic went their separate ways after January 1, 1993, an event sometimes called the Velvet Divorce.[45]

Slovakia has remained a close partner with the Czech Republic. Both countries cooperate with Hungary and Poland in the Visegrád Group, an alliance of four central European states—Czech Republic, Hungary, Poland, and Slovakia—for the purposes of furthering their European integration as well as advancing their military, economic, and energy cooperation with one another.[46] According to IMF, Slovakia is a high-income advanced economy.[47] The country joined the EU in 2004 as the 16th member of the Eurozone in January 2009, when it adopted the euro currency. The European commission in May 2008 approved the euro in Slovakia. The Slovak koruna was revalued at the time to 30.126 for 1 euro, which was also the exchange rate for the euro.[48] Slovakia is also a member of the Schengen Area, NATO, the UN, the OECD, and the WTO.

Slovakia is a parliamentary democratic republic with a multiparty system. The last parliamentary elections were held on March 10, 2012 and two rounds of presidential elections took place on March 15 and 29, 2014. The Slovak head of state is the president, elected by direct popular vote for a 5-year term. Most executive power lies with the head of

---

[45] The Breakup of Czechoslovakia (n.d.).

[46] "The Bratislava Declaration of the prime ministers of the Czech Republic, the Republic of Hungary, the Republic of Poland, and the Slovak Republic on the occasion of the 20th anniversary of the Visegrad Group (2011)."

[47] IMF (2006).

[48] Grajewski (2008).

government, the prime minister, who is usually the leader of the winning party, but he or she needs to form a majority coalition in the parliament. The president appoints the prime minister. The president on the recommendation of the prime minister appoints the remainder of the cabinet.

According to the European Commission, before the financial crisis of 2007 to 2008, Slovakia had experienced high and sustained economic growth. In 2007, 2008, and 2010 (with GDP growth of 10.5, 6, and 4 percent, retrospectively), Slovakia was the fastest growing economy in the EU.[49] In 2011 and 2012, Slovakia was the 2nd fastest growing Eurozone member after Estonia. In 2012, more than 75 percent of Slovakian exports went to, and more than 50 percent of Slovakian imports came from, other EU member states. The ratio of government debt to GDP in Slovakia reached 58 percent by the end of 2013.[50]

The Slovak economy is, nonetheless, a developed, high-income[51] economy, with a GDP per capita, as depicted in Figure A.10, at $26354.70 in 2014, when adjusted by PPP, equaling to 76 percent of the average of the EU in 2014.[52] The country used to be dubbed the "Tatra Tiger" before the recent global economic crisis. Slovakia successfully transformed from

SLOVAKIA GDP PER CAPITA PPP

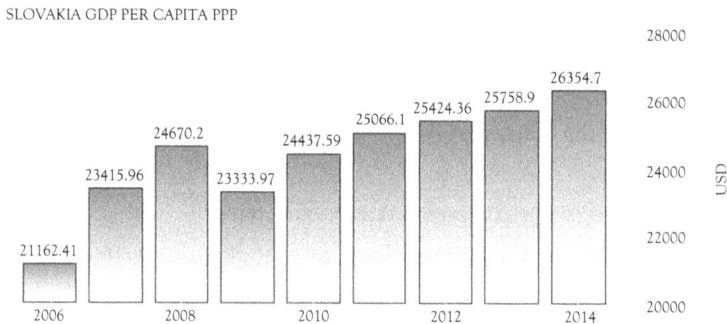

Figure A.10 Slovakia GDP per capita PPP

Source: tradingeconomics.com, World Bank.

---

[49] European Commission (2012).
[50] According to the MIT Observatory of Economic Complexity (n.d.).
[51] World Bank (2014).
[52] According to Eurostat (2015).

a centrally planned economy to a market-driven economy. Major privat-izations are nearly complete, the banking sector is almost completely in private hands, and foreign investment has risen.

Slovakia is an attractive country for foreign investors mainly because of its low wages, low tax rates, and well-educated labor force. In recent years, Slovakia has been pursuing a policy of encouraging foreign invest-ment. FDI inflow grew more than 600 percent from 2000 and cumu-latively reached an all-time high of $17.3 billion in 2006, or around $22,000 per capita by the end of 2008.

Although Slovakia's GDP comes mainly from the services sector, the industrial sector also plays an important role within its economy. The main industry sectors are car manufacturing and electrical engineering. Since 2007, Slovakia has been the world's largest producer of cars per capita,[53] with a total of 571,071 cars manufactured in the country in 2007 alone. There are currently three automobile assembly plants in the country, including Volkswagen's in Bratislava, PSA Peugeot Citroën's in Trnava, and Kia Motors' Žilina Plant. In 2018, Jaguar Land Rover is set to open the country's fourth automobile assembly plant in Nitra, a district in the Nitra Region of western Slovakia.[54]

Hungary

Hungary is a landlocked country in central Europe situated in the Carpathian Basin and, as illustrated in Figure A.11, bordered by Slovakia to the north, Romania to the east, Serbia to the south, Croatia to the southwest, Slovenia to the west, Austria to the northwest, and Ukraine to the northeast. The country's capital and largest city is Budapest. Hungary is a member of the EU, NATO, the OECD, the Visegrád Group, and the Schengen Area. The official language is Hungarian, which is the most widely spoken non-Indo-European language in Europe.

Hungary's current borders were first established by the Treaty of Trianon (1920) after WWI, when the country lost 71 percent of its

---

[53] IndustryWeek (2008).
[54] Pitas (2015).

Figure A.11 Hungary is bordered by Slovakia to the north, Romania to the east, Serbia to the south, Croatia to the southwest, Slovenia to the west, Austria to the northwest, and Ukraine to the northeast

Source: Worldtravels.com

territory, 58 percent of its population, and 32 percent of ethnic Hungarians. Following the interwar period, Hungary joined the Axis Powers in WWII, suffering significant damage and casualties. Hungary came under the influence of the Soviet Union, which contributed to the establishment of a four-decade-long communist dictatorship (1947 to 1989). The country gained widespread international attention regarding the Revolution of 1956 and the seminal opening of its previously restricted border with Austria in 1989, which accelerated the collapse of the Eastern Bloc. Hungary is today a democratic and developed country with an advanced high-income economy, a high quality of life and living standard, and a very high HDI.[55]

WWII left Hungary devastated, with more than 60 percent of the economy destroyed, which caused significant loss of life. As many as 280,000[56] Hungarians were raped, murdered, and executed or deported

---

[55] http://data.worldbank.org/income-level/OEC; Country and Lending Groups (n.d.).

[56] Prauser and Rees (2004).

for slave labor by Czechoslovaks,[57] Soviet Red Army troops,[58] and Yugoslavs.[59]

Hungary's economy is a medium-sized, high-income, structurally, politically, and institutionally open economy. Its economy experienced market liberalization in the early 1990s as part of the transition from a socialist economy to a market economy, similarly to most countries in the former Eastern Bloc.

The private sector accounts for more than 80 percent of the Hungarian GDP. Foreign ownership of and investment in Hungarian firms are widespread, with cumulative FDI worth more than $70 billion. Hungary's main industries are mining, metallurgy, construction materials, processed foods, textiles, chemicals, particularly pharmaceuticals, and motor vehicles. Hungary's main agricultural products are wheat, corn, sunflower seed, potatoes, sugar beets; pigs, cattle, poultry, and dairy products. In foreign investments, Hungary has seen a shift from lower-value textile and food industry to investment in luxury vehicle production, renewable energy systems, high-end tourism, and IT.

The currency of Hungary is called "forint," which was introduced in 1946. Hungary, as a member state of the EU, may seek to adopt the common European currency, the euro. To achieve this, the country would need to fulfill the Maastricht criteria. Hungary and the European Commission have been engaged in a legal and political battle over the independence of the country's central bank and other disagreements.

According to the World Bank Group,[60] Hungary's GDP was worth $137.10 billion in 2014, representing 0.22 percent of the world economy. GDP in Hungary averaged $52.28 billion from 1968 until 2014,

---

[57] Pogany (1997, 202); Rieber (2000, 50), Google Books—"A presidential decree imposing an obligation on individuals not engaged in useful work to accept jobs served as the basis for this action. As a result, according to documentation in the ministry of foreign affairs of the USSR, approximately 50,000 Hungarians were sent to work in factories and agricultural enterprises in the Czech Republic."

[58] Fenyvesi (2005, 50); Naimark (1995, 70).

[59] Cseres (1993).

[60] http://data.worldbank.org/income-level/OEC.

HUNGARY GDP

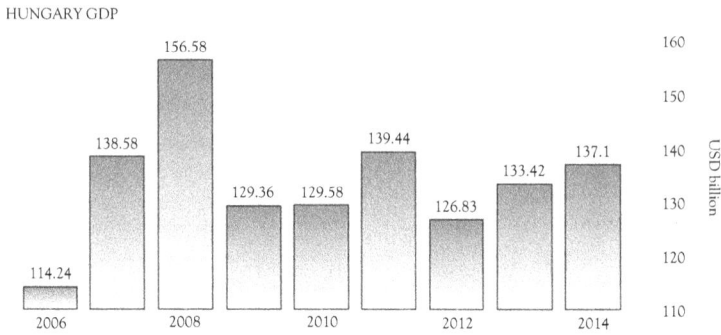

Figure A.12 Hungary GDP 2006–2014

Source: World Bank.

reaching an all time high of $156.58 billion in 2008 and a record low of $4.69 billion in 1968, as depicted in Figure A.12.[61]

The Hungarian economy was among the hardest hit by the global financial crisis, but with the help of a financial package from the IMF and EU, it recovered and in 2010 posting positive GDP growth. As on the first quarter of 2013, however, Hungary was still burdened by a large government debt to GDP ratio of over 82 percent.

Poland

Poland is a country in central Europe, as illustrated in Figure A.13, bordered by Germany to the west, the Czech Republic and Slovakia to the south, Ukraine and Belarus to the east, and the Baltic Sea, Kaliningrad Oblast—a Russian exclave—and Lithuania to the north. The country's population is slightly over 38.5 million.[62]

The establishment of a Polish state can be traced back to 966, when Mieszko I, ruler of a territory roughly coextensive with that of present-day Poland, converted to Christianity.[63] The Kingdom of Poland was founded in 1025, and in 1569 it cemented a longstanding political association with the Grand Duchy of Lithuania by signing the Union of Lublin.

---

[61] Eurostat (2013).

[62] Fawn (2013).

[63] Lukowski and Zawaszki (2001, 3).

Figure A.13 Poland is bordered by Germany to the west, the Czech Republic and Slovakia to the south, Ukraine and Belarus to the east, and the Baltic Sea, Kaliningrad Oblast and Lithuania to the north

Source: World Bank.

This union formed the Polish–Lithuanian Commonwealth, one of the largest and most populous countries of 16th- and 17th-century Europe. The Commonwealth ceased to exist in the years 1772 to 1795, when its territory was partitioned among Prussia, the Russian Empire, and Austria. Poland regained its independence at the end of WWI, in 1918.[64]

In September 1939, WWII started with the invasions of Poland by Nazi Germany and the Soviet Union. More than six million Polish citizens died in the war. In 1944, a Soviet-backed Polish provisional government was formed which, after a falsified referendum in 1947, took control of the country and Poland became a satellite state of the Soviet Union, as People's Republic of Poland. During the Revolutions of 1989,

---

[64] Lukowski and Zawaszki (2001, 9).

Poland's communist government was overthrown and Poland adopted a new constitution establishing itself as a democracy.[65]

Poland has undergone a remarkable transformation since the fall of the Iron Curtain. Employing some of the toughest economic measures right from the start in what was known as "shock therapy," initiated by Leszek Balcerowicz in the early 1990s, the country underwent its transformation from a socialist-style planned economy into a market economy, which generated a painful but relatively quick transition to an open market economy. As with other post-communist countries, Poland suffered slumps in social and economic standards, but it became the first post-communist country to reach its pre-1989 GDP levels, which it achieved by 1995 largely thanks to its booming economy.[66]

Since the fall of the communist government, Poland has pursued a policy of liberalization of the economy. It is an example of the transition from a centrally planned to a primarily market-based economy. Since then Poland has achieved a "very high" ranking in terms of human development,[67] as well as gradually improving economic freedom. Poland today is a democratic country with an advanced high-income economy, a high quality of life and a very high standard of living. According to a Credit Suisse report, Poles are the second wealthiest, after Czechs, of the central European countries.[68]

To date, there have been numerous improvements in human rights, such as the freedom of speech, Internet freedom (no censorship), civil liberties, and political rights, according to Freedom House. In 1991, Poland became a member of the Visegrád Group and joined the NATO alliance in 1999 along with the Czech Republic and Hungary.

The privatization of small and medium state-owned companies and a liberal law on establishing new firms have allowed the development of the private sector. As a consequence, consumer rights organizations have also appeared. Restructuring and privatization of "sensitive sectors" such as coal steel, rail transport, and energy has been continuing since 1990.

---

[65] Wandycz (2001, 66).
[66] Kowalik (2011).
[67] UNDP (2014).
[68] Iglicka (2008).

Although a member of the EU, Poland is still using its own currency, the zloty, and it has been reluctant to join the Eurozone. In one way this has been beneficial, keeping costs lower than in its eastern European neighbors, but hindering the ease of commerce in the zone. Unemployment is high, hovering just above 10 percent.

As depicted in Figure A.14, the country was the only EU member nation to escape a decline in GDP in consequence to the global financial crisis, as in recent years its economy was able to create probably the most varied GDP growth based on PPP per capita in its history.[69]

Poland's high-income economy is considered one of the healthiest of the post-communist countries and is one of the fastest growing within the EU.[70] According to the World Economic Forum (WEF), having a strong domestic market, low private debt, flexible currency, and not being dependent on a single export sector, Poland today has a strong economy.[71]

Poland's market liquidity is one of the highest among eastern Europe countries, which makes it more attractive for investors with a lower appetite for risk. Their main export partner is Germany, accounting for as much as a quarter of total exports. The country's most successful exports products include machinery, furniture, foods and meats, motorboats, light planes, hardwood products, casual clothing, shoes, and cosmetics. Other commodities produced in Poland include electronics, cars (Arrinera,

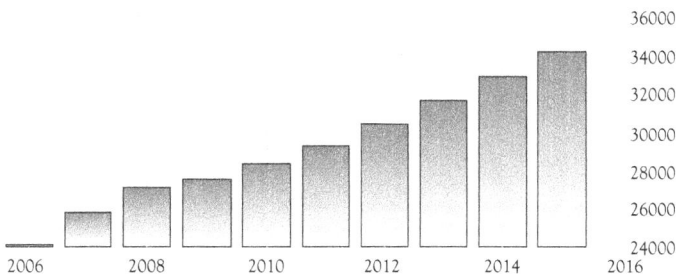

Figure A.14 Poland GDP based on PPP per capita 2006–2015

Source: tradingeconomics.com, IMF.

_____

[69] www.oanda.com/currency/iso-currency-codes/PLN (accessed March 1, 2016).
[70] SPI (2015).
[71] Schwab (n.d.).

Leopard), buses (Solaris, Solbus), helicopters (PZL Świdnik), transport equipment, locomotives, planes (PZL Mielec), ships, military engineering (including tanks, SPAAG systems), medicines (Polpharma, Polfa), food, clothes, glass, pottery (Bolesławiec), chemical products, and others.

Romania

Romania is located in the southeastern Europe region. As depicted in Figure A.15, it borders the Black Sea, between Bulgaria and Ukraine, also bordering Hungary, Serbia, and Moldova.

Modern Romania, a country member of the EU and NATO, and a unitary semi-presidential republic, emerged within the territories of the ancient Roman province of Dacia, and was formed in 1859 through a personal union of the Danubian Principalities of Moldavia and Wallachia. The new state, officially named Romania since 1866, gained independence from the Ottoman Empire in 1877. During WWII, Romania was an ally of Nazi Germany against the Soviet Union, fighting side by side

Figure A.15 Romania borders the Black Sea, between Bulgaria and Ukraine, also bordering Hungary, Serbia, and Moldova

Source: World Bank.

with the Wehrmacht until 1944, and then it joined the Allied powers after being occupied by the Red Army forces. After the war, Romania became a socialist republic and member of the Warsaw Pact.

Romania entered the EU along with Bulgaria on January 1, 2007. The two countries are still the poorest in the EU, according to their GDP per capita numbers, with Romania holding a slight edge. The Romanian market, though, is much bigger than Bulgaria's with a population of over 20 million, compared to Bulgaria's just over 7 million.

After the revolution, the National Salvation Front (NSF), led by Ion Iliescu, took partial multiparty democratic and free market measures.[72] In April 1990, a sit-in protest contesting the results of the elections and accusing the NSF, including Iliescu, of being made up of former communists and members of the *Securitate*, rapidly grew to become what was called the *Golaniad*. The peaceful demonstrations degenerated into violence, prompting the intervention of coal miners summoned by Iliescu. The subsequent disintegration of the NSF produced several political parties including the Social Democratic Party, and the Democratic Party. The former governed Romania from 1990 until 1996 through several coalitions and governments again with Iliescu as head of state. Since then, there have been several democratic changes of government with Emil Constantinescu elected president in 1996, Iliescu returning to power in 2000, Traian Băsescu being elected in 2004, and narrowly re-elected in 2009.

After the 1989 Revolution, the country experienced a decade of economic instability and decline, led in part by an obsolete industrial base and a lack of structural reform. In response, Romania not only began a transition back toward democracy but also a capitalist market economy. Following rapid economic growth in the 2000s, Romania became an economy predominantly based on services, and a producer and net exporter of machines and electric energy, featuring companies like Automobile Dacia and OMV Petrom. From 2000 onward, the country's economy was transformed into one of relative macroeconomic stability, characterized by high growth, low unemployment, and declining inflation.

---

[72] Hellman (1998).

In 2006, according to the Romanian Statistics Office,[73] GDP growth in real terms was recorded at 7.7 percent, one of the highest rates in Europe. However, a recession in 2008, following the global financial crisis that started in 2007 forced the government to borrow externally, including an IMF €20bn bailout program.[74] As depicted in Figure A.16, real GDP has been growing each year since then. According to IMF, the GDP per capita PPP grew from $14,875 in 2007 to an estimated $19,397 in 2014.

Industrial output has also grown reaching 6.5 percent year-on-year in February 2013, the highest in the EU-28.[75] The largest local companies include car maker Automobile Dacia, Petrom, Rompetrol, Ford Romania, Electrica, Romgaz, RCS & RDS (formerly Romanian Cable System & Romanian Data System), and Banca Transilvania. Exports have increased substantially in the past few years, with a 13 percent annual rise in exports in 2010. Romania's main exports are cars, software, clothing and textiles, industrial machinery, electrical and electronic equipment, metallurgic products, raw materials, military equipment, pharmaceuticals, fine chemicals, and agricultural products (fruits, vegetables, and flowers). Trade is mostly centered on the member states of the EU, with Germany and Italy being the country's single largest trading partners.

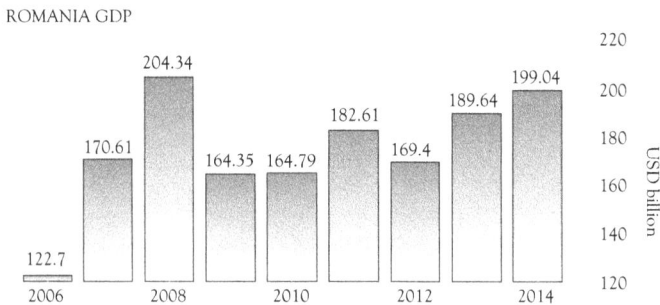

Figure A.16 Romania GDP 2006–2014

Source: tradingeconomics.com, World Bank.

[73] Romanian National Institute of Statistics (2007).
[74] *The New York Times* (2010).
[75] Eurostat (2013).

After a series of privatizations and reforms in the late 1990s and 2000s, government intervention in the Romanian economy is somewhat lower than in other European economies. In 2005, the government replaced Romania's progressive tax system with a flat tax of 16 percent for both personal income and corporate profit, among the lowest rates in the EU.[76] The economy is predominantly based on services, which account for 51 percent of GDP, even though industry and agriculture also have significant contributions, making up 36 and 13 percent of GDP, respectively. Since 2000, Romania has attracted increasing amounts of foreign investment, becoming the single largest investment destination in southeastern and central Europe.

Concerns about stability were raised after the resignation of the Victor Ponta government,[77] in November 2015. However, the effects of the current political uncertainty on the economy would depend on how quickly a new cabinet is formed and the measures it will take, according to central bank governor Mugur Isarescu, who believes the country is macro-economically stable.[78]

Bulgaria

Organized prehistoric cultures began developing on Bulgarian lands during the Neolithic period. Its ancient history saw the presence of the Thracians and later the Persians, Greeks, and Romans. The emergence of a unified Bulgarian state dates back to the establishment of the first Bulgarian empire in 681 AD, which dominated most of the Balkans and functioned as a cultural hub for Slavs during the middle ages.[79]

Bulgaria today is yet another country in the southeastern Europe region, as depicted in Figure A.17, bordered by Romania to the north, Serbia and Macedonia to the west, Greece and Turkey to the south, and the Black Sea to the east.

---

[76] Eurostat (2007).
[77] Gillet and Karasz (2015).
[78] Gillet and Karasz (2015).
[79] Roismanand Worthington (2011).

Figure A.17 *Bulgaria is bordered by Romania to the north, Serbia and Macedonia to the west, Greece and Turkey to the south, and the Black Sea to the east*

Source: RandMcNally.

With the downfall of the second Bulgarian empire in 1396, its territories came under Ottoman rule for nearly five centuries. The Russo-Turkish War (1877 to 1878) led to the formation of the third Bulgarian state. The following years saw several conflicts with its neighbors, which prompted Bulgaria to align with Germany in both the world wars. In 1946, it became a one-party socialist state as part of the Soviet-led Eastern Bloc. In December 1989, the ruling Communist Party allowed multi-party elections, which subsequently led to Bulgaria's transition into a democracy and a market-based economy.

Bulgaria's population of 7.4 million people is predominantly urbanized and mainly concentrated in the administrative centers of its 28 provinces. Most commercial and cultural activities are centered on the capital and the largest city Sofia. The strongest sectors of the economy are heavy industry, power engineering, and agriculture, all of which rely on local natural resources.

The country's current political structure dates to the adoption of a democratic constitution in 1991. Bulgaria is a unitary parliamentary republic with a high degree of political, administrative, and economic centralization. It is a member of the EU, NATO, and the Council of Europe, as well as a founding state of the Organization for Security and Co-operation in Europe (OSCE), while taking a nonpermanent seat at the UN Security Council three times. Corruption remains one of the biggest problems for doing business in the country. In addition, access to financing, inefficient government bureaucracies, policy and government instabilities are also serious concerns.

Prior to the WWII, Bulgaria was an agrarian economy with 80 percent of its labor force in agriculture. After WWII, the communists industrialized and ran Bulgaria as a centrally planned economy. Bulgaria, like Poland and Russia, tried "shock therapy" and abandoned it in short order. During 1991, retail prices were liberalized, which account for 90 percent of retail trade turnover. Prices on fuel and energy rose dramatically. The government retained control over the prices of 14 consumer staples using price ceilings. Once retail prices had been freed, it proved impossible to keep the wholesale prices of fuels and agricultural products under control. By the middle of 1991, these were also freed. This resulted in an annual rate of inflation of 334 percent in 1991 as measured by the Retail Price index (RPI). At the same time the government removed virtually all restrictions on imports and allowed the export of most goods to occur.[80]

Today, only 17 percent of its work force is in agriculture. After the Czech Republic, Bulgaria is the most urbanized country in CEE. Bulgaria has an emerging market economy in the upper middle-income range,[81] where the private sector accounts for more than 80 percent of GDP. From a largely agricultural country with a predominantly rural population in 1948, by the 1980s Bulgaria had transformed into an industrial economy with scientific and technological research at the top of its budgetary expenditure priorities.

Economic indicators have worsened amid the late-2000s financial crisis. After several consecutive years of high growth, as depicted in Figure A.18, GDP contracted again in 2009.[82] Positive growth was

---

[80] Levinson (1994).

[81] Levinson (1994).

[82] Eurostar (2011).

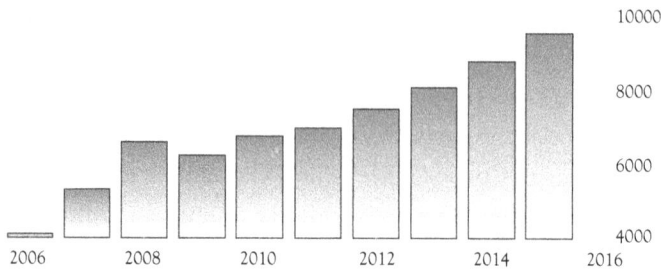

Figure A.18 Bulgaria GDP per capita 2006–2015

Source: tradingeconomics.com, World Bank.

restored in 2010, although investments and consumption continue to decline steadily due to rising unemployment.

After 2010, despite GDP per capita growth, intercompany debt exceeded €51 billion, meaning that 60 percent of all Bulgarian companies were mutually indebted.[83] By 2012, it had increased to €83 billion, or 227 percent of GDP.[84] The government implemented strict austerity measures with IMF and EU encouragement to some positive fiscal results, but the social consequences of these measures have been "catastrophic" according to the International Trade Union Confederation.

Corruption remains another obstacle to economic growth. Bulgaria is one of the most corrupt EU members and ranks 75th in the Corruption Perceptions Index.[85] Weak law enforcement and overall low capacity of civil service remain as challenges in curbing corruption. However, fighting against corruption has become the focus of the government because of the EU accession, and several anticorruption programs have been undertaken by different government agencies.

Economic activities are fostered by the lowest personal and corporate income tax rates in the EU,[86] and the second-lowest public debt of all member states at 16.5 percent of GDP in 2012. In 2013, GDP (PPP) was estimated at $119.6 billion, with a per capita value of $16,518. Sofia and

---

[83] Harizanova (2010).

[84] Harizanova (2010).

[85] "Corruption Perceptions Index: Transparency International" (2012).

[86] Novinite (2010).

the surrounding Yugozapaden planning area is the most developed region of the country with a per capita PPP GDP of $27,282 in 2011.

Slovenia

Slovenia, as depicted in Figure A.19, is a nation state in southern central Europe, located at the crossroads of main European cultural and trade routes. It is bordered by Italy to the west, Austria to the north, Hungary to the northeast, Croatia to the south and southeast, and the Adriatic Sea to the southwest. It is a parliamentary republic and a member of the UN, EU, and NATO. The capital and largest city is Ljubljana.[87]

The Slavic, Germanic, Romance, and Hungarian languages meet here. Although the population is not homogeneous, the majority is Slovene. Slovene is the official language throughout the country, whereas

Figure A.19 Slovenia is bordered by Italy on west, Austria to the north, Hungary to the northeast, Croatia to the southeast, and the Adriatic Sea to the southwest

Source: Britannica.com.

---

[87] Vuk Dirnberk and Valantič (n.d.).

Italian and Hungarian are co-official regional minority languages in those municipalities where the Italian and the Hungarian minority are present. Slovenia is a largely secularized country, but Catholicism as well as Lutheranism has significantly influenced its culture and identity.[88]

Historically, the current territory of Slovenia was part of many different state formations, including the Roman Empire and the Holy Roman Empire, followed by the Habsburg Monarchy. In October 1918, the Slovenes exercised self-determination for the first time by co-founding the internationally unrecognized State of Slovenes, Croats, and Serbs, which merged in December 1918 with the Kingdom of Serbia into the Kingdom of Serbs, Croats, and Slovenes (renamed Kingdom of Yugoslavia in 1929). During WWII, Slovenia was occupied and annexed by Germany, Italy, and Hungary, with a tiny area transferred to the Independent State of Croatia, a Nazi puppet state.[89]

Afterward, it was a founding member of the Federal People's Republic of Yugoslavia, later renamed the Socialist Federal Republic of Yugoslavia (SFRY), a communist state that was the only country in the Eastern Bloc not part of the Warsaw Pact. In June 1991, after the introduction of multiparty representative democracy, Slovenia split from Yugoslavia and became an independent country.[90] In 2004, it entered NATO and the EU; in 2007 became the first former communist country to join the Eurozone; and in 2010 joined the OECD, a global association of high-income developed countries.

Slovenia is a parliamentary democracy republic with a multiparty system. The head of state is the president, who is elected by popular vote and has an important integrative role. He is elected for 5 years and at maximum for two consecutive terms. He has mainly a representative role and is the commander-in-chief of the Slovenian military forces.[91]

Corruption, while less extensive than in some other central European countries, remains a problem, usually involving conflicts of interest and contracting links between government officials and private businesses.

---

[88] Armstrong and Anderson (2007, 165).
[89] Katzenstein (1997, 4).
[90] Katzenstein (1997, 4).
[91] Furtlehner (2008).

The judicial system is sound and transparent but remains comparatively inefficient, understaffed, and plagued by a large case backlog. Private property rights are constitutionally guaranteed, but enforcement is slow. The government of Slovenian Democratic Party Prime Minister Janez Janša collapsed in February 2013. Janša was subsequently convicted of corruption and began serving a 2-year prison sentence in June 2014. In July 2014, Miro Cerar's new SMC party won a plurality of seats in parliament with about 35 percent of the popular vote. Privatizations and efforts to reduce the public sector have been slowed by instability. The government still controls about half of the economy. A government bailout of over €3 billion went to banks carrying bad loans in December 2013. Slovenia joined the EU and NATO in 2004, adopted the euro in 2007, and joined the OECD in 2010.[92] The country has excellent infrastructure and an educated workforce.

The labor market remains rigid despite reform efforts, and the lack of overall regulatory efficiency limits private-sector growth. While property rights are respected, the level of perceived corruption has increased. Nonetheless, Slovenia has a developed economy and its per capita income is the second richest of the Slavic countries after Czech Republic.[93] Slovenia was in the beginning of 2007 the first new member to introduce the euro as its currency, replacing the tolar.[94] There is a big difference in prosperity between the various regions. The economically most prosperous regions are the central Slovenia regions, which includes the capital Ljubljana, and the western Slovenian regions of Goriška and Coastal–Karst. The poorest regions are Mura, the central Sava, and the Littoral–Inner Carniola.

As shown in Figure A.20, during 2004 to 2006, Slovenia's GDP grew at an average of 5 percent a year, reaching almost 7 percent by 2007. The growth surge was fuelled by debt, particularly among firms, and especially in construction. After the global financial crisis of 2007 and the European sovereign-debt crisis in 2008, the price for a boom that veered

---

[92] Furtlehner (2008).

[93] Eurostar (2015).

[94] Eurostar (2015).

SLOVENIA GDP

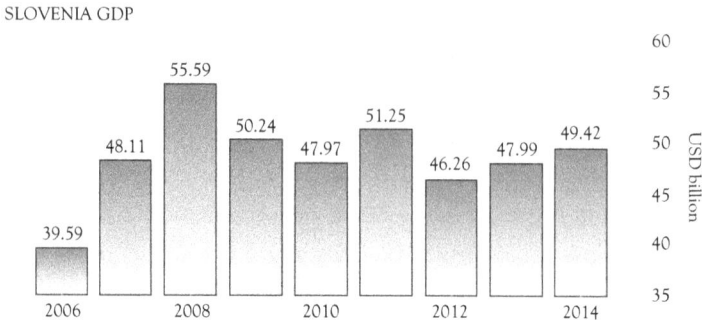

Figure A.20 Slovenia's GDP per capita 2006–2014

Source: tradingeconomics, World Bank.

out of control had to be paid.[95] The construction industry was severely hit in 2010[96] and in 2009 and 2010 Slovenian GDP per capita shrunk by 8 percent, the biggest decline in the EU after the Baltic countries and Finland.

According to Heritage,[97] Slovenia's total national debt at the end of September 2011 amounted to €15,884 million or 44.4 percent of GDP.[98] In August 2012, the three main ratings agencies have all downgraded Slovenian sovereign debt.

Slovenia's economic freedom score is 60.3, making its economy the 88th freest in the world, according to 2015 Index. Its score has decreased by 2.4 points since last year, reflecting a combined decline in the management of public spending, business freedom, and freedom from corruption that dwarfs improvements in labor freedom and monetary freedom. Slovenia is ranked 36th out of 43 countries in the Europe region, and its overall score is just below the world average.

Croatia

Croatia is at the crossroads of central and southeast Europe and the Mediterranean. As illustrated on the map in Figure A.21, its capital city

---

[95] *The Economist* (2012).

[96] *The Economist* (2012).

[97] www.heritage.org/index/country/slovenia.

[98] STA (2012).

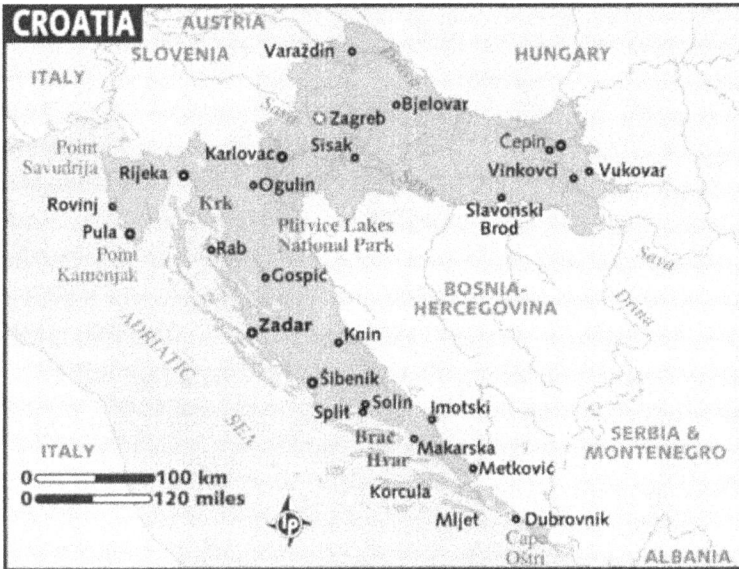

Figure A.21 Croatia borders the Adriatic Sea coast on the west, Slovenia on the northwest, Hungary on the northeast, and Bosnia-Herzegovina on the southeast

Source: lonelyplanet.com.

is Zagreb, which forms one of the country's primary subdivisions, along with its 20 other counties. The country borders the Adriatic Sea coast, in which it has more than a thousand islands. Croatia also borders Slovenia on the northwest, Hungary on the northeast, and Bosnia-Herzegovina on the southeast. Croatia has a population of about 4.28 million, most of whom are Croats, with the most common religious denomination being Roman Catholicism.

In 1918, after WWI, Croatia was included in the unrecognized State of Slovenes, Croats, and Serbs, which seceded from Austria-Hungary and merged into the Kingdom of Yugoslavia. A fascist Croatian puppet state existed during WWII. After the war, Croatia became a founding member and a federal constituent of SFRY, a constitutionally socialist state. In June 1991, Croatia declared independence. The Croatian War of Independence was fought successfully during the 4 years following the declaration.

Croatia is a republic governed under a parliamentary system. The IMF classifies Croatia as an emerging and developing economy, and the

World Bank identifies it as a high-income economy. Croatia is a member of the EU, the UN, the Council of Europe, NATO, the WTO, as well as a founding member of the Union for the Mediterranean. As an active participant in the UN peacekeeping forces, Croatia has contributed troops to the NATO-led mission in Afghanistan and took a nonpermanent seat on the UN Security Council for the 2008 to 2009 term.

Though still one of the wealthiest of the former Yugoslav republics, Croatia's economy suffered significantly during the war, from 1991 to 1995. As a result, the country's economic infrastructure sustained massive damage, particularly the revenue-rich tourism industry. The country's output during that time collapsed, and Croatia missed the early waves of investment in CEE that followed the fall of the Berlin Wall. From 1989 to 1993, the GDP fell by 40.5 percent.

As depicted in Figure A.22, between 2000 and 2008, however, Croatia's economic fortunes began to improve with moderate but steady GDP growth between 4 and 6 percent, led by a rebound in tourism and credit-driven consumer spending. The economy retracted again during 2009 and 2010 in consequence of the global financial crisis, but began to recover in 2011. Strong capital inflows, partly channeled through Croatia's largely foreign-owned banking sector, underpinned the robust growth up to the 2008 global financial crisis. FDI, including cross-border intercompany lending from parent holdings, was also sizable. To a greater extent than peer economies in the region, the sizeable FDI inflows largely bypassed the tradable sector.

In a context of a tightly managed euro exchange rate, cost competitiveness losses accumulated, and the already poor export performance

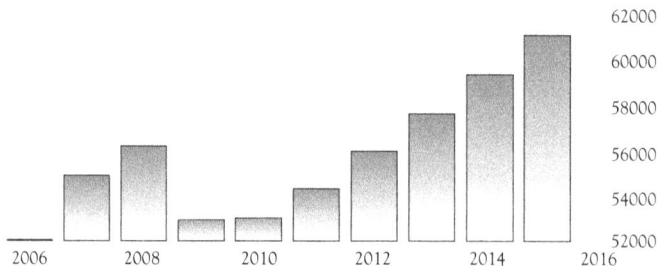

Figure A.22 Croatia's GDP per capita in USD 1992–2008

Source: statinfo.biz, World Bank.

deteriorated further. As a result, by 2008 Croatia registered an overall negative net international investment position (NIIP) of over 75 percent of GDP and a record current account deficit of 8.9 percent of GDP. At 110.8 and 36 percent of GDP, respectively, corporate and household debt and general government debt were not particularly high when the crisis flared up, though gross external debt was already in excess of 100 percent of GDP.

In 2010, economic output was dominated by the service sector, which accounted for 66 percent of GDP, followed by the industrial sector with 27.2 percent and agriculture accounting for 6.8 percent of GDP.[99] Shipbuilding, food processing, pharmaceuticals, IT, and biochemical and timber industry dominate the industrial sector in Croatia. In 2010, Croatian exports were valued at 64.9 billion kuna (€8.65 billion) with 110.3 billion kuna (€14.7 billion) worth of imports. The Croatian state still controls a significant part of the economy, with government expenditures accounting for as much as 40 percent of GDP.[100] A backlogged judiciary system, combined with inefficient public administration, especially on issues of land ownership and corruption, are particular concerns.

Inflation over the same period remained tame and the currency, the kuna, stable. Other difficult problems still remain, including a stubborn high unemployment rate, uneven regional development, and a challenging investment climate. Croatia continues to face reduced foreign investment. On July 1, 2013, Croatia joined the EU, following a decade-long application process. EU accession has increased pressure on the government to reduce Croatia's relatively high public debt, which triggered the EU's excessive deficit procedure for fiscal consolidation. Zagreb has cut spending since 2012, and the government also raised additional revenues through more stringent tax collection and by raising the value added tax. The government has also sought to accelerate privatization of nonstrategic assets, with mixed success.

The service sector dominates Croatia's economy, followed by the industrial sector and agriculture. Tourism is a significant source of revenue during the summer, with Croatia ranked the 18th most popular

---

[99] Eurostat (2011).
[100] U.S. Department of State (2015).

tourist destination in the world. The state controls a part of the economy, with substantial government expenditure. The EU is Croatia's most important trading partner. Since 2000, the Croatian government has invested in infrastructure, especially transport routes and facilities along the pan-European corridors. Internal sources produce a significant portion of energy in Croatia; the rest is imported. Croatia provides a universal health care system and free primary and secondary education, while supporting culture through numerous public institutions and corporate investments in media and publishing.

Despite not joining the EU until 2013, Croatia experienced similar adverse macroeconomic trends in the pre-crisis years. The investment-led internal demand contributed to rapid import penetration. Though price and wages dynamics were contained in relative terms, subdued productivity dynamics resulted in increasing unit labor costs. In addition, it still suffers from other difficulties typically facing other transitional economies. An independent judiciary has not been fully established, and there are delays and backlogs in adjudicating cases.

Corruption is perceived as prevalent in major public companies, the health sector, universities, public procurement systems, the construction sector, and land registry offices. In 2014, a former prime minister was found guilty of masterminding a scheme to siphon off $2.7 million from state companies. Although some reforms are being implemented, the court system is cumbersome, inefficient, and time-consuming. Land registry offices need further reform to guarantee clearly defined property rights. An uncertain civic environment and fiscal pressures will continue to challenge efforts to build on Croatia's modest improvements in economic freedom over the past 5 years. Reforms to open up the investment regime should help the country to integrate more fully into the European market.

In March 2014, the European Commission[101] concluded that Croatia was experiencing excessive macroeconomic imbalances. More specifically the risks stemming from high external liabilities, declining export performance, highly leveraged firms, and fast increasing general government debt, all in a context of low growth and poor adjustment capacity, required specific monitoring and strong policy action.

---

[101] European Commission (2015).

Albania

Albania is a country in southeastern Europe. As depicted in Figure A.23, Albania borders Montenegro on the northwest, Kosovo to the northeast, the Republic of Macedonia to the east, and Greece to the south and southeast. It also has a coast on the Adriatic Sea to the west and on the Ionian Sea to the southwest, and it is less than 72 km (45 miles) from Italy, across the Strait of Otranto, which connects the Adriatic Sea to the Ionian Sea.

Albania declared independence in 1912 and was recognized the following year. It then became a principality, republic, and kingdom until being invaded by Italy in 1939, which formed Greater Albania. The latter eventually turned into a Nazi German protectorate in 1943.[102] Albania experienced widespread social and political transformations during the

Figure A.23 Albania borders Montenegro on the northwest, Kosovo to the northeast, the Republic of Macedonia to the east, Greece to the south and southeast, the Adriatic Sea to the west, and on the Ionian Sea to the southwest

Source: operationworld.org

---

[102] Zolo (2002).

communist era, as well as isolationism from much of the international community.

The socialist reconstruction of Albania was launched immediately after the annulling of the monarchy and the establishment of a "People's Republic." In 1947, Albania's first railway line was completed, with the second completed eight months later. New land reform laws were passed granting the land to the workers and peasants who tilled it. Agriculture became cooperative, and production increased significantly, leading to Albania's becoming agriculturally self-sufficient. By 1955, illiteracy was eliminated among Albania's adult population.[103]

During this period Albania became industrialized and saw rapid economic growth, as well as unprecedented progress in the areas of education and health. The average annual rate of Albania's national income was 29 percent higher than the world average and 56 percent higher than the European average.[104] Albania's communist constitution did not allow taxes on individuals; instead, taxes were imposed on cooperatives and other organizations, with much the same effect.

After protests beginning in 1989 and reforms made by the communist government in 1990, the People's Republic was dissolved in 1991 to 1992 and the Republic of Albania was founded. The communists retained a stronghold in parliament after popular support in the elections of 1991. However, in March 1992, amid liberalization policies resulting in economic collapse and social unrest, a new front led by the new Democratic Party took power. In 1991, the socialist republic was dissolved and the Republic of Albania was established.

Albania is today a parliamentary republic. The country's capital, Tirana, represents its financial and industrial heartland, with a metropolitan population of almost 800,000 people out of around 2.9 million Albanians.[105] Albania has made progress in its democratic development since first holding multiparty elections in 1991, but deficiencies remain. International observers judged elections to be largely free and fair since the restoration of political stability following the collapse of pyramid schemes

---

[103] Pllumi (1948).

[104] Dalakoglou (n.d.).

[105] INSTAT (2015).

in 1997; however, most of Albania's post-communist elections have been marred by claims of electoral fraud. Albania joined NATO in April 2009 and in June 2014 became a candidate for EU accession. Albania is also a member of the UN, the OSCE in Europe, the Council of Europe, and the WTO. It is one of the founding members of the Energy Community, Organization of the Black Sea Economic Cooperation, and the Union for the Mediterranean. It is also an official candidate for membership in the EU.

Albania, a formerly closed, centrally planned state, is a developing country with a modern open-market economy. Free-market reforms have opened the country to foreign investment, especially in the development of energy and transportation infrastructure. Notwithstanding, a large informal economy and an inadequate energy and transportation infrastructure remain obstacles.

Although Albania's economy continues to grow, it has slowed, and the country is still one of the poorest in Europe. Albania managed to weather the first waves of the global financial crisis but, more recently, its negative effects have put some pressure on the Albanian economy, resulting in a significant economic slowdown. While the government is focused on establishing a favorable business climate through the simplification of licensing requirements and tax codes, it entered into a new arrangement with the IMF for additional financial and technical support.

Remittances, a significant catalyst for economic growth, declined from 12 to 15 percent of GDP before the 2008 financial crisis to 5.7 percent of GDP in 2014, mostly from Albanians residing in Greece and Italy. The agricultural sector, which accounts for almost half of the employment but only about one-fifth of GDP, is limited primarily to small family operations and subsistence farming, because of a lack of modern equipment, unclear property rights, and the prevalence of small, inefficient plots of land.

Complex tax codes and licensing requirements, a weak judicial system, endemic corruption, poor enforcement of contracts and property issues, and antiquated infrastructure contribute to Albania's poor business environment and make attracting foreign investment difficult. Inward FDI has significantly increased in recent years as the government has embarked on an ambitious program to improve the business climate through fiscal and legislative reforms. Albania's electricity supply is uneven despite upgraded transmission capacities with neighboring countries. Technical and non-technical losses in electricity—including theft and nonpayment—continue to undermine the financial viability of the entire system, although the government has taken steps to stem nontechnical losses and begin to upgrade the distribution grid. Also, with help from international donors, the government is taking steps to improve the poor national road and rail network, a long-standing barrier to sustained economic growth.

The country will continue to face challenges from increasing public debt, having exceeded its former statutory limit of 60 percent of GDP in 2013 and reaching 72 percent in 2014. Strong trade, remittance, and banking sector ties with Greece and Italy make Albania vulnerable to spillover effects of debt crises and weak growth in the Eurozone. The government will face critical tests in 2015 as it works to implement IMF-mandated reforms, especially those aimed at improving the electricity sector.

Bosnia-Herzegovina

Bosnia and Herzegovina, also known informally as Bosnia, is a country in southeastern Europe located on the Balkan Peninsula. As illustrated on the map in Figure A.24, the country is bordered by Croatia to the north, west, and south, Serbia to the east, Montenegro to the southeast, and the Adriatic Sea to the south. Sarajevo is the capital and the largest city.

Bosnia and Herzegovina is a region that traces permanent human settlement back to the Neolithic age, during and after which it was populated by several Illyrian and Celtic civilizations. Culturally, politically, and socially, the country has one of the richest histories in the region, having been first settled by the Slavic peoples that populate the area today from the 6th through to the 9th centuries AD. They then established the first independent banate in the region, known as the Banate of Bosnia,[106] in the early 12th century upon the arrival and convergence of peoples that would eventually come to call themselves Dobri Bošnjani.[107] This

---

[106] Mojzes (2000).
[107] Meaning "Good Bosnians."

Figure A.24 Bosnia is bordered by Croatia to the north, west, and south, Serbia to the east, Montenegro to the southeast, and the Adriatic Sea to the south

Source: Encyclopedia Britannica

evolved into the Kingdom of Bosnia in the 14th century, after which it was annexed into the Ottoman Empire, under whose rule it remained from the mid-15th to the late-19th centuries.

The Ottomans brought Islam to the region, and altered much of the cultural and social outlook of the country. This was followed by annexation into the Austro-Hungarian Monarchy, which lasted up until WWI. In the interwar period, Bosnia was part of the Kingdom of Yugoslavia and after WWII, the country was granted full republic status in the newly formed SFRY.

Bosnia and Herzegovina declared sovereignty in October 1991 and independence from the former Yugoslavia on March 3, 1992, after a referendum boycotted by ethnic Serbs. Following the dissolution of Yugoslavia, the country proclaimed independence in 1992, which was followed by the Bosnian War, lasting until late 1995. The Bosnian Serbs—supported by neighboring Serbia and Montenegro—responded with armed resistance aimed at partitioning the republic along ethnic lines and joining Serb-held areas to form a "Greater Serbia." In March 1994, Bosniaks and Croats reduced the number of warring factions from three to two by signing an agreement creating a joint Bosniak-Croat Federation of Bosnia and Herzegovina. On November 21, 1995, in Dayton, Ohio, the warring parties initialed a peace agreement that ended 3 years of interethnic civil strife.[108]

Bosnia has a transitional economy with limited market reforms. The economy relies heavily on the export of metals, energy, textiles, and furniture as well as on remittances and foreign aid. A highly decentralized government hampers economic policy coordination and reform, while excessive bureaucracy and a segmented market discourage foreign investment. Interethnic warfare in Bosnia and Herzegovina caused production to plummet by 80 percent from 1992 to 1995 and unemployment to soar, but the economy made progress until 2009, when the global economic crisis caused a downturn. Foreign banks, primarily from Austria and Italy, now control most of the banking sector. The konvertibilnamarka, the national currency introduced in 1998, is pegged to the euro, and confidence in the currency and the banking sector has remained stable.

Today, the country maintains high literacy, life expectancy, and education levels and is one of the most frequently visited countries in the region,[109] projected to have the third highest tourism growth rate in the world between 1995 and 2020. Bosnia and Herzegovina is regionally and internationally renowned for its natural beauty and cultural heritage inherited from six historical civilizations, its cuisine, winter sports, its eclectic and unique music, architecture and its festivals, some of which are the largest and most prominent of their kind in southeastern Europe.

The country is home to three main ethnic groups or, officially, constituent peoples, a term unique for Bosnia and Herzegovina. Bosniaks are the largest group of the three, with Serbs second and Croats third. Regardless of ethnicity, a citizen of Bosnia and Herzegovina is often identified in English as a Bosnian. The terms Herzegovinian and Bosnian are maintained as a regional rather than ethnic distinction, and the region of

---

[108] The final agreement was signed in Paris on December 14, 1995.
[109] Lonely Planet (n.d.).

Herzegovina has no precisely defined borders of its own. Moreover, the country was simply called "Bosnia" until the Austro-Hungarian occupation at the end of the 19th century.[110]

Bosnia and Herzegovina has a bicameral legislature and a three-member presidency composed of a member of each major ethnic group. However, the central government's power is highly limited, as the country is largely decentralized and comprises two autonomous entities: the Federation of Bosnia and Herzegovina and Republika Srpska, with a third region, the Brčko district, governed under the local government.

The Federation of Bosnia and Herzegovina is itself complex and consists of 10 federal units, also known as cantons. The country is a potential candidate for membership to the EU and has been a candidate for NATO membership since April 2010, when it received a Membership Action Plan at a summit in Tallinn. In addition, the country has also been a member of the Council of Europe since April 2002 and has been a founding member of the Mediterranean Union upon its establishment since July 2008.

Bosnia faces the dualproblem of rebuilding a war-torn country and introducing transitional liberal market reforms to its formerly mixed economy. One legacy of the previous era is a strong industry, which under former republic President Džemal Bijedić and SFRY President Josip Broz Tito, metal industries were promoted in the republic, resulting in the development of a large share of Yugoslavia's plants. Bosnia and Herzegovina had a very strong industrial export-oriented economy in the 1970s and 1980s, with large-scale exports.

The war in the 1990s, however, caused a dramatic and very negative change for the Bosnian economy.[111] The country's total GDP fell sharply by about 60 percent. The large destruction of physical infrastructure also contributed to devastated the economy.[112] With much of the production capacity unrestored, the Bosnian economy still faces considerable difficulties.

---

[110] Crayne (2000).

[111] Malcolm (1996).

[112] Malcolm (1996).

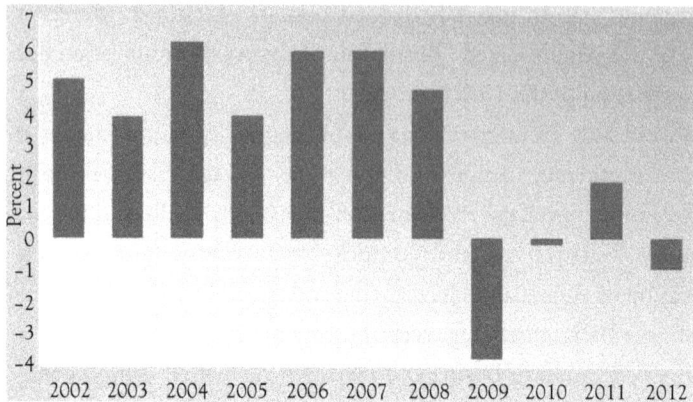

Figure A.25 Bosnia GDP 2002–2012

Source: IMF.

As depicted in Figure A.25, the country's GDP contracted by –3.9 percent in 2009. The worsening conditions across Europe and the Eurozone in particular did not help Bosnia's economy. In real terms, since 2009, the Bosnian economy has experienced what is effectively a depression.

The seemingly successful drive toward economic prosperity in the early 2000s came to a crashing halt after the global financial crisis of 2008. Like most countries in the EU's capital and trade-dependent periphery, the crisis hit the economy of Bosnia hard. The crisis depressed private sector activity and placed strains on already burdened public budgets. Wage growth, which benefited the working middle classes during the first half of the 2000s, has remained relatively flat. Unemployment shot up to 46 percent, including the portion of long-term unemployed, which grew from 20 to 25 percent Youth unemployment grew from its 2008 low of 47 to 63 percent in 2012. Moreover, the burden of inflation, which has plagued most of the Balkans after 2008, has added to the difficulties of vulnerable groups.

Implementation of privatization, however, has been slow, and local entities only reluctantly support national-level institutions. Banking reform accelerated in 2001 as all foreign banks, primarily from western Europe, now control most of the banking sector. Successful implementation of a value-added tax in 2006 provided a steady source of revenue for the government and helped rein in gray-market activity.

National-level statistics have also improved over time but a large share of economic activity remains unofficial and unrecorded. Bosnia and Herzegovina became a full member of the Central European Free Trade Agreement in September 2007, but despite that fact, foreign investment has dropped sharply since 2007 and a sizable current account deficit, as well as a very high unemployment rate remain the two most serious economic problems.

Government spending, including transfer payments, also remains high, at roughly 40 percent of GDP, because of redundant government offices at the national, subnational, and municipal level. The country has a disproportionately large public sector, which dates back to Yugoslav times and has only been partly reformed since. Public expenditures amount to nearly half of GDP and, if state-owned enterprises (SOEs) and costs from corruption are added in, the public sector may be as large as 70 percent of GDP. That's not much smaller than in the 1980s! Though public spending is high, it is not pro-poor.

For instance, high social protection spending benefits the wealthy almost as much as the poor. While SOEs maintain employment, even in some extreme cases when factories no longer operate, they also generate bills, which ultimately are paid by the taxpayer.

In turn, this created a negative spiral: taxes are high and biased against employment. A large tax wedge swallows over a third of even the lowest paid workers' salaries, making it almost impossible for employers to create formal jobs. And employers are hit by the region's worst business environment—partly the result of a plethora of regulatory regimes and a rent seeking rather than public service oriented public sector.

In addition, Bosnia is still based on an economy of consumption rather than production. During the post-war economic recovery, the country did not create new foundations for sustainable economic growth. Today, consumption remains at over 100 percent of GDP, with only a handful of countries having higher figures. To sustain high levels of income, create prosperity, and eliminate poverty, Bosnia will need to shift toward an economic model built on production of goods and services rather than consumption.

The country receives substantial amounts of reconstruction assistance and humanitarian aid from the international community but will have to prepare for an era of declining assistance. Bosnia and Herzegovina's top economic priorities, therefore, are focused on the acceleration of integration into the EU, the strengthening of the fiscal system, the public administration reforms, becoming a member of WTO, and securing economic growth by fostering a dynamic and competitive private sector. Flooding caused significant damage in the spring of 2014, and Bosnia will struggle to recover from it in 2015.

Bosnia's shift to an entirely non- or antinationalist politics as a whole seems like a long shot given the still living memory of the civil war, the post-Dayton ethno political institutions, which not only privilege, but premise the entire political process as one of rule by ethno nationalist consensus. In addition, it benefit the existing nationalist parties, which had already seized the opportunity upon the protests to stir up conspiracy theories about how the alleged real goal behind the protestors was to undermine the power and standing of one owns or the other national group.

The potential for a non-nationalist political solidarity across all of Bosnia that would entirely and categorically reject this approach seems possible, but it will take more than a few symbolic gestures to overcome the divisions that have been sewn by the civil war and entrenched institutionally and politically in post-Dayton Bosnia. Indeed, what has united the grieving populations of all three groups is the belief that parties of all stripes have used political power in Bosnia chiefly for personal enrichment at the expense of the rest. The mass protests, which have already produced radical institutional innovation at the local and regional level, are clearly also a call for a much-empowered Bosnian central state that not only does away with the logic of ethno politics, but also possesses the means to steer the country toward more meaningful and more inclusive economic development.

Kosovo

Kosovo, also known as Kosova by Albanians and Косово by Serbians, is a disputed territory[113] and partially recognized state in southeastern Europe that declared its independence from Serbia in February 2008 as the Republic of Kosovo, with its capital and largest city being Pristina.

---

[113] Rossi (2014).

While Serbia recognizes the Republic's governance of the territory, it still continues to claim it as its own Autonomous Province of Kosovo and Metohija.[114] As depicted in Figure A.26, the country is landlocked in the central Balkan Peninsula, bordered by the Republic of Macedonia and Albania to the south, Montenegro to the west, and the uncontested territory of Serbia to the north and east.

After being part of the Ottoman Empire from the 15th to the early-20th century, in the late-19th century Kosovo became the center of the Albanian independence movement with the League of Prizren.[115] As a result of the defeat in the First Balkan War (1912 to 1913), the

Figure A.26 Kosovo is bordered by the Republic of Macedonia and Albania to the south, Montenegro to the west, and the uncontested territory of Serbia to the north and east

Source: BBC.

---

[114] Engjellushe (2014).

[115] The League for the Defense of the Rights of the Albanian Nation, commonly known as the League of Prizren, was an Albanian political organization founded on January 5, 1877, in the old town of Prizren, in the Kosova Vilayet of the Ottoman Empire.

Ottoman Empire ceded the Vilayet of Kosovo to the Balkan League. At the time, the Kingdom of Serbia took its larger part, while the Kingdom of Montenegro annexed the western part before both countries became a part of the Kingdom of Yugoslavia after WWI. After a period of Yugoslav unitarianism in the Kingdom of Yugoslavia, the post-WWII Yugoslav constitution established the Autonomous Province of Kosovo and Metohija within the Yugoslav constituent republic of Serbia.

Long-term severe ethnic tensions between Kosovo's Albanian and Serb populations left Kosovo ethnically divided, resulting in interethnic violence, including the Kosovo War of 1998 to 1999.[116] The war ended with a military intervention of NATO, which forced the Federal Republic of Yugoslavia to withdraw its troops from Kosovo, which became a UN protectorate. On February 17, 2008 Kosovo's Parliament declared independence. It has since gained diplomatic recognition as a sovereign state by 108 UN member states. Serbia refuses to recognize Kosovo as a state,[117] although with the Brussels Agreement of 2013[118] it has accepted the legitimacy of Kosovo institutions. The agreement solidified that Kosovo's elected government, and not Serbia's exclusively, would operate the public institutions in Kosovo.

Kosovo lacks diplomatic recognition from 85 UN member states.[119] The country is not itself a member of the UN, but is recognized by 23 of the 28 members, and is a potential candidate for future enlargement of the EU. Kosovo is, however, a member of IMF, as well as the World Bank, the International Road and Transport Union (IRU), Regional Cooperation Council, Council of Europe Development Bank, Venice Commission, and the European Bank for Reconstruction and Development.[120]

---

[116] Schabnel and Thakur (2001).

[117] Smith (2015).

[118] The Brussels Agreement was made between the governments of Serbia and Kosovo on the normalization of their relations. It was negotiated and concluded, although not signed by either party, in Brussels under the auspices of the EU. The agreement was concluded on April 19, 2013.

[119] Smith (2015).

[120] Sinani (2013).

Kosovo was the poorest part of the former SFRY, and in the 1990s its economy suffered from the combined results of political upheaval, the Yugoslav wars, Serbian dismissal of Kosovo employees, and international sanctions on Serbia, of which it was then part. After 1999, it had an economic boom as a result of postwar reconstruction and foreign assistance. Despite the global financial crisis of 2009 and the subsequent Eurozone crisis, as depicted in Figure A.27, in the period from 2003 to 2011, notwithstanding declining foreign assistance, growth of GDP averaged over 5 percent a year, and inflation was low.[121]

Most of this economic development since 1999 has taken place in the trade, retail, and construction sectors. The private sector, which has emerged since 1999, has been mainly small-scale. The industrial sector has remained weak. The economy, and its sources of growth, is therefore geared far more to demand than production, which was in 2011 in deficit by about 20 percent of GDP. Consequently, Kosovo is highly dependent on remittances from the diaspora, most of them from Germany and Switzerland, as well as FDI, which a high proportion also comes from the diaspora, in addition to other capital inflows.[122]

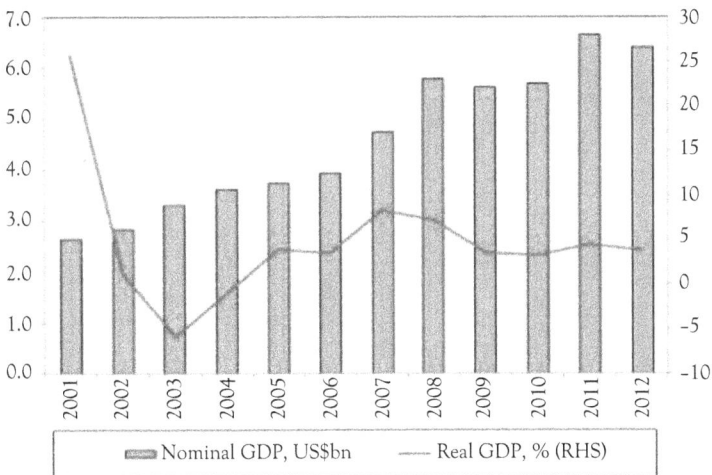

Figure A.27 Kosovo's nominal versus real GDP for period 2001–2012

Source: BMI Research.

---

[121] www.worldbank.org/en/country/kosovo

[122] IMF (2012a).

A major deterrent to foreign manufacturing investment in Kosovo was removed in 2011 when the European Council accepted a convention allowing Kosovo to be accepted as part of its rules for diagonal cumulative origination, allowing the label of Kosovo origination to goods, which have been processed there but originated in a country elsewhere in the convention. Since 2002 the European Commission has compiled a yearly progress report on Kosovo, evaluating its political and economic situation. Kosovo became a member of the World Bank and the IMF on June 29, 2009.

Government revenue is also dependent on demand rather than production. Only 14 percent of revenue comes from direct taxes and the rest mainly from customs duties and taxes on consumption. In part this reflects low levels of production, but it also reflects very low direct taxation rates. In 2009, corporation tax was halved from 20 to 10 percent.

Kosovo adopted the German mark in 1999 to replace the Serbian dinar, and later replaced it with the euro, although the Serbian dinar is still used in some Serb-majority areas, mostly in the north. This means that Kosovo has no levers of monetary policy over its economy, and must rely on a conservative fiscal policy to provide the means to respond to external shocks. The World Bank has pointed out, however, that informal employment is widespread, and the ratio of wages to per capita GDP is the second highest in southeast Europe; the true rate may therefore be lower.[123]

The dispute over Kosovo's international status, and the interpretation, which some nonrecognizing states place on symbols that may or may not imply sovereignty, continues to impose economic costs on Kosovo. Examples include flight diversions because of a Serbian ban on flights to Kosovo over its territory, loss of revenues because of a lack of a regional dialing code (end-user fees on fixed lines accrue to Serbian Telecoms, while Kosovo has to pay Monaco and Slovenia for use of their regional codes for mobile phone connections, no international bank account number (IBAN) code for bank transfers until 2015, and no regional Kosovo code for the Internet. Nevertheless, information and communications

---

[123] IMF (2012a).

technology in Kosovo has developed very rapidly and one survey has suggested that broadband Internet penetration is comparable to the EU average.

Macedonia

Macedonia is a country located in the central Balkan Peninsula in southeast Europe. As illustrated in Figure A.28, the country is a landlocked country bordered by Kosovo to the northwest, Serbia to the north, Bulgaria to the east, Greece to the south, and Albania to the west. It is one of the successor states of the former Yugoslavia, from which it declared independence in 1991. It became a member of the UN in 1993, but, as a result of an ongoing dispute with Greece over use of the name Macedonia, it was admitted under the provisional description of "the former Yugoslav Republic of Macedonia."[124]

Figure A.28 Macedonia is a landlocked country bordered by Kosovo to the northwest, Serbia to the north, Bulgaria to the east, Greece to the south, and Albania to the west

---

[124] United Nations (1993).

Macedonia's economy has almost always been completely agricultural in nature from the beginning of the Ottoman Empire when it was part of the District of Skopje and Province of Salonika. It concentrated on pasture farming and vineyard growing. Opium poppy, introduced into the region in 1835, became an important crop as well by the late-19th century, and remained so until the 1930s. The role of industry in the region's economy, however, increased during the industrial era. Macedonia was responsible for large outputs of textiles and several other goods in the Ottoman Empire; despite the fact outdated techniques to produce the goods persisted.

The stagnation of Macedonian economy began under the ruling of the Kingdom of Serbia. When WWII ended, the country's economy began to experience revitalization by way of subsidies from Serbia. The subsidies assisted Macedonia to redevelop its lost industry and shift its agricultural-centered economy to an industry-centered economy with new hearts of industry emerging all over the country in Veles, Bitola, Stip, and Kumanovo. Previously, Skopje was the only industrial center in Macedonia, this expanded to several other cities during Socialist Yugoslavia.

The breakup of Yugoslavia in 1991 depressed Macedonia's economy. An absence of infrastructure, UN sanctions on its largest market Federal Republic of Yugoslavia,[125] and a Greek economic embargo hindered economic growth until 1996. After the fall of Socialist Yugoslavia, the economy experienced several shocks that damaged the local economy. Starting with the western embargo on the Yugoslavian common market, and ending with the Greek embargo on Macedonia over the country's name.

The economy began to recover in 1995 and experienced a full recovery after the 2001 insurgency by ethnic Albanians. Worker remittances and foreign aid have softened the subsequent volatile recovery period. GDP growth suffered in 1999 due to the severe regional economic dislocations caused by the Kosovo war.

As depicted in Figure A.29, however, Macedonia's nominal and real GDP has increased each year after that by an average of 6 percent on a yearly basis, except in 2001—due to the insurgency by ethnic

---

[125] World Bank (2015).

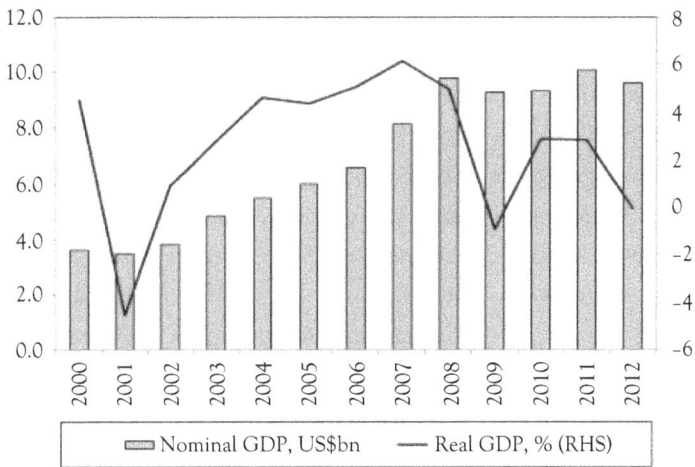

Figure A.29 Macedonia's nominal and real GDP growth 2000–2012

Source: BMI Research (bmiresearch.com).

Albanians—and then again in 2008 due to the economic crisis when its economy contracted with the rest of the world in 2009 and 2010. In the wake of the global economic crises, Macedonia has experienced decreased FDI inflows, a lowering of credit availability, and a large trade deficit. As a result of conservative fiscal policies and a sound financial system, however, in 2010 the country credit rating improved slightly and was kept at that level in 2011. The global financial crisis, therefore, had actually little impact on the country due to Macedonian banks' stringent rules, allowing GDP to grow again in 2011. Macedonia today maintains a low debt-to-GDP ratio and is experiencing a revitalized investment interest by companies from Germany, France, Austria, and others.

Real GDP in the first half of 2011 increased significantly, driven by 23.6 percent growth in the construction sector, 13.2 percent in mining, quarrying, and manufacturing, 12.4 percent in wholesale and retail trade, and 4.2 percent in transport and communication services. Industrial output in the first 8 months of 2011 was 7.5 percent higher than in the same period of 2010. Low public and external debt and a comfortable level of foreign exchange reserves allowed for further relaxation of monetary policy, with the reference interest rate of the central bank decreasing to 4 percent.

Successful privatization in 2000 boosted the country's reserves to over $700 million. Also, the leadership demonstrated a continuing commitment to economic reform, free trade, and regional integration. The economy can meet its basic food needs but depends on outside sources for all of its oil and gas and most of its modern machinery and parts.

Macedonia is significantly vulnerable to economic developments in Europe, due to strong banking and trade ties, and dependent on regional integration and progress toward EU membership for continued economic growth. Macedonia has maintained macroeconomic stability with low inflation, but it has so far lagged the region in attracting FDI and creating jobs, despite making extensive fiscal and business sector reforms. Macroeconomic stability has been maintained by a prudent monetary policy, which keeps the domestic currency pegged against the euro.

In October 2010, the World Bank board of directors approved a new Country Partnership Strategy (CPS) with Macedonia for the period 2011 to 2014. This CPS will provide the country assistance of about $100 million in funding for the first 2 years to improve competitiveness, strengthen employability and social protection, and increase the use of sustainable energy. This assistance also includes a commitment of $30 million in direct budget support in the form of a policy-based guarantee by the World Bank to the government to facilitate its access to financing from international capital markets, a process that had been started in November 2011.

Macedonia became the first country eligible for the IMF's Precautionary Credit Line in January 2011. This program gives Macedonia a line of credit worth €475 million (about $675 million) over 2 years, to be accessed only in case of need brought about by external shocks. The credit line was approved after extensive consultations with the IMF in October and December 2010. The IMF expects that there will be no additional withdrawals from the PCL. Macedonia has the best economic freedom in the region, according to the 2012 Index of Economic Freedom, released in January 2012 by the conservative U.S. think tank Heritage Foundation and the Wall Street Journal.[126]

---

[126] Ristic (2012).

Montenegro

Montenegro is a sovereign state in southeastern Europe. As illustrated in Figure A.30, the country as bordered by the Adriatic Sea to the southwest, Croatia to the west, Bosnia and Herzegovina to the northwest, Serbia to the northeast, and Albania to the southeast. Its capital and largest city is Podgorica, while Cetinje is designated as the Prijestonica, meaning the former Royal Capital City.[127]

Since 1918, Montenegro used to be part of Yugoslavia. In April 1941, Nazi Germany and Italy attacked and occupied the Kingdom of Yugoslavia. Italian forces occupied the country and established a puppet Kingdom of Montenegro. An uprising against Italian occupation broke out in July 1941. Unexpectedly, the uprising took sway and by July 20,

Figure A.30 Montenegro as bordered by the Adriatic Sea to the southwest, Croatia to the west, Bosnia and Herzegovina to the northwest, Serbia to the northeast, and Albania to the southeast

Source: Montenegromap.net.

---

[127] Monstat (2011).

1918, 32,000 men and women joined the fight. As a result, beside the coast and major towns, which were besieged, Montenegro was mostly liberated. In a month of fighting, the Italian army had 5000 dead, wounded, and captured. Fighters who remained under arms split into two groups. Most of them joined the Yugoslav Partisans, consisting of communists and those inclined toward active resistance. Those loyal to the Karađorđević dynasty and opposing communism went on to become Chetniks,[128] and turned to collaboration with Italians against the Partisans. The uprising lasted until mid-August, when it was suppressed by a counter-offensive numbering 67,000 Italian troops brought in from Albania. Faced with new and overwhelming Italian forces, many of the fighters lay down their arms and returned home.

Then, war broke out between Partisans and Chetniks during the first half of 1942. Pressured by Italians and Chetniks, the core of the Montenegrin Partisans left to Serbia and Bosnia where they joined with other Yugoslav Partisans. Fighting between Partisans and Chetniks continued through the war. Chetniks with Italian backing controlled most of the country from mid-1942 to April 1943. Montenegrin Chetniks received the status of "anti-communist militia" and received weapons, ammunition, food rations, and salaries from Italy. Most of them were moved to Mostar where they participated in the Battle of Neretva against the Partisans but were dealt with a heavy defeat.

During the German operation *Schwartz*[129] against the Partisans in May and June 1943, Germans disarmed a large number of Chetniks without fighting, as they feared they would turn against them in case of an Allied invasion of the Balkans. After the capitulation of Italy in September 1943, Partisans managed to take hold of most of Montenegro

---

[128] The Chetniks were armed bands of Serbs active in Yugoslavia during its occupation (1941–1945). They had in common their loyalty to the Yugoslav royal house, aiming to restore it to the throne after the war.

[129] Name of German operation to engage and destroy the remaining partisan formations that had escaped into northern Montenegro with their wounded. It was critical for the Germans at this moment in time to wipe out the partisan menace and secure their lines of communication in the Balkans due to a rapidly building fear of an Allied invasion in Greece or along the Adriatic coast following the surrender of Axis forces in Tunisia.

for a brief time, but German forces soon occupied Montenegro and fierce fighting continued during late-1943 and entire 1944. The Partisans liberated Montenegro in December 1944.

The Yugoslav Partisans liberated Montenegro, and the rest of the Yugoslavia, in 1944. But a second uprising in Nazi-occupied Europe happened in July 1941 in Montenegro, when Montenegrins stood up against the fascists and joined communist Partisans. As a result, Montenegro became a constituent of the six republics of the communist SFRY, and its capital became Podgorica, renamed Titograd in honor of President Josip Broz Tito. After the war, the infrastructure of Yugoslavia was rebuilt, industrialization began, and the University of Montenegro was established. Greater autonomy was established until the Socialist Republic of Montenegro ratified a new constitution 1974.

In 1992, on a referendum of whether to remain as part of Yugoslavia, most voters' chose in favor to stay with Serbia. The Muslim, Albanian, and Catholic minorities as well as the pro-independence Montenegrins boycotted the referendum. The opponents claimed that the poll was organized under antidemocratic conditions with widespread propaganda from the state-controlled media in favor of a pro-federation vote. There is no impartial report on the fairness of the referendum, as it was unmonitored, unlike in 2006 when EU observers were present.

During the 1991 to 1995 Bosnian and Croatian War, Montenegrin police and military forces joined Serbian troops in the attacks to Dubrovnik, in Croatia. These operations, aimed at acquiring more territory, were characterized by a consistent pattern of large-scale violations of human rights.[130] Montenegrin General Pavle Strugar was convicted for his part in the bombing of Dubrovnik. Bosnian refugees were arrested by Montenegrin police and transported to Serb camps in Foča, where they were subjected to systematic torture and executed.[131]

In 1996, Milo Đukanović's government severed ties between Montenegro and the Serbian regime, which was then under Slobodan Milošević. Montenegro formed its own economic policy and adopted the German Deutsche Mark as its currency and subsequently adopted the euro,

---

[130] United Nations (1992).

[131] United Nations (1992).

although not part of the Eurozone currency union. Subsequent governments have pursued pro-independence policies and political tensions
with Serbia simmered despite the political changes in Belgrade. NATO
forces bombed targets in Montenegro during Operation Allied Force in
1999, although the extent of these attacks was very limited in both time
and area affected.[132]

In 2002, Serbia and Montenegro came to a new agreement regarding continued cooperation and entered into negotiations regarding the
future status of the Federal Republic of Yugoslavia. In 2003, the Yugoslav
federation was replaced in favor of a more decentralized state union
named Serbia and Montenegro. Such status of the union between Montenegro and Serbia was decided by a referendum on Montenegrin independence on May 21, 2006. A total of 419,240 votes were cast, representing
86.5 percent of the total electorate. About 55.5 percent were for independence and 44.5 percent were against.[133] The difference narrowly surpassed
the 55 percent quorum needed to validate the referendum under the rules
set by the EU. According to the electoral commission, the 55 percent
threshold was passed by only 2,300 votes. Serbia, the member states of
the EU, and the permanent members of the UN Security Council, all
recognized Montenegro's independence. On June 3, 2006, the Montenegrin Parliament declared the independence of Montenegro,[134] formally
confirming the result of the referendum. Serbia did not object to the
declaration.

Classified by the World Bank as an upper middle-income country,
Montenegro is a member of the UN, the WTO, the OSCE in Europe,
the Council of Europe, the Central European Free Trade Agreement, and
a founding member of the Union for the Mediterranean.

The economy of Montenegro is mostly a service-based economy,
currently in the process of economic transition. The economy of this
small Balkan state is recovering from the impact of the Yugoslav Wars
and the decline of industry following the breakup of the SFRY. The loss
of previously guaranteed markets and suppliers following the breakup of

---

[132] BBC (1999).
[133] BBC (2006).
[134] BBC (2006).

Yugoslavia left the Montenegrin industrial sector reeling as production was suspended and the privatization program, which had begun in 1989, was interrupted. The disintegration of the Yugoslav market, and the imposition of UN sanctions in May 1992 were the causes of the greatest economic and financial crisis in Montenegro since WWII.

During 1993, two-third of the Montenegrin population lived below the poverty line, while frequent interruptions in relief supplies caused the health and environmental protection to drop below the minimum of international standards. The financial losses under the adverse effects of the UN sanctions on the overall economy of Montenegro are estimated to be approximately $6.39 billion. This period was marked by the second highest hyperinflation in the history of humankind, which reached 3 million percent in January 1994.

Due to its favorable geographical location with a large coast to the Adriatic Sea, and a water-link to Albania across Lake Skadar, Montenegro became a hub for smuggling activity. The entire Montenegrin industrial production had stopped, and the country's main economic activity became the smuggling of user goods, especially those in short supply such as gasoline and cigarettes, both of which skyrocketed in price.

As depicted in Figure A.31 and according to the World Bank, Montenegro's GDP was worth $4.58 billion in 2014. The country entered a recession in 2008 as a part of the global financial crises, with GDP contracting by 4 percent. However, Montenegro remained a target for FDI, becoming the only country in the Balkans able to increase it. The country

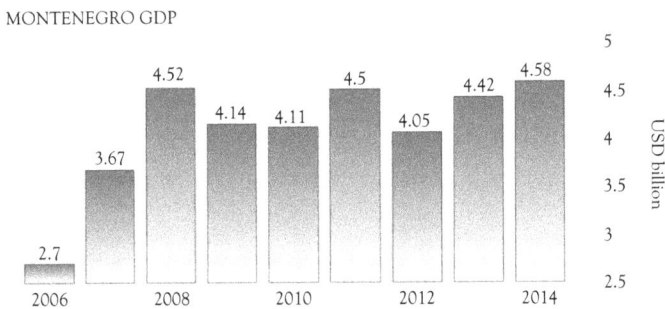

Figure A.31 Montenegro GDP 2006–2014

Source: World Bank, tradingeconomics.

exit the recession in 2010 and GDP has continued to grow since.[135] However, the significant dependence of the Montenegrin economy on FDI leaves it susceptible to external shocks and a high export and import trade deficit. The GDP value of Montenegro represents 0.01 percent of the world economy. GDP in Montenegro averaged $3.08 billion from 2000 until 2014, reaching an all time high of $4.58 billion in 2014 and a record low of $0.98 billion in 2000.

In 2007, the service sector made up for 72.4 percent of GDP, with industry and agriculture making up the rest at 17.6 and 10 percent, respectively. There are 50,000 farming households in Montenegro that rely on agriculture to fill the family budget.

Aluminum, steel production, and agricultural processing make up for most of the industrial output. Tourism is an important contributor to the Montenegrin economy. Approximately one million tourists visited Montenegro in 2007, resulting in €480 million of tourism revenue. Tourism is considered the backbone of future economic growth, and government expenditures on infrastructure improvements are largely targeted toward that goal.

Serbia

Serbia is a sovereign state situated at the crossroads between central and southeast Europe, covering the southern part of the Pannonian Plain and the central Balkans. As depicted in Figure A.32, Serbia is a landlocked country bordered by Hungary to the north, Romania and Bulgaria to the east, Macedonia to the south, and Croatia, Bosnia, and Montenegro to the west, in addition to claim a border with Albania through the disputed territory of Kosovo. The capital of Serbia, Belgrade, is one of the largest cities in southeast Europe. Serbia numbers around 7 million residents.[136]

By the mid-16th century, the entire territory of modern-day Serbia was annexed by the Ottoman Empire, at times interrupted by the

---

[135] Tanner (2009).
[136] Global Edge (n.d.).

Figure A.32 Serbia is bordered by Hungary to the north, Romania and Bulgaria to the east, Macedonia to the south, and Croatia, Bosnia, and Montenegro to the west, in addition to claim a border with Albania through the disputed territory of Kosovo

Source: Britannica.

Habsburgs.[137] In the early-19th century, the Serbian Revolution established the nation-state as the region's first constitutional monarchy, which subsequently expanded its territory. Following disastrous casualties in WWI, and subsequent unification of Habsburg crown land of Vojvodina with Serbia, the country cofounded Yugoslavia with other south Slavic peoples, which would exist in various political formations until

---

[137] The House of Habsburg, or House of Austria, was one of the most important royal houses of Europe. The Habsburgs, between 1438 and 1740, continuously occupied the throne of the Holy Roman Empire.

the Yugoslav Wars of the 1990s, which had devastating effects for the region. As a result, Serbia formed a union with Montenegro in 1992, which broke apart in 2006, when Serbia again became an independent country. In 2008 the parliament of Kosovo, Serbia's southern province with an Albanian ethnic majority, declared independence, with mixed responses from the international community.

Serbia is a member of the UN, Council of Europe (CoE), OSCE, The Partnership for Peace[138] (PfP), the Black Sea Economic Cooperation (BSEC), and Central European Free Trade Agreement (CEFTA). As a membership candidate,[139] Serbia is currently negotiating its EU accession.[140] The country is acceding to the WTO[141] and is a militarily neutral state. Serbia is an upper-middle income economy with dominant service sector, followed by the industrial sector and agriculture.

Serbia became a stand-alone sovereign republic in the summer of 2006 after Montenegro voted in a referendum for independence from the Union of Serbia and Montenegro. When the vote was followed by a formal declaration of independence by Montenegro, a special session of parliament in Belgrade declared Serbia to be the legal successor to the now defunct Union. Serbia and Montenegro, the two republics still left in the old Yugoslav federation, had agreed in 2002 to scrap remnants of the ex-communist state and create the new, looser Union of Serbia and Montenegro.

The EU-brokered deal under which the union came into being in 2003 was intended to stabilize the region by settling Montenegrin demands for independence and preventing further changes to Balkan borders. The same agreement also contained the seeds of the Union's dissolution. It stipulated that after 3 years, the two republics could hold referendums on whether to keep or scrap it. Montenegro duly voted for independence in a referendum in May 2006. The two republics had been united in one form

---

[138] A NATO program aimed at creating trust between NATO and other states in Europe.

[139] BBC (2012).

[140] BBC (2013).

[141] WTO News (2013).

or another for nearly 90 years. With separation from Montenegro, Serbia is cut off from the Adriatic Sea and becomes landlocked.

The end of the Union of Serbia and Montenegro marked the closing chapter in the history of the separation of the six republics of the old Socialist Republic of Yugoslavia which was proclaimed in 1945 and comprised Serbia, Montenegro, Slovenia, Croatia, Bosnia-Herzegovina, and Macedonia. Under Yugoslavia's authoritarian communist leader, Josip Broz Tito, the lid was kept on ethnic tensions. The federation lasted for over 10 years after his death in 1980, but under Serbian nationalist leader Slobodan Milosevic, it fell apart through the 1990s. The secession of Slovenia and Macedonia came relatively peacefully, but there were devastating wars in Croatia and Bosnia. Serbia and Montenegro together formed the Federal Republic of Yugoslavia between 1992 and 2003.

In 1998, violence flared in the autonomous province of Kosovo in Serbia. The Kosovo Liberation Army, supported by the majority ethnic Albanians, came out in open rebellion against Serbian rule. International pressure on Milosevic[142] grew amid the escalating violence. NATO launched air strikes in Kosovo and Serbia in March 1999. An exodus of ethnic Albanians to neighboring countries gathered pace. The UN took over administration of the region after Serbian forces had been driven out. Kosovo declared independence in February 2008 after the failure of UN-brokered talks on the status of the province. Serbia said the declaration was illegal, and other countries are divided as to whether to recognize it.

In late 2005, the EU began talks with Belgrade on the possibility of reaching a Stabilization and Association Agreement. These were called off some months later because of the continuing failure of the Serbian authorities to arrest several war crimes suspects. One of the most notorious of these, the former Bosnian Serb leader Radovan Karadzic, was arrested in Belgrade in July 2008 by Serbian security forces and extradited to The Hague, weeks after a pro-Western government took office. European foreign ministers praised the arrest as a significant step for Serbia in its efforts to join the EU.

---

[142] Milosevic was the Serbian and Yugoslav politician who was the president of Serbia.

In December 2009, Serbia formally submitted its application to join the EU. The beginning of accession talks was delayed while two major Serbian war crimes suspects were still at large, but with the arrest of former Bosnian Serb military commander Ratko Mladic and Croatian Serb leader Goran Hadzic in 2011, this block to Serbia gaining EU candidate status was removed.

The European Commission duly recommended Serbia for EU candidate status in a report in October 2011, but insisted that the opening of membership talks was conditional on Serbia normalizing its ties with Kosovo. The deadlock over this issue was finally broken with the signing of a EU-brokered deal between Belgrade and Kosovo in April 2013. However, Serbia insists that the normalization agreement, which grants a high degree of autonomy to Serb-majority areas in northern Kosovo, does not mean that it has recognized its former province's independence. Serbia's EU accession talks began in January 2014.

Although the current Serbian government is pro-Western and sees eventual membership of the EU as being in the country's best interests, Serbia is traditionally an ally of Russia, which supported its opposition to Kosovo's independence. In 2008, the signing of a major energy deal further strengthened Serbia-Russia ties, and in October 2009 Russia granted Serbia a 1-billion euro (£0.9 billion) loan to help it cover its budget deficit after the economy was hit hard by the global downturn. When the nationalist Tomislav Nikolic became president in 2012, he declared his intention of developing ties with both the EU and Moscow.

Serbia economy is mostly based on services with 55 percent of the GDP, industry with about 37 percent, and agriculture, with about 8 percent.[143] In the late 1980s, at the beginning of the process of economic transition from a planned economy to a market economy, Serbia's economy had a favorable position, but it was gravely impacted by economic sanctions from 1992 to 1995.[144]

After the ousting of former Yugoslav President Slobodan Milošević in October 2000, the country went through an economic

---

[143] CIA (2016).
[144] Dobbs (1999).

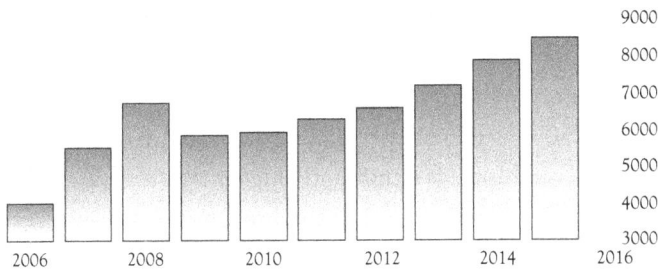

Figure A.33 Serbia per capita GDP 2006–2015

Source: tradingeconomics.com, World Bank.

liberalization process, and experienced fast economic growth. As depicted in Figure A.33, GDP per capita (nominal) grew significantly from 2000 to 2014. After years of economy decline due to world financial crisis, in 2011, the economy GDP growth was 2 percent.[145] Serbia entered a second recession in 2012, causing GDP to decline 1.5 percent for that year. In 2013 and 2014, Serbia was among the top 10 of European countries in regard to GDP growth.[146] GDP (nominal) growth for 2014 was very significant.[147]

Since the 1990s, Serbia has experienced a serious "brain drain," especially during the wars at that time.[148] Each year, more than 32,000 people emigrate. Despite the loss, the Serbian diaspora's transfers account between 10 and 15 percent of Serbia's GDP and significantly increase living standards in some parts of the country.

In recent years, Serbia has seen an increasingly swift FDI trend, including auto industry (Fiat), metal processing (U.S. Steel), building materials (Lafarge), food and beverages (Carlsberg, Coca Cola, and Nestle), textiles (Golden Lady, Pompea), leather (Progetti Company, Falc East), and the information and communications technology (ICT) sector (Microsoft and Siemens).

---

[145] Filipovic (2012).

[146] Filipovic (2012, 2).

[147] Filipovic (2012, 4).

[148] Bibić (2015).

Most of the FDI during 2000 to 2012 period came, in ascending order, from Italy, Austria, Norway, Belgium, and Greece, while other major investor countries also include the United States, Russia, and Germany. The actual amount of investments from countries such as the United States and Israel is significantly higher than the official figure due to their companies investing primarily through European affiliates.

APPENDIX B

A Brief Scanning of the CIS Countries

The following is a brief scanning of the Commonwealth of Independent State (CIS) countries to help in the understanding of their challenges and competitive advantages in furthering their economies and global market integrations that are discussed in this book.

The CIS, as discussed in Chapter 3, is a regional organization, which was created in December 1991 by the former Soviet Republics. In the adopted *Declaration*, the participants of the *Commonwealth* declared their interaction on the basis of sovereign equality.

Originally, there were 12 member states that were part of the CIS, including Azerbaijan, Armenia, Belarus, Kazakhstan, Kyrgyzstan, Moldova, Russia, Tajikistan, Turkmenistan, Uzbekistan, Ukraine, and Georgia. Both Ukraine and Georgia left the CIS in 2014 and 2009, respectively.

Armenia

Armenia is a unitary, multiparty, democratic nation-state with an ancient cultural heritage. The Satrapy of Armenia was established in the sixth century BC, after the fall of Urartu. In the first century BC, the Kingdom of Armenia reached its height under Tigranes the Great. Armenia became the first country in the world to adopt Christianity as its official religion[1] in between late third century to early years of the fourth century, becoming the first Christian nation.[2] As a result, previously predominant Zoroastrianism and paganism in Armenia gradually declined.

---

[1] Garsoïan (1997).

[2] Stringer (2005).

Figure B.1 Armenia is bordered by Turkey to the west, Georgia to the north, the de facto independent Nagorno-Karabakh Republic and Azerbaijan to the east, and Iran and the Azerbaijani exclave of Nakhchivan to the south

Source: Magellan Geographix.

As depicted in Figure B.1, Armenia is a landlocked country in the South Caucasus region of Eurasia, bordered by Turkey to the west, Georgia to the north, the de facto independent Nagorno-Karabakh Republic and Azerbaijan to the east, and Iran and the Azerbaijani exclave of Nakhchivan to the south. Armenia is the second most densely populated country of the former Soviet Republics because of its small size.

Between the 16th century and first half of the 19th century, the traditional Armenian homeland was composed of eastern Armenia, while the western side of Armenia came under rule of the rivaling Ottoman and successively Iranian Empires, being partially occupied by the two over the centuries. By the mid-19th century, eastern Armenia had been conquered by Russia from Qajar Iran, while most of the western parts of the traditional Armenian homeland still remained under Ottoman rule.

During World War I (WWI), the Armenians living in their ancestral lands in the Ottoman Empire were systematically exterminated in the

Armenian genocide in two phases: the wholesale killing of the able-bodied male population through massacre and subjection of army conscripts to forced labor, followed by the deportation of women, children, the elderly, and infirm on death marches leading to the Syrian desert. Driven forward by military escorts, the deportees were deprived of food and water and subjected to periodic robbery, rape, and massacre.[3] The Armenian genocide is acknowledged to have been one of the first modern genocides.[4] According to the research conducted by Arnold J. Toynbee, an estimated 600,000 Armenians died during deportation from 1915 to 1916. This figure, however, accounts for solely the first year of the genocide and does not take into account those who died or were killed after the report was compiled on May 24, 1916.[5] The International Association of Genocide Scholars places the death toll at "more than a million."[6] The total number of people killed has been most widely estimated at between 1 and 1.5 million.[7]

In 1918, during the Russian Revolution, all non-Russian countries were granted independence from the dissolved empire, leading to the establishment of the first Republic of Armenia. By 1920, the state was incorporated into the Transcaucasian Socialist Federative Soviet Republic (TSFSR), a founding member of the Soviet Union in 1922. In 1936, the Transcaucasian state was dissolved, leaving its constituent states, including the Armenian Soviet Socialist Republic, as full Union republics. The modern Republic of Armenia became independent in 1991 during the dissolution of the Soviet Union.

Until its independence, Armenia's economy was based largely on industries including chemicals, electronic products, machinery, processed food, synthetic rubber, and textiles. It has also been highly dependent on outside resources. Agriculture accounted for only 20 percent of net material product and 10 percent of employment before the breakup of the Soviet Union in 1991. Armenian mines produce copper, zinc, gold, and

---

[3] Kieserand Schaller (2002); Walker (1980).
[4] Ferguson (2006).
[5] Robert (1992).
[6] BBC (2008).
[7] BBC (2008).

lead. The vast majority of energy is produced with imported fuel, including gas and nuclear fuel from Russia, to power its single nuclear power plant. The main domestic energy source is hydroelectric. Small amounts of coal, gas, and petroleum have not yet been developed.

Like other former states, Armenia's economy suffers from the legacy of a centrally planned economy and the breakdown of former Soviet trading patterns. Soviet investment in the country and the support of Armenian industry has virtually disappeared; only a few major enterprises are still able to function. In addition, the effects of the 1988 earthquake, which killed more than 25,000 people and left more than 500,000 people homeless, are still being felt. Although a cease-fire has been held since 1994, the conflict with Azerbaijan over Nagorno-Karabakh has not been resolved. The consequent blockade along both the Azerbaijani and Turkish borders has devastated the economy, because of Armenia's dependence on outside supplies of energy and most raw materials. Land routes through Azerbaijan and Turkey are still closed, while routes through Georgia and Iran are adequate and reliable.

In 1992 to 1993, the gross domestic product (GDP) had fallen nearly 60 percent from its 1989 level. The national currency, the dram, suffered hyperinflation for the first few years after its introduction in 1993. Nonetheless, Armenia has registered strong economic growth since 1995 and inflation has been negligible for the past several years. New sectors, such as precious stone processing and jewelry making, as well as communication technology have experienced significant growth in the country. This steady economic progress has earned Armenia increasing support from international institutions. The government has made major strides toward joining the World Trade Organization (WTO), which it joined in 2003. The government also launched in 1994 an ambitious International Monetary Fund (IMF)-sponsored economic liberalization program that resulted in positive growth rates from 1995 to 2005.

Armenia also has managed to slash inflation, stabilize its currency, and privatize most small and medium-sized enterprises (SMEs). Armenia's unemployment rate, however, remains high, despite strong economic growth. Armenia is now a net energy exporter, although it does not have sufficient generating capacity to replace its nuclear power plant in

Metsamor, which is under international pressure to shut down. The electricity distribution system was privatized in 2002.

The IMF, World Bank, the European Bank for Reconstruction and Development (EBRD), as well as other international financial institutions and foreign countries have been extending considerable grants and loans to the country, targeting a reduction of the budget deficit, stabilization of the local currency, development of private businesses, energy sources, agriculture, food processing, transportation, and health and education sectors. Hence, Armenia's severe trade imbalance has been offset somewhat by international aid, remittances from Armenians working abroad, and foreign direct investment (FDI).

According to the World Bank, the GDP per capita in Armenia was last recorded at $7,763.39 in 2014, when adjusted by purchasing power parity (PPP). The GDP per capita, in Armenia, when adjusted by PPP, as shown in Figure B.2, is equivalent to 44 percent of the world's average. GDP per capita PPP in Armenia averaged $4,464.91 from 1990 until 2014, reaching an all time high of $7,763.39 in 2014 and a record low of $1,841.72 in 1993.

Continued progress will depend on the ability of the government to strengthen its macroeconomic management, including increasing revenue collection, improving the investment climate, and accelerating privatization. A liberal foreign investment law was approved in June

ARMENIA GDP PER CAPITA PPP

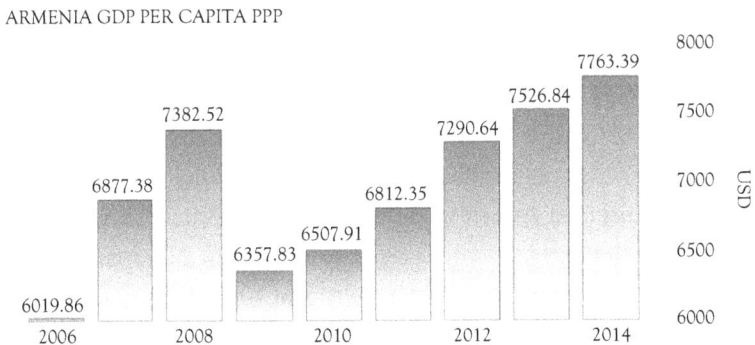

Figure B.2 Armenia GDP per capita

Source: World Bank, tradingeconomics.com

1994, and a law on privatization was adopted in 1997, as well as a program on state property privatization.

Azerbaijan

Located in the South Caucasus, Azerbaijan is a transcontinental country situated at the crossroads of eastern Europe and western Asia. While often politically aligned with Europe, Azerbaijan is generally considered to be at least mostly in southwest Asia geographically with its northern part bisected by the standard Asia-Europe divide, the Greater Caucasus. The United Nations (UN) and the U.S. Central Intelligence Agency (CIA) classification of the country differs, with the UN placing Azerbaijan in western Asia, while the CIA World Factbook places it mostly in southwest Asia, and the *Merriam-Webster's Collegiate Dictionary* places them in both! We'll let you take a pick! Nonetheless, the country, as depicted in Figure B.3, bordered by the Caspian Sea to the east, Russia to the north, Georgia to the northwest, Armenia to the west, and Iran to the south. In addition, the exclave of Nakhchivan is bounded by Armenia to the north and east, Iran to the south and west, while having a short border with Turkey in the northwest.

The country proclaimed its independence in 1918 and became the first Muslim-majority democratic and secular republic to have operas, theaters, and modern universities.[8] The Constitution of Azerbaijan does not declare an official religion, and all major political forces in the country are secularist, but the majority of people and some opposition movements adhere to Shia Islam.[9] Azerbaijan was incorporated into the Soviet Union in 1920 as the Azerbaijan Soviet Socialist Republic, proclaiming its independence from the Union of Soviet Socialist Republics (USSR) in August 1991, before the official dissolution of the USSR.[10] In September 1991, the disputed Armenian-majority Nagorno-Karabakh region reaffirmed its willingness to create a separate state as the Nagorno-Karabakh Republic. The region, effectively independent since the beginning of the

---

[8] Swietochowski (1995); Schulze (2000).

[9] Cornell (2010).

[10] King (2006).

Figure B.3 Azerbaijan is bordered by the Caspian Sea to the east, Russia to the north, Georgia to the northwest, Armenia to the west, and Iran to the south

Source: CDC.

Nagorno-Karabakh War in 1991, is internationally recognized as part of Azerbaijan until a final solution to its status is found through negotiations facilitated by the Organization for Security and Cooperation in Europe (OSCE).[11]

Azerbaijan is a unitary semi-presidential republic. The country is a member state of the Council of Europe, the OSCE, and the NATO Partnership for Peace (PfP) program. It is one of the six independent Turkic-speaking states, being an active member of the Turkic Council and the TÜRKSOY community. The country has diplomatic relations with 158 countries and holds membership in 38 international organizations. It is one of the founding members of the CIS[12] and Organization for the Prohibition of Chemical Weapons. Also a member of the UN since 1992,

---

[11] King (2006).
[12] Europa Publications Limited (1998).

Azerbaijan was elected to membership in the newly established Human Rights Council by the United Nations General Assembly in May 2006. The country is also a member state of the Non-Aligned Movement, holds observer status in WTO, and is a correspondent at the International Telecommunication Union.

Economically, Azerbaijan has completed its post-Soviet transition into a major oil-based economy from one where the state played the major role. Economic growth has been spurred by the exploration and development of oil and gas reserves, high levels of public expenditure, and substantial reforms to support a market-based economy. Despite robust growth, the economy of Azerbaijan remains largely dependent upon the extraction and production of fossil fuels. Today, however, the country is an oil-rich economy whose gross national income per capita has increased approximately tenfold since 2001.

As depicted in Figure B.4, Azerbaijan's GDP per capita in Azerbaijan was last recorded at $16,710.30 in 2014, when adjusted by PPP. The country's GDP per capita when adjusted by PPP is equivalent to 94 percent of the world's average. GDP per capita PPP in Azerbaijan averaged $8,777.13 from 1990 until 2014, reaching an all time high of $16,710.30 in 2014 and a record low of $3,319.77 in 1995.[13] Such rates cannot be sustained, but despite reaching 26.4 percent in 2005 (second highest GDP growth in the world in 2005 only to Equatorial Guinea), and 2006

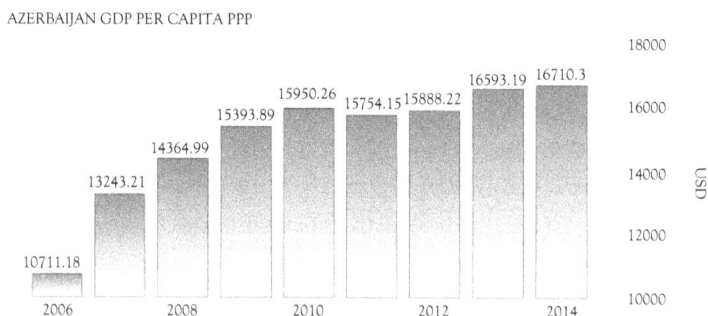

AZERBAIJAN GDP PER CAPITA PPP

Figure B.4 Azerbaijan GDP growth

Source: World Bank, trendingeconomics.com

---

[13] RosBusinessConsulting—News Online (n.d.).

over 34.6 percent (world highest), in 2008 dropped to 10.8 percent, and dropped further to 9.3 percent in 2009.[14] The national currency, the Azerbaijani manat, was stable in 2000, depreciating 3.8 percent against the dollar. The budget deficit equaled 1.3 percent of GDP in 2000.

Progress on economic reform has generally lagged behind macroeconomic stabilization. The government has undertaken regulatory reforms in some areas, including substantial opening of trade policy, but inefficient public administration, in which commercial and regulatory interests are comingled, limit the impact of these reforms. The government has largely completed privatization of agricultural lands and SMEs. In August 2000, the government launched a second-stage privatization program, in which many large state enterprises will be privatized. Since 2001, the ministry of economic development of Azerbaijan Republic regulates the economic activity in the country.

The manat tumbled by more than 30 percent following Azerbaijan's switch from a currency peg to a free-floating exchange rate. The move, which represented the second drastic devaluation of the currency in 2015, is aimed at protecting the country's dwindling foreign exchange reserves, which have come under pressure from falling oil prices and the economic crisis in Russia, and to restore export competitiveness. Oil and gas account for more than 90 percent of Azerbaijan's exports and 70 percent of government revenues. While the devaluation seemed inevitable against the backdrop of tumbling foreign reserves, it will likely have a negative impact on salaries, pensions, and savings in local currency, fuel inflation, and increase concerns over the Azerbaijani banking sector, which has a large share of bank deposits denominated in foreign currency.

In 2015, Azerbaijan's economy rebounded, however, with robust growth of 5.7 percent in the first half of the year, up from 2.1 percent in the same period in 2014. Boosted mainly by government capital expenditure, the economy outside of the large petroleum sector was the major driver of growth. The public investment program remains a key source of economic expansion and employment, but budget revenues are under pressure from lower oil prices.

---

[14] Today.Az (2009).

Official foreign currency reserves fell by more than 30 percent from January to August 2015 because the central bank intervened to maintain the new exchange rate after the February 2015 devaluation of the Azerbaijan manat. Oil prices, key to local currency stability, have fallen dramatically over the past year, from $103.08 per barrel of Azeri light crude in August 2014 to $46.23, a year later.

To limit inflation, the central bank has reduced local currency liquidity. With tepid domestic demand largely offsetting price pressures from the devaluation, year-on-year inflation rose to only 3.5 percent in the first half of 2015, which was nevertheless up from 1.6 percent for the same period in 2014. The devaluation will continue to put inflationary pressure on imports other than food.

Azerbaijan faces a multifaceted crisis from 2016 to 2017. Low oil prices led to a major currency devaluation in 2015, which will depress consumption and investment and push up inflation. Pressure on the currency remains high, and the authorities imposed currency controls in mid-January 2016. The banking sector will suffer major losses this year, and depend heavily on state support. Falling incomes and rising unemployment will lead to protests in some areas and a rise in political uncertainty.

Belarus

Belarus, as depicted in Figure B.5, is a landlocked country in eastern Europe bordered by Russia to the northeast, Ukraine to the south, Poland to the west, and Lithuania and Latvia to the northwest. Minsk, the capital, count with over 40 percent of its 207,600 square kilometers (80,200 sq mi) of forested area. Its strongest economic sectors are service industries and manufacturing.

Until the 20th century, different states at various times controlled the lands of today's Belarus. In the aftermath of the 1917 Russian Revolution, Belarus declared independence as the Belarusian People's Republic, succeeded by the Socialist Soviet Republic of Byelorussia, which became a founding constituent republic of the Soviet Union in 1922, then renamed as the Byelorussian Soviet Socialist Republic. The country lost almost half of its territory to Poland after the Polish-Soviet war of 1919 to 1921,

Figure B.5 Belarus is a landlocked country in eastern Europe bordered by Russia to the northeast, Ukraine to the south, Poland to the west, and Lithuania and Latvia to the northwest

Source: globalsecurity.org

with most of the borders of Belarus adopting their modern shape in 1939 when some lands of the Second Polish Republic were reintegrated into it after the Soviet invasion of Poland and were finalized after World War II (WWII).[15]

During WWII, military operations devastated Belarus, which lost about a third of its population and more than half of its economic resources.[16] The republic was redeveloped in the post-war years. In 1945, Belarus became a founding member of the UN, along with the Soviet Union and the Ukrainian Soviet Socialist Republic (SSR). Later on, during the dissolution of the Soviet Union, the parliament of the republic declared the sovereignty of Belarus, in July 1990, becoming independent on August 25, 1991.

According to data from the U.S. government,[17] most of the Belarusian economy remains state-controlled and has been described as "Soviet-style."[18] In 2006, a little more of 50 percent of Belarusians were employed

---

[15] A Taylor & Francis Group (2004); Abdelal (2001).

[16] Axell (2002).

[17] U.S. State Department (2014).

[18] Press Service of the President of the Republic of Belarus (2004).

by state-controlled companies, while a little more than 47 percent were employed by the private sector, of which about 6 percent were partially foreign-owned. Important agricultural products include potatoes and cattle byproducts, including meat.[19]

After the fall of the Soviet Union, all former Soviet Republics faced a deep economic crisis. Belarus has however chosen its own way of overcoming this crisis. After the 1994 election of Alexander Lukashenko as the first president, the country launched itself into a path of "market socialism" as opposed to what Lukashenko considered the "wild capitalism" chosen by Russia at that time. In keeping with this policy, administrative controls over prices and currency exchange rates were introduced. Also the state's right to intervene in the management of private enterprises was expanded, but on March 4, 2008, the president issued a decree abolishing the golden share rule in a clear movement to improve its international rating regarding the foreign investment.

Historically, textiles and wood processing had constituted a large part of the industrial activity in the country. Belarus's main exports included heavy machinery, agricultural products, and energy products. At the time of the dissolution of the Soviet Union in 1991, Belarus was one of the world's most industrially developed states by percentage of GDP as well as the richest CIS member-state. Economically, Belarus involved itself in the CIS, Eurasian Economic Community, and Union with Russia.

The currency, the Belarusian ruble (BYR[20]), was introduced in May 1992, replacing the Soviet ruble. The first coins of the Republic of Belarus were issued on December 27, 1996. The ruble was reintroduced with new values in 2000 and has been in use ever since. As part of the Union of Russia and Belarus, both states have discussed using a single currency along the same lines as the euro. This led to a proposal that the Belarusian ruble be discontinued in favor of the Russian ruble (RUB), starting as early as January 1, 2008. The National Bank of Belarus abandoned pegging the Belarusian ruble to the Russian ruble in August 2007. A new currency, the new Belarusian ruble (BYN) will be introduced in July 2016, replacing the Belarusian ruble in a rate of 1:10,000 (10,000 old rubles = 1

---

[19] *Al Jazeera* (2009).

[20] The symbol for the ruble is Br and the ISO 4217 code is BYR.

new ruble). This redenomination can be considered as an effort to fight the high inflation rate.

Regarding GDP growth, back in the 1990s industrial production had plunged due to decreases in imports, investment, and demand for Belarusian products from its trading partners, which impacted GDP growth. But as depicted in Figure B.6, GDP began rising again in 1996, when Belarus became the fastest-recovering former Soviet Republic in terms of its economy. The GDP per capita in Belarus was last recorded at $17,348.77 in 2014, when adjusted by PPP, which is equivalent to 98 percent of the world's average.[21]

In 2006, Belarus's largest trading partner was Russia, which accounted for nearly half of total trade, with the EU being the next largest trading partner, with nearly a third of foreign trade. In 2005, about a quarter of the population was employed by industrial factories but employment was, and continues to be, high in agriculture, manufacturing sales, trading goods, and education. Because of its failure to protect labor rights for a labor force of more than 4 million people, among whom women hold slightly more jobs than men, Belarus lost its EU Generalized System of Preferences status in June 2007, which raised tariff rates to their prior most favored nation levels.[22]

Weak external demand from the key trading partners of Russia and Ukraine has depressed Belarus's output in early 2015. In addition,

BELARUS GDP PER CAPITA PPP

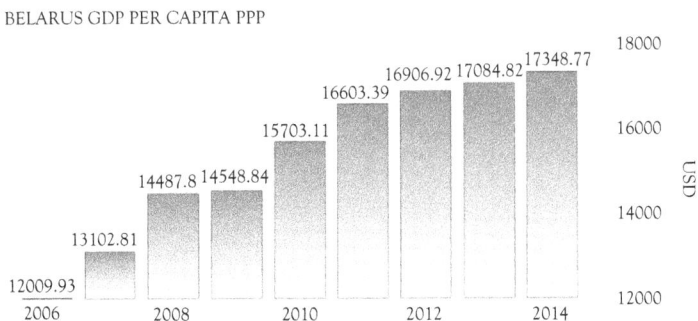

Figure B.6 Belarus GDP per capital in PPP terms 1990–2015

Source: World Bank, tradingeconomics.

---

[21] Blejer and Kreb (2002).

[22] WTO (2012).

despite tightening of monetary policy, inflation has been high due to the impact from exchange rate depreciation. Although net exports slightly improved, foreign exchange reserves declined due to large external debt repayments. Despite the weaker economy, the government has managed to keep fiscal policy prudent. Stability-oriented macroeconomic tightening has occurred in response to a deteriorating external environment. The economy was expected to enter into a recession during 2015, which was likely to endure in 2016. The current economic challenges and domestic structural constraints reinforce the need for a comprehensive economic transformation.

Georgia

Georgia is a country in Eurasia, located on the crossroads of eastern Europe and west Asia. As depicted in Figure B.7, the country is nestled between the Greater Caucasus and Lesser Caucasus mountain ranges. It is bordered to the west by the Black Sea, to the north and northeast by Russia, to the south by Turkey and Armenia, and to the southeast by Azerbaijan. The capital and the largest city is Tbilisi. Georgia covers a territory of

Figure B.7 Georgia is bordered by the Black Sea on the west, to the north and northeast by Russia, to the south by Turkey and Armenia, and to the southeast by Azerbaijan

Source: RandMcnally.

69,700 square kilometers (26,911 sq miles), and its 2015 population is about 3.75 million. Georgia is a unitary, semi-presidential republic, with the government elected through a representative democracy.

During classical antiquity, several independent kingdoms became established in what is now Georgia, including the kingdoms of Colchis and Iberia, which adopted Christianity as their state religion in the early fourth century, leading to the decline and elimination of previously dominant paganism, Zoroastrianism, and Mithraism. Thereafter and throughout the early modern period, Georgia became fractured and fell into decline due to the onslaught of various hostile empires, including the Mongols, the Ottoman Empire, and successive dynasties of Iran. After a brief period of independence following the Russian Revolution of 1917, the first Georgian Republic was occupied by Soviet Russia in 1921, and absorbed into the Soviet Union as the Georgian Soviet Socialist Republic in 1922. After restoring its independence in 1991, post-communist Georgia suffered from a civil unrest and economic crisis for most of the 1990s. After a peaceful change of power in the Rose Revolution of 2003, Georgia pursued a strong pro-Western foreign policy, introducing a series of political and economic reforms.

Georgia is a member of the Council of Europe and the GUAM (Georgia, Ukraine, Azerbaijan, and Moldova) Organization for Democracy and Economic Development. It contains two de facto independent regions, Abkhazia and South Ossetia, which gained limited international recognition after the 2008 Russo-Georgian War. Georgia and a major part of the international community consider the regions to be part of Georgia's sovereign territory under Russian military occupation.

In February 1921, the Red Army attacked Georgia defeating the Georgian army and prompting the social-democratic government to flee the country. By the end of February 1921, the Red Army entered Tbilisi and installed a communist government loyal to Moscow, led by a Georgian Bolshevik named Filipp Makharadze. There remained, however, significant opposition to the Bolsheviks, which culminated in the August 1924 Uprising. Soviet rule was firmly established only after this uprising was suppressed.[23] Georgia was then incorporated into the TSFSR, which united

---

[23] Knight (n.d.).

Georgia, Armenia and Azerbaijan. Later, in 1936, the TSFSR was disaggregated into its component elements and Georgia became the Georgian SSR.

Joseph Stalin, an ethnic Georgian, born of Ioseb Besarionis Dze Jugashvili in Gori, was prominent among the Bolsheviks. Stalin was to rise to the highest position, leading the Soviet Union from April 3, 1922 until his death on March 5, 1953. Few years later, for most of the WWII period, during 1941 to 1945, almost 700,000 Georgians fought in the Red Army against Nazi Germany, even though a few fought on the German side. About 350,000 Georgians died in the battlefields of the Eastern Front.

Georgia's main economic activities include cultivation of agricultural products such as grapes, citrus fruits, and hazelnuts, as well as mining of manganese, copper, and gold. It also produces alcoholic and nonalcoholic beverages, metals, machinery, and chemicals in small-scale industries. The country imports nearly all its needed supplies of natural gas and oil products. It has sizeable hydropower capacity that now provides most of its energy needs. Georgia has overcome the chronic energy shortages and gas supply interruptions of the past by renovating hydropower plants and by increasingly relying on natural gas imports from Azerbaijan instead of from Russia.

Despite the severe damage, the economy of Georgia suffered due to civil strife in the 1990s. The country has been able to recover significantly by 2000, with the help of the IMF and the World Bank. As depicted in Figure B.8, robust GDP growth has been achieved since then. GDP

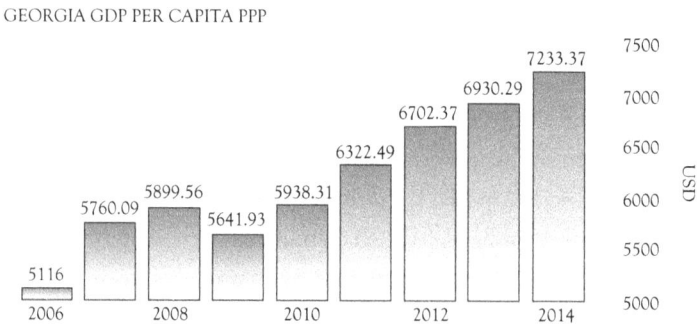

GEORGIA GDP PER CAPITA PPP

Figure B.8 Georgia GDP growth in PPP, 2006–2014

Source: World Bank, tradingeconomics.

growth, spurred by gains in the industrial and service sectors, remained in the 9 to 12 percent range in 2005 to 2007, but during 2006 and in 2008, the World Bank named Georgia the top reformer in the world.[24]

Favorable domestic conditions and strong external demand supported economic growth in the first half of this year, demonstrating that regional economic tensions have not yet adversely affected Georgia. The large Russian market, which opened up for Georgian products in July 2013, helped increase exports, particularly of wine. Greater consumer and business confidence gave a boost to manufacturing and trade. In addition, the construction sector benefited from renewed public infrastructure projects and resumption in business related investments. The agricultural sector grew at a relatively modest pace compared with industry and services.

GDP growth did slow in the first quarter of 2015 to 3.2 percent from 4.8 percent for the whole of 2014. Preliminary data show a further slowdown to 2.6 percent in the first half of 2015. The slowdown largely reflects declines of 5.2 percent in manufacturing and 2.5 percent in trade, and it came despite strong growth of 22.9 percent in mining and 17.2 percent in construction. After expanding by 12.2 percent in the first quarter, bank credit fell by 1.5 percent in the second in line with slower growth.

Annual average inflation in August 2015 amounted to 3.2 percent as large increases for tobacco and alcoholic beverages and furnishings, household equipment, and maintenance offset smaller declines for transport and clothing and footwear. Continuing moderate inflation, despite depreciation of the Georgia lari by nearly 33 percent since November 2014, reflects weakening domestic demand and reduced profit margins for firms, along with lower prices for imported food and energy. Inflationary expectations have recently increased, however, with the depletion of inventories accumulated at cheaper prices, rising production costs, and extensive dollarization in the economy.

Though export data for the first 6 months of 2015 suggested a further cut in exports of nearly 24 percent, reflecting a drop in vehicle exports by nearly two-third, lower oil prices helped cut imports by about 9 percent. In addition, sharp declines in remittances, from the Russian Federation

---

[24] World Bank (2015).

and Greece by 41 and 19 percent, respectively, caused total remittances to fall by almost 23 percent in the first half of 2015.

Despite planned fiscal consolidation, capital spending is expected to contribute to growth in the second half of 2015 and in 2016. However, net exports will remain a drag on growth, as recession in the Russian Federation and Ukraine weakens the external outlook. Inflation is expected to accelerate to about 6 percent by the end of 2016. With tighter monetary policy, according to the Asian Development Bank[25] outlook for Georgia in 2015 and 2016, the current account deficit may reach 14.1 percent of GDP in the first quarter of 2016 as the trade deficit widened and the regional economic slowdown trimmed remittances. The deficit was funded largely through FDI inflows and official development assistance.

Georgia has a developed, stable, and reliable energy sector but efforts are required to improve the efficiency in domestic energy use. The most promising source of additional energy generation is hydropower and the government is focused on securing private investments for construction of new hydropower stations. Currently, only 12 percent of Georgia's hydropower potential is being utilized.

One of the potential drivers of economic growth in cities and regions is tourism, which recently saw rapid growth in Georgia and has become an important source of job creation. The number of visitors increased from 560,000 in 2005 to 5 million in 2013, with 6.3 million expected in 2015. An integrated and demand-driven approach to regional development has been designed with the support of the Bank and is currently seen as critical in spurring growth and job creation in historic cities and cultural villages.

Kazakhstan

Kazakhstan, the world's largest landlocked country by land area, is a country in central Asia, with a minor part west of the Ural River and thus in Europe. As depicted in Figure B.9, the country borders Russia on the

---

[25] www.adb.org/countries/georgia/economy

Figure B.9 Kazakhstan borders Russia on the north, China on the east, Kyrgyzstan, Uzbekistan, and Turkmenistan on the south, and the Caspian Sea on the west

Source: Eurasianet.org

north, China on the east, Kyrgyzstan, Uzbekistan, and Turkmenistan on the south, and the Caspian Sea on the west.

The terrain of Kazakhstan includes flatlands, steppe, taiga, rock canyons, hills, deltas, snow-capped mountains, and deserts. With an estimated 18 million people as of 2014, Kazakhstan is the 61st most populous country in the world. Given its large land area, its population density is among the lowest, at less than 6 people per square kilometer (15 people per sq miles). The capital is Astana, where it was moved in 1997 from Almaty. Nomadic tribes have historically inhabited the territory of Kazakhstan. This changed in the 13th century, when Genghis Khan occupied the country as part of the Mongolian Empire.

Following internal struggles among the conquerors, power eventually reverted to the nomads. By the 16th century, the Kazakh emerged as a distinct group, divided into three jüz (ancestor branches occupying specific territories). The Russians began advancing into the Kazakh steppe in the 18th century, and by the mid-19th century, they nominally ruled all of Kazakhstan as part of the Russian Empire. Following the 1917 Russian Revolution and subsequent civil war, the territory of Kazakhstan was reorganized several times. In 1936, it was made the Kazakh Soviet Socialist Republic, considered an integral part of the Soviet Union.

Kazakhstan was the last of the Soviet Republics to declare independence following the dissolution of the Soviet Union in 1991. Kazakhstan has worked to develop its economy, especially its dominant hydrocarbon industry.[26] *Human Rights Watch* says that "Kazakhstan heavily restricts freedom of assembly, speech, and religion,"[27] and other human rights organizations regularly describe Kazakhstan's human rights situation as poor.

The country is populated by 131 ethnicities, including Kazakhs (who make up 63 percent of the population), Russians, Uzbeks, Ukrainians, Germans, Tatars, and Uyghurs. Islam is the religion of about 70 percent of the population, with Christianity practiced by 26 percent. Kazakhstan officially allows freedom of religion, but religious leaders who oppose the government are suppressed. The Kazakh language is the state language, and Russian has equal official status for all levels of administrative and institutional purposes, reflecting the long history of Russian dominance in the region.

Kazakhstan is an upper-middle-income country with per capita GDP adjusted for PPP, as depicted in Figure B.10, of nearly $22,469 thousand in 2013. Its per capita GDP grew in 2014 although real GDP dropped due to internal capacity constraints in the oil industry, less favorable terms

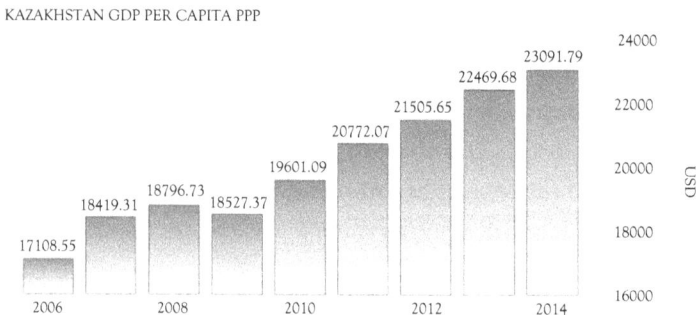

Figure B.10 Kazakhstan GDP per capita PPP 2006–2014

Source: World Bank, tradingeconomics.

---

[26] Zarakhovich (2006).

[27] Human Rights Watch, World Report (2015).

of trade, and an economic slowdown in Russia. The contribution of net exports to GDP growth improved materially followed by a sharp devaluation of the Kazakhstan tenge in February 2014, leading to a strong drop in imports of goods that became more costly. As a result of the devaluation, domestic inflation, as measured by the consumer price index (CPI), increased from 4.8 percent year-on-year in December 2013 to 6.9 percent in August 2014, due to higher imported input prices.

Income growth in the country had a positive impact on poverty indicators, with prosperity shared broadly. The share of the Kazakhstan population living in poverty went down from 47 percent in 2001 to about 3 percent in 2013, as measured by the national poverty line. Similarly, at the international poverty line, as measured by the PPP-corrected $2.50 per capita per day, poverty in Kazakhstan fell from 41 percent in 2001 to 4 percent in 2009.

However, against a benchmark of a higher poverty line at the PPP-corrected $5 per capita per day (which is more appropriate for countries with a higher level of income per capita), some 42 percent of Kazakhstan's population were still living in poverty in 2009, though down from 79 percent in 2001. Kazakhstan's performance in the World Bank's indicator of shared prosperity also shows progress, with growth rate of consumption per capita of the bottom 40 percent of households of about 6 percent, while the average consumption growth for all households was about 5 percent from 2006 to 2010.

Trade policy will remain a central instrument to help the country integrate into the global economy, but Kazakhstan will face a complex trade policy environment in the medium-term. The economy is adjusting to the Eurasia Customs Union, which it joined in 2010, and is pursuing an accelerated schedule of further integration into the Common Economic Space by 2015. Kazakhstan is also expected to join the WTO in the near future while its trade strategy lists several free trade agreements to be negotiated.

Education is a high priority for Kazakhstan, and in 2011, Kazakhstan ranked first on UNESCO's "Education for All Development Index" by achieving near-universal levels of primary education, adult literacy, and gender parity. These results have reflected Kazakhstan's efforts of expanding pre-school access and free, compulsory secondary education. For the next 10 years, Kazakhstan is embarking on further major reforms across all education levels.

Kazakhstan faces challenges in restructuring its health care system. The country's health outcomes lag behind its rapidly increasing income. The major causes of adult mortality are noncommunicable diseases such as cancer, cardiovascular disease, and other tobacco and alcohol-related diseases and injuries. The new State Health Care Development Program recognizes health as one of the country's major priorities and a prerequisite for sustainable socioeconomic development.

Looking forward, despite the short-term vulnerabilities accentuated by the uncertain regional economic outlook, Kazakhstan's medium-term prospects look promising. In the medium term, the economy will continue to grow on the back of the expanding oil sector, while growth of the non-oil economy will be lower due to lower domestic demand. In the longer run, Kazakhstan's development objective of joining the rank of the top 30 most developed countries by 2050 will depend on its ability to sustain balanced and inclusive growth. Enhancing medium- to long-term development prospects depends on Kazakhstan's success in diversifying its endowments, namely, creating highly skilled human capital, improving the quality of physical capital, and more importantly, strengthening institutional capital—all of the necessary ingredients for the development and expansion of the private sector in the country.

Kyrgyzstan

Kyrgyzstan's history spans over 2,000 years, encompassing a variety of cultures and empires. Although geographically isolated by its highly mountainous terrain, which has helped preserve its ancient culture, Kyrgyzstan has historically been at the crossroads of several great civilizations, namely as part of the Silk Road and other commercial and cultural routes. Though long inhabited by a succession of independent tribes and clans, Kyrgyzstan has periodically come under foreign domination and attained sovereignty as a nation-state only after the breakup of the Soviet Union in 1991.

Figure B.11 Kyrgyzstan is bordered by Kazakhstan to the north, Uzbekistan to the west, Tajikistan to the southwest, and China to the east

Source: Google.

The country, officially known as Kyrgyz Republic, is a country located in central Asia. As depicted in Figure B.11, the country is landlocked and mountainous, bordered by Kazakhstan to the north, Uzbekistan to the west, Tajikistan to the southwest, and China to the east. Its capital and largest city is Bishkek.

Since independence, Kyrgyzstan has officially been a unitary parliamentary republic, although it continues to endure ethnic conflicts, revolts, economic troubles, transitional governments, and political party conflicts.[28] Kyrgyzstan is a member of the CIS, the Eurasian Economic Union (EEU), the Collective Security Treaty Organization (CSTO), the Shanghai Cooperation Organization (SCO), the Organization of Islamic Cooperation, the Turkic Council, the TÜRKSOY community, and the UN.

---

[28] The Economist (2011).

Ethnic Kyrgyz make up the majority of the country's 5.7 million people, followed by significant minorities of Uzbeks and Russians. The official language, Kyrgyz, is closely related to the other Turkic languages, although Russian remains widely spoken, a legacy of a century-long policy of *Russification*. The majority of the population, about 64 percent, is nondenominational Muslims. In addition to its Turkic origins, Kyrgyz culture bears elements of Persian, Mongolian, and Russian influence.

After independence in 1992, the Kyrgyz Republic's economy and public services were hit hard by the break-up of the Soviet economic zone and the end of subsidies from Moscow. Thanks to the adoption of market-based economic reforms in the 1990s, the economy has nearly recovered to its pre-independence level of output, but infrastructure and social services have suffered from low investment. With a per capita PPP GDP of $2,920.60 in 2011, as depicted in Figure B.12, the Kyrgyz Republic remains a low-income country. Moreover, the global economic crisis, the political unrest of April and June 2010, and food price increases in 2011 and 2012 have reversed earlier gains in poverty reduction with GDP dropping to $2,869.82. The absolute poverty rate increased from 33.7 percent in 2010 to 36.8 percent in 2011.

A series of reform-oriented government policies since the political crises of 2010 have sought to restore economic and social stability, and to address shortcomings in public governance and the investment climate. Following strong growth in 2013, the Kyrgyz economy was hit by a significant decline in gold production due to geological movements at the

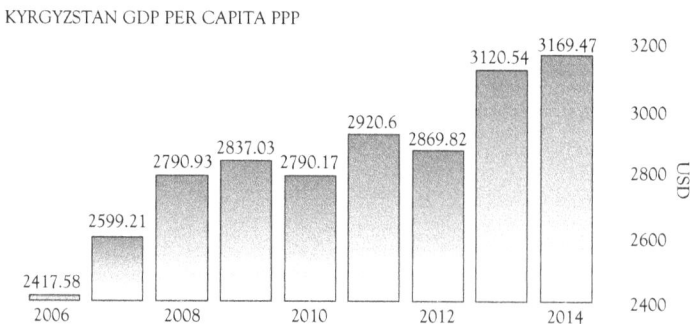

Figure B.12 Kyrgyzstan per capita GDP 2006–2014

Source: World Bank, tradingeconomics.

Kumtor gold mine. Real GDP in the first half of 2012 contracted by 5.6 percent as gold production at Kumtor fell by 60 percent. Excluding Kumtor, real output grew moderately at 3.9 percent with growth across all sectors.

Weak economic governance and a high level of perceived corruption remain key obstacles to development in the Kyrgyz Republic, and were considered causes of the political unrest of 2010. The government's Medium Term Development Program, adopted in 2011, stated improving governance and fighting corruption to be its top priority.

The agricultural sector, which accounts for about a quarter of the country's GDP and about one-third of employment, expanded rapidly between 1996 and 2002. The government successfully completed a land reform, created a rural bank and agribusiness and rural advisory services, and established water-user associations and pasture committees. The energy sector is one of the largest in the Kyrgyz economy, accounting for around 3.9 percent of GDP and 16 percent of industrial production. The bulk of the country's current generating capacity is hydropower. The key challenges faced by the sector are high commercial losses and low tariffs, leading to inadequate funding for maintenance and investment, winter energy shortages, and governance issues. All these led to significant deterioration of energy assets and poor sector performance. Mining constitutes about 26 percent of tax revenues, about 10 percent of GDP, and 50 percent of export earnings. The country has been reviewing mining legislation and mineral licensing procedures. To address governance issues in mining, the Kyrgyz Government started implementing the Extractive Industries Transparency Initiative in 2004.

The road network connects remote communities and links the Kyrgyz Republic to neighboring countries. Rehabilitating strategic road corridors is on the government's priority list, given their importance in providing access to international markets and basic public services. However, basic preventative maintenance is seriously underfunded.

Improving education, healthcare, and social protection is another top priority for the Kyrgyz Republic. The government is currently implementing medium-term reforms in these sectors.

Moldova

Moldova, as depicted in Figure B.13, is a landlocked country in eastern Europe, bordered by Romania to the west and Ukraine to the north, east, and south. The capital city is Chişinău. Moldova is a parliamentary republic with the president as the head of state and the prime minister as the head of government. It is a member state of the UN, the Council of Europe, the WTO, the OSCE, the GUUAM (Georgia, Ukraine, Uzbekistan, Azerbaijan and Moldova), the CIS, and the Organization of the Black Sea Economic Cooperation (BSEC) and aspires to join the EU.

Moldova declared independence on August 27, 1991 as part of the dissolution of the Soviet Union. The current Constitution of Moldova was adopted in 1994. A strip of Moldovan territory on the east bank of

Figure B.13 Moldova is a landlocked country in Eastern Europe, bordered by Romania to the west and Ukraine to the north, east, and south

Source: Magellan Geographix.

the river Dniester has been under the de facto control of the breakaway government of Transnistria since 1990, which includes a large proportion of predominantly russophone East Slavs of Ukrainian (28 percent) and Russian (26 percent) descent (altogether 54 percent as of 1989), while Moldovans (40 percent) have been the largest ethnic group, and where the headquarters and many units of the Soviet 14th Guards Army were stationed, an independent Pridnestrovian Moldavian Soviet Socialist Republic was proclaimed on August 16, 1990, with its capital in Tiraspol.

The motives behind this move were fear of the rise of nationalism in Moldova and the country's expected reunification with Romania upon secession from the USSR. In the winter of 1991 to 1992, clashes occurred between Transnistrian forces, supported by elements of the 14th Army, and the Moldovan police. Between March 2 and July 26, 1992, the conflict escalated into a military engagement.

After the breakup from the USSR in 1991, energy shortages, political uncertainty, trade obstacles and weak administrative capacity contributed to the decline of economy. In January 1992, Moldova introduced a market economy, liberalizing prices, which resulted in rapid inflation. As a part of an ambitious economic liberalization effort, Moldova introduced a convertible currency, liberalized all prices, stopped issuing preferential credits to state enterprises, backed steady land privatization, removed export controls, and liberalized interest rates. The government entered into agreements with the World Bank and the IMF to promote growth. The economy reversed from decline in late 1990s.

From 1992 to 2001, the country suffered a serious economic crisis, leaving most of the population below the poverty line. In 1993, a national currency, the Moldovan leu, was introduced to replace the temporary cupon. The economy of Moldova began to change in 2001, and until 2008 the country saw a steady annual growth of between 5 and 10 percent.

The early 2000s also saw a considerable growth of emigration of Moldovans looking for work in Russia, Italy, Portugal, Spain, Greece, Cyprus, Turkey, and other countries. As a result, remittances from Moldovans abroad account for almost 38 percent of Moldova's GDP, the second-highest percentage in the world, after Tajikistan. Due to a decrease in industrial and agricultural output following the dissolution of the Soviet Union, the service sector has grown to dominate Moldova's economy and currently composes over 60 percent of the nation's GDP. However, Moldova remains the poorest country in Europe.

Moldova's economic performance over the last few years, as depicted in Figure B.14, has been relatively strong, aided by improved fiscal, monetary, and exchange rate policy. Moldova experienced the highest cumulative per capita PPP GDP growth, relative to the pre-crisis year of 2007, in the region. However, growth has been volatile because of climatic and global economic conditions. The GDP per capita in Moldova was last recorded at $4,753.55 in 2014, when adjusted by PPP. The GDP per capita, in the country, when adjusted by PPP is equivalent to 27 percent of the world's average. GDP per capita PPP in Moldova averaged $3,476.80 from 1990 until 2014, reaching an all time high of $6,416.46 in 1990 and a record low of $2,267.88 in 1999.

However, the economy decreased 3.7 percent in the third quarter of 2015. Due to a bad harvest, agriculture decreased 17.4 percent and on the expenditure side, the internal demand was weak due to low remittances. Nonetheless, good economic performance in the first half of the year, maintained Moldova's GDP growth positive, increasing 0.5 percent, year-on-year, in January to September 2015.

The existing macroeconomic framework is considered broadly adequate, even though macroeconomic risks associated with the financial sector, vulnerabilities to external and climatic shocks, institutional weaknesses and related slippages in the implementation of macroeconomic and

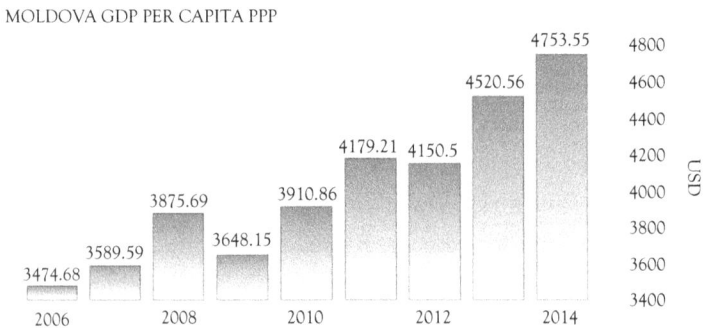

Figure B.14 Moldova's per capita PPP GDP 2006–2015

Source: World Bank, tradingeconomics.com.

structural reforms will continue to be substantial over the medium-term. European integration anchors the government's policy reform agenda, but political tensions and weak governance pose risks to reforms.

Moldova's recent economic performance reduced poverty and promoted shared prosperity. The national poverty and extreme poverty rates, using national poverty definitions, fell from 30.2 and 4.5 percent in 2006 to 16.6 and 0.6 percent, respectively in 2012, making Moldova one of the world's top performers in terms of poverty reduction. Similarly, consumption growth among the bottom 40 percent of the population outpaced average consumption growth.

Despite a sharp decline in poverty, however, Moldova remains one of the poorest countries in Europe. The most vulnerable groups at risk of poverty in Moldova remain those with low education levels, households with three or more children, those in rural areas, families relying on self-employment, the elderly, and Roma. Additionally, the reduction in remittances could negatively impact consumption and poverty. Moldova performs well in some areas of gender equality, yet disparities persist in education, health, economic opportunity, agency, and violence against women. Human trafficking is a serious problem; Moldova is a source, and to a lesser extent a transit and destination country, for both sex trafficking and forced labor.

Considering the fragile economic and political external environment, the pace of reforms must be accelerated. Key challenges include fighting corruption, improving the investment climate, removing obstacles for exporters, channeling remittances into productive investments, and developing a sound financial sector. Moldova needs to improve the efficiency and equity of its public spending, in particular through better management of public capital investments, which are crucial for higher growth. Administrative and judicial reforms remain a challenge for improving public sector governance, which is a precondition for European integration and economic modernization.

Russia

Russia, a federal semi-presidential republic, is a country in northern Eurasia, the largest country in the world, covering more than one-eighth of the Earth's inhabited land area. Russia is the world's ninth most populous country with over 144 million people at the end of 2015. Extending across the entirety of northern Asia and much of eastern Europe, Russia spans 11 time zones and incorporates a wide range of environments and landforms. As depicted in Figure B.15, from northwest to southeast, Russia is boarded by Norway, Finland, Estonia, Latvia, Lithuania, Poland, Belarus, and Ukraine on the west, Georgia, Azerbaijan, Kazakhstan, China, Mongolia, and North Korea to the south, and the North Pacific Ocean to the east. It shares maritime borders with Japan by the Sea of Okhotsk and the U.S. state of Alaska across the Bering Strait.

The nation's history began with that of the East Slavs, who emerged as a recognizable group in Europe between the third and eighth centuries AD (anno Domini). Founded and ruled by a Varangian warrior elite and their descendants, the medieval state of Rus arose in the ninth century. In 988, it adopted orthodox Christianity from the Byzantine Empire, beginning the synthesis of Byzantine and Slavic cultures that defined Russian culture for the next millennium. Rus' ultimately disintegrated into a

Figure B.15 Russia is boarded by Norway, Finland, Estonia, Latvia, Lithuania, Poland, Belarus, and Ukraine to the west; Georgia, Azerbaijan, Kazakhstan, China, Mongolia, and North Korea to the south; and the North Pacific Ocean to the east. It shares maritime borders with Japan by the Sea of Okhotsk and the U.S. state of Alaska across the Bering Strait

Source: Russialist.org

number of smaller states; most of the Rus' lands were overrun by the Mongol invasion and became tributaries of the nomadic Golden Horde in the 13th century.

The Grand Duchy of Moscow gradually reunified the surrounding Russian principalities, achieved independence from the Golden Horde, and came to dominate the cultural and political legacy of Kievan Rus'. By the 18th century, the nation had greatly expanded through conquest, annexation, and exploration to become the Russian Empire, which was the third largest empire in history, stretching from Poland in Europe to Alaska in North America.[29]

Following the Russian Revolution, the Russian Soviet Federative Socialist Republic (SFSR) became the largest and leading constituent of the Soviet Union, the world's first constitutionally socialist state and a recognized world superpower, and a rival to the United States,[30] which played a decisive role in the Allied victory in WWII. The Soviet era saw some of the most significant technological achievements of the 20th century, including the world's first human-made satellite, and the first man in space. By the end of 1990, the Soviet Union had the world's second largest economy, largest standing military in the world, and the largest stockpile of weapons of mass destruction.

Following the partition of the Soviet Union in 1991, 14 independent republic nations emerged from the USSR, including Armenia, Azerbaijan, Belarus, Estonia, Georgia, Kazakhstan, Kyrgyzstan, Latvia, Lithuania, Moldova, Tajikistan, Turkmenistan, Ukraine, and Uzbekistan. As the largest, most populous, and most economically developed republic, the SFSR reconstituted itself as the Russian Federation and is recognized as the continuing legal personality of the Soviet Union.

The Russian economy ranks as the 10th largest by nominal GDP and sixth largest by PPP as of 2015.[31] Russia's extensive mineral and energy resources, the largest reserves in the world, have made it one of the largest producers of oil and natural gas globally.[32] The country is one of the five recognized nuclear weapons states and possesses the largest stockpile

---

[29] Taagepera (1997).
[30] Adelman and Gibson (1989).
[31] IMF (2015).
[32] International Energy Agency (2012).

of weapons of mass destruction. Russia was the world's second biggest exporter of major arms from 2010 to 2014, according to Stockholm International Peace Research Institute (SIPRI) data.[33]

Russia is a great power and a permanent member of the UN Security Council, a member of the G20, the Council of Europe, the Asia-Pacific Economic Cooperation (APEC), the SCO, the OSCE, and the WTO, as well as being the leading member of the CIS, the CSTO and one of the five members of the EEU, along with Armenia, Belarus, Kazakhstan, and Kyrgyzstan.

Russia has a developed, high-income market economy with enormous natural resources, particularly oil and natural gas. It has the 15th largest economy in the world by nominal GDP and the 6th largest by PPP. As depicted in Figure B.16, since the turn of the 21st century, higher domestic consumption and greater political stability have bolstered economic growth in Russia. The GDP per capita in Russia was last recorded at $23,292.91 in 2014, when adjusted by PPP. The GDP per capita, in Russia, when adjusted by PPP is equivalent to 131 percent of the world's average. GDP per capita PPP in Russia averaged $17,196.23 from 1990 until 2014, reaching an all time high of $23,561.37 in 2013 and a record low of $11,173.03 in 1998.

The country ended 2008 with its ninth straight year of growth, but growth has slowed with the decline in the price of oil and gas. Nontraded

RUSSIA GDP PER CAPITA PPP

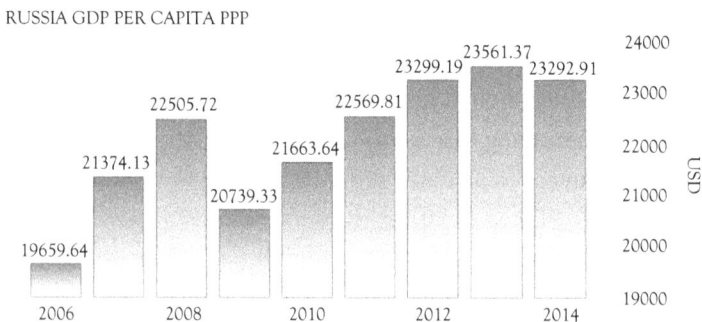

Figure B.16 Russia's per capita PPP GDP 2006–2015

Source: World Bank, tradingeconomics.com.

---

[33] Stockholm International Peace Research Institute (2014).

services and goods for the domestic market, as opposed to oil or mineral extraction and exports, primarily drove growth. Approximately 12.8 percent of Russians lived below the national poverty line in 2011, significantly down from 40 percent in 1998 at the worst point of the post-Soviet collapse. Unemployment in Russia was 5.4 percent in 2014, down from about 12.4 percent in 1999. The middle class has grown from just 8 million persons in 2000 to 104 million persons in 2013. However, after U.S.-led sanctions since 2014 and a collapse in oil prices, the proportion of middle-class could halve to 20 percent. Sugar imports reportedly dropped 82 percent between 2012 and 2013 as a result of the increase in domestic output.

Russia's recession deepened in the first half of 2015 with a severe impact on households. The economy continues to adjust to the 2014 terms-of-trade shock amid a tense geopolitical context marked by ongoing international sanctions. Oil and gas prices remained low through the first half of 2015, further underscoring Russia's vulnerability to volatile global commodity markets. The weakening of the ruble created a price advantage for some industries, boosting a narrow range of exports and encouraging investment in a certain sectors, but this was not sufficient to generate an overall increase in nonenergy exports. Investment demand continued to contract for a third consecutive year.

Economic policy uncertainty arising from an unpredictable geopolitical situation and the continuation of the sanctions regime caused private investment to decline rapidly as capital costs rose and consumer demand evaporated. The record drop in consumer demand was driven by a sharp contraction in real wages, which fell by an average of 8.5 percent in the first 6 months of 2015, illustrating the severity of the recession. However, the deterioration of real wages was also the primary mechanism through which the labor market adjusted to lower demand, and unemployment increased only slightly from 5.3 percent in 2014 to 5.6 percent in the first half of 2015. The erosion of real income significantly increased the poverty rate and exacerbated the vulnerability of households in the lower 40 percent of the income distribution.

The policy response by the authorities successfully stabilized the economy. The transition to a free-floating exchange rate allowed imports to adjust to 17 percent depreciation in the real effective exchange rate during the first half of 2015, strengthening the current-account balance.

Meanwhile, measures to support the financial sector appear to have contained systemic risks, and there are early signs of stabilization. Nevertheless, the pass-through effect of the December 2014 depreciation boosted inflation to levels not seen since 2002.

Even as the recession deepened in the first half of 2015, controlling inflation became the central bank's main policy challenge. Low oil prices continue to put downward pressure on federal revenue, ushering in a period of difficult fiscal consolidation. Real public spending is expected to fall by 5 percent in 2015, notwithstanding a temporary increase in the first half of the year caused by frontloaded expenditures as part of the government's anticrisis plan to cushion some of the fiscal consolidation impact. Falling oil revenues constrained the government's ability to counter the decline in real income, and nominal increases in pensions and social benefits were below the headline inflation rate. This accelerated an already troubling rise in the poverty rate, which climbed from 13.1 percent in the first half of 2014 to 15.1 percent in the first half of 2015.

Turkmenistan

Turkmenistan, as depicted in Figure B.17, is a country in central Asia, bordered by Kazakhstan to the northwest, Uzbekistan to the north and east, Afghanistan to the southeast, Iran to the south and southwest, and the Caspian Sea to the west.

Turkmenistan has been at the crossroads of civilizations for centuries. In medieval times, Merv was one of the great cities of the Islamic world and an important stop on the Silk Road, a caravan route used for trade with China until the mid-15th century. Annexed by the Russian Empire in 1881, Turkmenistan later figured prominently in the anti-Bolshevik movement in central Asia. In 1924, Turkmenistan became a constituent republic of the Soviet Union, Turkmen Soviet Socialist Republic (Turkmen SSR). The country became independent upon the dissolution of the Soviet Union in 1991. Turkmenistan possesses the world's fourth largest reserves of natural gas resources.[34] Since 1993, citizens have received government-provided electricity, water, and natural gas free of charge.

---

[34] Fox News (2006).

Figure B.17 Turkmenistan is bordered by Kazakhstan to the northwest, Uzbekistan to the north and east, Afghanistan to the southeast, Iran to the south and southwest, and the Caspian Sea to the west

Source: Encyclopedia Britannica.

President for Life Saparmurat Niyazov ruled Turkmenistan until his death in 2006. Gurbanguly Berdimuhamedow was elected president in 2007. According to *Human Rights Watch*,

> Turkmenistan remains one of the world's most repressive countries. The country is virtually closed to independent scrutiny, media and religious freedoms are subject to draconian restrictions, and human rights defenders and other activists face the constant threat of government reprisal.

President Berdymukhamedow promotes a personality cult in which he, his relatives, and associates enjoy unlimited power and total control over all aspects of public life.[35]

---

[35] HRW (2014).

TURKMENISTAN GDP PER CAPITA PPP

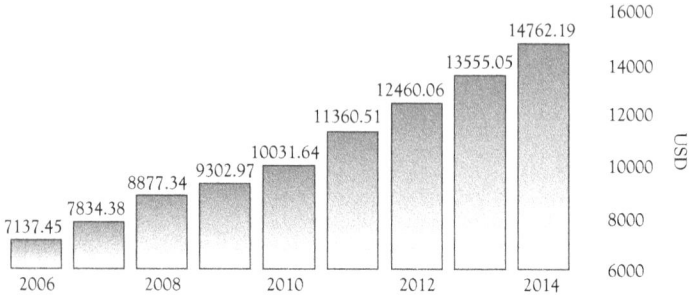

Figure B.18 Turkmenistan GDP per capita PPP 2006–2014

Source: World Bank, tradingeconomics.com.

The Turkmen economy, as depicted in Figure B.18, continued strong growth performance in 2012, expanding by 11.1 percent. High growth performance sustained over an extended period of time led to a steady increase in income levels and moved the country to an upper middle-income status. Preliminary outcomes of the annual economic developments demonstrate that the Turkmen economy remains resilient to the global uncertainties stemming from the Eurozone crisis. The GDP per capita in Turkmenistan was last recorded at $14,762.19 in 2014, when adjusted by PPP. The GDP per capita, in Turkmenistan, when adjusted by PPP is equivalent to 83 percent of the world's average. GDP per capita PPP in Turkmenistan averaged $7,471.40 from 1990 until 2014, reaching an all time high of $14,762.19 in 2014 and a record low of $4,221.14 in 1997.

The country possesses the world's fourth-largest reserves of natural gas and substantial oil resources. Turkmenistan has taken a cautious approach to economic reform, hoping to use gas and cotton sales to sustain its economy. In 2004, the unemployment rate was estimated to be 60 percent. However, between 1998 and 2002, Turkmenistan suffered from the continued lack of adequate export routes for natural gas and from obligations on extensive short-term external debt. At the same time, however, the value of total exports has risen sharply because of increases in international oil and gas prices. Economic prospects in the near future are discouraging because of widespread internal poverty and the burden of foreign debt.

The government maintains a large portfolio of social transfers and budget subsidies. Currently, all 17 subsidies have a universal character and are guaranteed until 2030, after which time the government may decide to move to a more targeted public social transfer policy. Social indicators have showed improvements commensurate with the country's economic performance. According to the State Statistics Committee of Turkmenistan, wages and salaries have increased by 11.2 percent during 2012 compared to 2011. After adjusting for inflation, the real rate of wage increase still makes up 6 percent.

The Government's National Socio-Economic Development Program for 2011 to 2030 and the National Rural Development Program focus on inclusive economic growth while preserving economic independence, modernizing the country's infrastructure, and promoting FDI.

Tajikistan

Tajikistan is a mountainous landlocked sovereign country in central Asia, with an estimated 8 million people in 2013, it is the 98th most populous country and with an area of 143,100 square kilometer (55,300 sq miles). It is the 96th largest country in the world. The territory that now constitutes the country was previously home to several ancient cultures, including the city of Sarazm of the Neolithic and the Bronze Age, and was later home to kingdoms ruled by people of different faiths and cultures, including the Oxus civilization, Andronovo culture, Buddhism, Nestorian Christianity, Zoroastrianism, and Manichaeism.

As depicted in Figure B.19, the country is bordered by Afghanistan to the south, Uzbekistan to the west, Kyrgyzstan to the north, and China to the east. Pakistan lies to the south separated by the narrow Wakhan Corridor. Traditional homelands of Tajik people included present-day Tajikistan, Afghanistan, and Uzbekistan.

Numerous empires and dynasties, including the Achaemenid Empire, Sassanian Empire, Hephthalite Empire, Samanid Empire, Mongol Empire, Timurid dynasty, and the Russian Empire, have ruled the area. As a result of the breakup of the Soviet Union, Tajikistan became an independent nation in 1991. A civil war was fought almost immediately after independence, lasting from 1992 to 1997. Since the end of the war, newly

Figure B.19 *Tajikistan is bordered by Afghanistan to the south, Uzbekistan to the west, and Kyrgyzstan to the north, and China to the east*

Source: Operationworld.com.

established political stability and foreign aid have allowed the country's economy to grow.

Tajikistan is a presidential republic consisting of four provinces. Most of Tajikistan's 8 million people belong to the Tajik ethnic group, who speak Tajik (Persian), although many people also speak Russian. Mountains cover more than 90 percent of the country. It has a transition economy that is dependent on aluminum and cotton production. Its economy is the 126th largest in the world in terms of purchasing power and 136th largest in terms of nominal GDP.

As a result of the economic recession in Russia, weakening of the Russian ruble and tightening of migration regulations, economic growth in Tajikistan slowed from an average of 7.5 percent a year over the past decade to 6.4 percent in the first 6 months of 2015. The U.S. dollar value of remittances, about 80 percent of which originate from Russia, fell by 32 percent from January to June 2015, compared to the same period in 2014, largely due to the sharp depreciation of the Russian ruble. The slowdown in remittances affected domestic demand, which in turn depressed growth in services, the major contributor to economic growth in the past.

Growth is projected to significantly slow down in the medium term, with a very gradual recovery, putting Tajikistan's poverty reduction gains of the last decade at great risk. As this trend in the economy is likely to persist in the medium term, it is even more important that Tajikistan implements sound macroeconomic policies and structural reforms that are necessary to create the foundation for more domestically generated inclusive growth, while investing in quality public services. The current situation should be seen as an opportunity to reform the economy and to adopt new engines of growth—private investment and export—to generate more and better-paying jobs in the country.

To date, Tajikistan has done a remarkable job in reducing poverty. During the period 1999 to 2014, poverty fell from over 80 percent to about 32 percent in the country. Tajikistan's pace of poverty reduction over the past 15 years has been among the top 10 countries in the world. However, the country has done less well in reducing nonmonetary poverty. Recently available micro-data suggests that limited or no access to education (secondary and tertiary), heating, and sanitation is the main contributor to nonmonetary poverty. These three are the most unequally distributed services, with access to education varying by income level and heating and sanitation according to location.

As depicted in Figure B.20, Tajikistan's GDP per capita was last recorded at $2,532.51 in 2014, when adjusted by PPP. The GDP per capita, in Tajikistan, when adjusted by PPP is equivalent to 14 percent of the world's average. GDP per capita PPP in Tajikistan averaged $1,849.28

TAJIKISTAN GDP PER CAPITA PPP

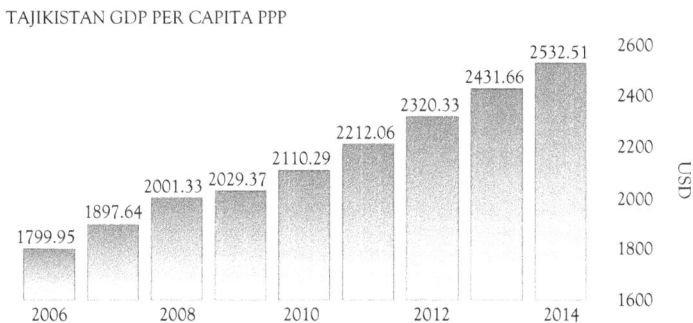

Figure B.20 Tajikistan GDP per capita PPP 2006–2015

Source: World Bank, tradingeconomics.com.

from 1990 until 2014, reaching an all time high of $3,635.34 in 1990 and a record low of $1,040.23 in 1996.

The Government of Tajikistan has set ambitious goals to be reached by 2020: to double GDP, to reduce poverty to 20 percent, and to expand the middle class. To achieve higher growth, Tajikistan needs to implement a deeper structural reform agenda designed to (a) reduce the role of the state and enlarge that of the private sector in the economy through a more conducive business climate, thus increasing private investment and generating more productive jobs; (b) modernize and improve the efficiency and social inclusiveness of basic public services; and (c) enhance the country's connectivity to regional and global markets and knowledge.

The difficult environment for doing business in Tajikistan, as well as obstacles to FDI, have discouraged private investment and limited overall investment. Averaging about 15 percent of GDP annually since 2008, total investment is low by regional and international standards.

Public investment accounts for 80 percent of the total, or 12 percent of GDP, and private investment for 20 percent, or only 3 percent of GDP—much lower than the Europe and central Asia developing country average. The main obstacles cited by both local and foreign entrepreneurs are inadequate infrastructure, in particular insufficient and unreliable energy supply, the weak rule of law, especially as regards property rights, and tax policy and administration. Increased private investment and new business development are crucial prerequisites for increased job creation.

With 20 percent of GDP and 53 percent of employment, the agriculture sector in Tajikistan offers a solid foundation for economic development. The Government of Tajikistan displays a strong commitment to the agricultural reform program, which includes the resolution of the cotton debt crisis, accelerated land reform, freedom to farm, improved access to rural finance, and increased diversification of agriculture.

Efforts are underway to make investment in agriculture more profitable, especially for exports, by enhancing access to markets and by empowering farmers through strengthening their land-use rights, improving their access to credit and inputs, and enabling them to make their own cropping decisions. The recent growth of noncotton agricultural exports indicates the potential for growth in agro-processing, including storage of fruit and vegetables, which holds great promise for development, along with textiles and clothing.

Meeting Tajikistan's energy demand will be an important part of the agenda to reduce poverty and create an enabling environment for private businesses. Approximately 70 percent of the population suffers from extensive electricity shortages during winter. The shortages increased considerably starting in 2009, when Tajikistan's power network was severed from the Central Asia Power System and power trade with central Asian countries stopped. Electricity shortages in winter are estimated to be at least 2,000 gigawatt-hours, or about 20 percent of winter electricity demand.

Tajikistan is also faced with a young and rapidly growing population. Recent estimates show that 55 percent of the population in Tajikistan is under the age of 25, making improved public services in social sectors (education, health, and social protection), as well as job creation, imperative components of government's poverty reduction strategy.

Ukraine

The territory of modern Ukraine has been inhabited since 32,000 BC. During the middle ages, the area was a key center of East Slavic culture, with the powerful state of Kievan Rus' forming the basis of Ukrainian identity. The country is currently in dispute with Russia over the Crimean, which Russia annexed back in 2014, although Ukraine and most of the international community still do not recognize it as Russian. If we include Crimea, Ukraine has a total area of 603,628 square kilometer (233,062 sq miles), which makes the country the largest within the entire Europe and the 46th largest country in the world. With a total population of about 44.5 million, Ukraine is the 32nd most populous country in the world. Ukraine, as depicted in Figure B.21, is a country in eastern Europe bordered by Russia to the east and northeast, Belarus to the northwest, Poland and Slovakia to the west, Hungary, Romania, and Moldova to the southwest, and the Black Sea and Sea of Azov to the south and southeast, respectively.

Following its fragmentation in the 13th century, the territory was contested, ruled, and divided by a variety of powers, including Lithuania, Poland, the Ottoman Empire, Austria-Hungary, and Russia. A Cossack republic emerged and prospered during the 17th and 18th centuries, but its territory was eventually split between Poland and the Russian Empire,

Figure B.21 Ukraine is a country in eastern Europe bordered by Russia to the east and northeast, Belarus to the northwest, Poland and Slovakia to the west, Hungary, Romania, and Moldova to the southwest, and the Black Sea and Sea of Azov to the south and southeast, respectively

Source: Worldtravels.com.

and later submerged fully into Russia. Two brief periods of independence occurred during the 20th century, once near the end of WWI and another during WWII, but both occasions would ultimately see Ukraine's territories conquered and consolidated into a Soviet Republic, a situation that persisted until 1991, when Ukraine gained its independence from the Soviet Union in the aftermath of its dissolution at the end of the Cold War.

Following independence, Ukraine declared itself a neutral state.[36] Nonetheless, the country formed a limited military partnership with the Russian Federation, other CIS countries, and a partnership with NATO since 1994. In the 2000s, the government began leaning toward NATO, and the NATO-Ukraine Action Plan signed in 2002 set a deeper cooperation with the alliance. It was later agreed that the question of joining NATO should be answered by a national referendum at some point in the future.

---

[36] Parliament of Ukraine (2007).

Former President Viktor Yanukovych considered the current level of co-operation between Ukraine and NATO sufficient, and was against Ukraine joining NATO. In 2013, protests against the government of President Yanukovych broke out in downtown Kiev after the government made the decision to suspend the Ukraine-European Union Association Agreement and seek closer economic ties with Russia. This began a several-months-long wave of demonstrations and protests known as the Euromaidan, which later escalated into the 2014 Ukrainian revolution that ultimately resulted in the overthrowing of Yanukovych and the establishment of a new government. These events precipitated the annexation of Crimea by the Russian Federation in February 2014, and the war in Donbass in March 2014; both are still ongoing as of December 2015. On January 1, 2016, Ukraine joined the Deep and Comprehensive Free Trade Area with the EU.[37]

Ukraine has long been a global breadbasket because of its extensive, fertile farmlands, and it remains one of the world's largest grain exporters. The diversified economy of Ukraine includes a large heavy industry sector, particularly in aerospace and industrial equipment.

Ukraine is a unitary republic under a semi-presidential system with separate powers: legislative, executive, and judicial branches. Its capital and largest city is Kiev. Ukraine maintains the second-largest military in Europe, after that of Russia, when reserves and paramilitary personnel are taken into account. The country is home to 45.4 million people (including Crimea), 77.8 percent of whom are Ukrainians by ethnicity, followed by a sizeable minority of Russians (17.3 percent) as well as Romanians and Moldovans, Belarusians, Crimean Tatars, and Hungarians. Ukrainian is the official language of Ukraine; its alphabet is Cyrillic. The dominant religion in the country is Eastern Orthodoxy, which has strongly influenced Ukrainian architecture, literature, and music.

Ukraine's GDP per capita PPP, as depicted in Figure B.22, was last recorded at $8,267.07 in 2014, when adjusted by PPP. The GDP per capita, in Ukraine, when adjusted by PPP is equivalent to 47 percent of the world's average. GDP per capita PPP in Ukraine averaged $6,996.86

---

[37] Balmforth (2010).

UKRAINE GDP PER CAPITA PPP

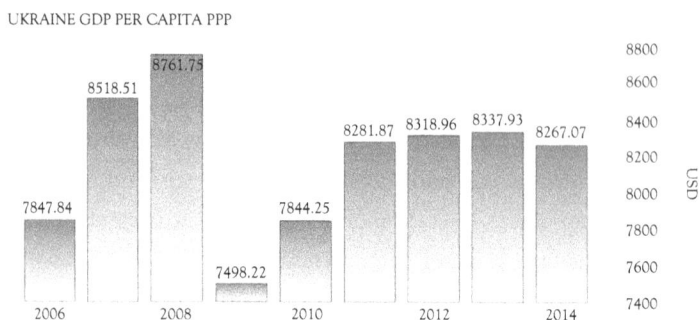

Figure B.22 Ukraine GDP per capita PPP 2006–2015

Source: World Bank, tradingeconomics.com.

from 1990 until 2014, reaching an all time high of $10,490.37 in 1990 and a record low of $4,462.78 in 1998.

Ukraine posted zero economic growth over 2012 and 2013 because serious macroeconomic and structural weaknesses remain unaddressed. A combination of de-facto fixed exchange rate policy, loose fiscal policy together with considerable quasi-fiscal subsidies in the energy sector has led to further widening of the budget and the external imbalances and threatens sustainability.

Top concerns for Ukraine now are the developments in the Eurozone and the state of the global economy together with resolution of the political crisis in the country. Confidence in the government and the state institutions is low. Economic growth remained weak for the last 2 years. After five consequent quotes of economic slowdown started in the second half of 2012, Ukraine's GDP posted growth of 3.7 percent year-on-year in the fourth quarter of 2013, driven by good harvest and low statistical base. This brought fiscal year (FY) GDP growth to 0.0 percent (after 0.2 percent in 2012). Performance of the key sectors remained weak due to weak external conditions and delays in domestic policy adjustment.

Economic growth is expected to recover slightly in 2014; however the risks for this forecast are still substantial. On the external side, the main risk is a protracted crisis in Europe, leading to lower demand for exports and more difficult access to global capital markets. Domestically, the main risk is a failure to implement macroeconomic rebalancing (preferably anchored in a program with the IMF). Delays in macroeconomic adjustment could mean that the forced adjustment will be much sharper. Ukraine's access to financing is already limited by investor concerns over the sustainability of its macro framework, political situation, and the poor investment climate.

To support the banking industry, World Bank is actively working with the government and the National Bank of Ukraine and other financial regulators on strengthening the policy and regulatory role of the state in the financial sector, while consolidating state ownership of financial institutions.

Evidence shows Ukraine is facing a health crisis, and the country needs to make urgent and extensive measures to its health system to reverse the progressive deterioration of citizens' health. Crude adult death rates in Ukraine are higher than its immediate neighbors, Moldova and Belarus, and among the highest not only in Europe, but also in the world.

The unemployment rate increased to 9.5 percent at the beginning of 2009 as a result of the global financial crisis, and today stands at 7.5 percent. While firms in the country face a shortage of skilled workers, many university graduates can't find employment or end up in jobs that do not use their skills due to skills mismatch.

Literacy and school enrollment rates are high in Ukraine. However, larger budget allocations to education have not resulted in improvements in the quality of education. Ukraine's priority should be to make better use of the resources allocated for the sector by significantly downsizing the school network to fit the smaller (current and projected) cohorts of students.

Ukraine has tremendous agricultural potential and could play a critical role in contributing to global food security. This potential has not been fully exploited due to depressed farm incomes and a lack of modernization within the sector. The establishment of a legal framework for secure land ownership, development of an efficient registration system, and ensuring free and transparent land markets are important elements of a policy framework that could facilitate agricultural development in Ukraine.

Ukraine is one of the most energy-inefficient countries in the region and restructuring and upgrading its energy sector continues to be one of the key development challenges for the government. The sector faces problems maintaining security, reliability, and quality of supply due to delays in energy sector reform, poor financial condition of energy sector enterprises, lack of investments, and deferred maintenance in aging infrastructure. These factors threaten the sustainability of economic growth, degrade the environment, and increase the cost of social services. Improving them is among Ukraine's top strategic priorities.

The municipal and services sector in Ukraine suffers from decades of underinvestment and poor maintenance. The need to invest in water and wastewater utilities is growing dramatically and the existing low tariff levels are a major limitation to the sustainability of utilities. The need for rehabilitation is exacerbated by the overall high-energy consumption in water production and wastewater treatment. Improving service delivery through rehabilitation of infrastructure and promotion of energy efficiency solutions offers the possibility of driving utilities toward financial sustainability while providing improved services.

Uzbekistan

Eastern Turkic-speaking nomads conquered once part of the Turkic Khaganate and later Timurid Empires, the region that today includes the Republic of Uzbekistan, in the early 16th century. The area was gradually incorporated into the Russian Empire during the 19th century, and in 1924 what is now Uzbekistan became a bordered constituent republic of the Soviet Union, known as the Uzbek Soviet Socialist Republic (Uzbek SSR). Following the breakup of the Soviet Union, it declared independence as the Republic of Uzbekistan on August 31, 1991 (officially celebrated the following day).

Uzbekistan is a doubly landlocked country in central Asia. It is a unitary, constitutional, presidential republic, comprising 12 provinces, one autonomous republic, and one capital city. As depicted in Figure B.23, Uzbekistan is bordered by Kazakhstan to the north, Tajikistan to the southeast, Kyrgyzstan to the northeast, Afghanistan to the south, and Turkmenistan to the southwest.

Uzbekistan is officially a democratic, secular, unitary, constitutional republic with a diverse cultural heritage. The country's official language is Uzbek, a Turkic language written in Latin alphabet and spoken natively by

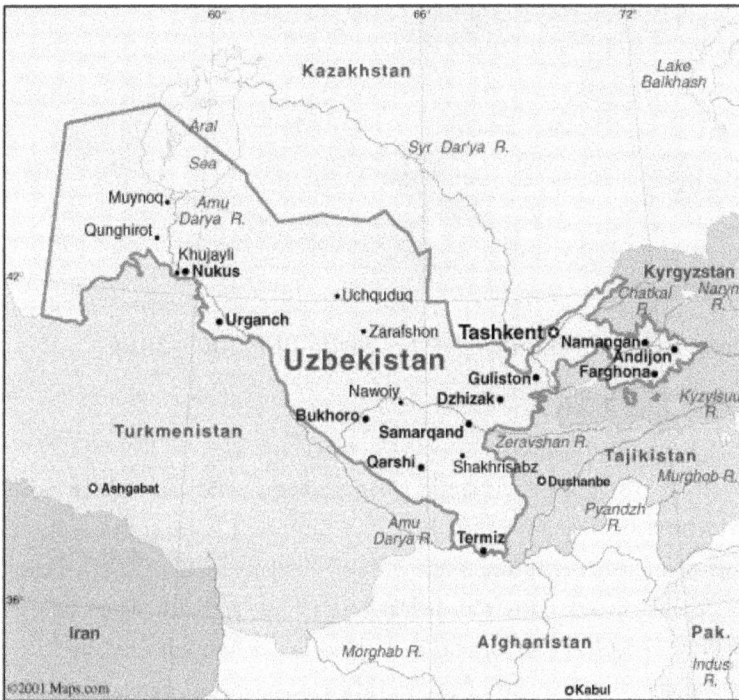

Figure B.23 Uzbekistan is bordered by Kazakhstan to the north, Tajikistan to the southeast, Kyrgyzstan to the northeast, Afghanistan to the south, and Turkmenistan to the southwest

Source: maps.com.

approximately 85 percent of the population; however, Russian remains in widespread use. Uzbeks constitute 81 percent of the population, followed by Russians (5.4 percent), Tajiks (4.0 percent), Kazakhs (3.0 percent), and others (6.5 percent). A majority of Uzbeks are nondenominational Muslims. Uzbekistan is a member of the CIS, OSCE, UN, and the SCO.

Uzbekistan's economy relies mainly on commodity production, including cotton, gold, uranium, and natural gas. Despite the declared objective of transition to a market economy, its government continues to maintain economic controls, which imports in favor of domestic "import substitution."

As depicted in Figure B.24, since the mid-2000s, Uzbekistan has enjoyed robust GDP growth, thanks to favorable trade terms for its key export commodities like copper, gold, natural gas, cotton, the

UZBEKISTAN GDP PER CAPITA PPP

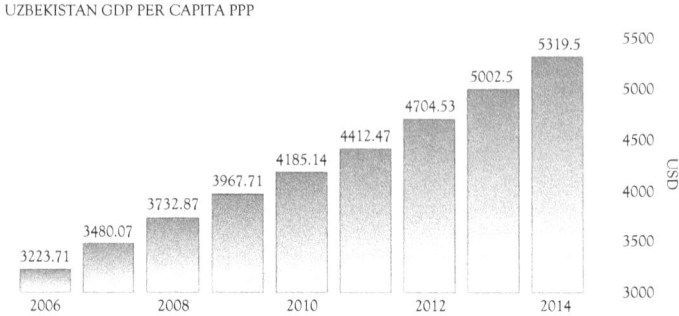

Figure B.24 Uzbekistan GDP per capita PPP 2008–2014

Source: World Bank, tradingeconomics.

government's macro-economic management, and limited exposure to international financial markets that protected it from the economic downturn. Still, the future is not without challenges. The GDP per capita in Uzbekistan was last recorded at $5,319.50 in 2014, when adjusted by PPP. The GDP per capita, in Uzbekistan, when adjusted by PPP is equivalent to 30 percent of the world's average. GDP per capita PPP in Uzbekistan averaged $3,164.74 from 1990 until 2014, reaching an all time high of $5,319.50 in 2014 and a record low of $2,216.68 in 1996.

Since the mid-2000s, Uzbekistan has enjoyed robust GDP growth due to its favorable trade terms for its key export commodities, the government's economic management, and limited exposure to international financial markets that protected it from the economic downturn.

Overall growth for Uzbekistan is projected to continue at around 7 to 8 percent annually from 2011 to 2014, supported by net exports and a large capital investment program. World prices for Uzbekistan's principal exports are projected to remain favorable at least through the first half of the 2012 to 2015 FY Country Partnership Strategy (CPS) period.

The impact of recent increases in global food and energy prices is expected to be limited given Uzbekistan's policy of self-sufficiency in both food grains and energy. Given the government's plans to finance up to two-third of their investment program from external sources, including loans, external debt is expected to increase gradually.

The country has to contend with a combination of risk factors going forward, including deteriorating security conditions due to the situation in

Afghanistan, and increasing tensions between its neighbors over regional issues, especially the management and use of transboundary energy and water resources. Domestically, Uzbekistan has to work to minimize its economy's vulnerability to possible external shocks affecting commodity prices and the anticipated inflow of FDI and external loans to finance the large public investment program.

Uzbekistan, with the goal of becoming an industrialized, high middle-income country by around 2050, is continuing to transition to a more market-oriented economy to ensure equitable distribution of growth between regions and to maintain infrastructure and social services. The country's policy goals and priorities are: to increase the efficiency of infrastructure, especially of energy, transport, and irrigation; to enhance the competitiveness of specific industries, such as agro-processing, petro-chemicals, and textiles; to diversify the economy and thereby reduce its reliance on commodity exports; and to improve access to and the quality and outcomes of education, health, and other social services.

Endorsements

"Eastern European Economies: A Region in Transition" is a comprehensive and unbiased analysis of the region's economic transformation. "This is a must-read for anyone interested in Eastern Europe's past and also in its future."

Andrey Kortunov, Director General, Russian International Affairs Council, Russia Federation.

"I have found this book a great resource of Eastern European Economy and its development. Its geopolitical breadth and scope, including my country Kosovo, is very accurate and I recommend it to all the readers as it is a great support to them for its unique variety of different strategies of countries in attempts to European integration."

Valentina Gara, Master of Philological Science, Public Relations Manager at Prishtina International Airport, Kosovo.

"This book is very recommendable for anyone seeking a clearer understanding of the Eastern European economies and their transition into larger economic frameworks of Europe and globalized state of the world economy. It is informative in terms of basic information and synthetic overviews it provides, covering both joint phenomena and particularities or details not to be missed of different economies seen from perspectives of two experienced global academic thinkers and practitioners. The book is sorted in an orderly thematic fashion supported by up-to-date statistics and explained in a manner that makes it accessible to a wide range of audiences, business and academic alike, being also useful as an informative guide for private or institutional investors interested in the potential of this growing and transforming region."

Dr. Mario Svigir, Economics Lecturer and Institutional Consultant, University EFFECTUS, Zagreb, Croatia.

"I highly recommend this book as a well-balanced and easy-to-follow source of economic thinking for Central and Eastern Europe transition. It demonstrates how economics and politics are connected to everyday life in the region."

Sergey Komyagin, IHS CEE Regional Business Executive, Moscow, Russia.

"It's not easy to understand the uniqueness of Eastern Europe countries. This part of the world had to face communism, geopolitical issues, and transition from state-centered economy to free market. Moreover, it was also challenged with finding its own way to build relations with the European Union. This book provides a thorough analysis of Eastern European economy, which has been skillfully explained with regard to political and social changes. I highly recommend it as a compendium of knowledge for students and businessmen alike. Not only does it provide an excellent overview of the subject, but also an insightful stance on expanding economy of this region."

Ewelina Kroll, Law Firm MichałZołubak M&As, Warsaw, Poland.

"With *Eastern European Economies: A Region in Transition* Marcus Goncalves and Erika Cornelius Smith have written a very useful book for business people like me, who frequently travel to Eastern Europe in their work. Winston Churchill coined the expression 'the iron curtain' in a famous speech in 1946, and for more than 40 years it was. The nations in the east of Europe were trapped in a communist system, which brought many absurd aspects and totalitarian societies. Today, soon 30 years after the wall fell, the people of the Eastern economies still live in the remnants of these systems, through outdated commercial laws and structures that are very different from what we are used to in the West. Yet the people of Eastern Europe are friendly and inviting to business, and to successfully do business in the East, this book can be a treasure trove of knowledge for the business traveler. Seldom have I found people so inviting to business and knowledge as in the Eastern countries, yet one needs to understand their history, transition, and economic conditions to interact respectfully and well with them. For such depth and breath, Goncalves' and Smith's book offers a great help in understanding this region in transition."

Jörgen Eriksson, Founding Partner, Bearing Group Ltd, London, UK.

References

Abdelal, R. 2001. *National Purpose in the World Economy: Post-Soviet States in Comparative Perspective.* Ithaca, NY: Cornell University Press.

Aceves, R. 2016. "Economic Snapshot for Central and Eastern Europe." *Focus Economics*, January 13. Retrieved from www.focus-economics.com/regions/central-and-eastern-europe

Adelman, J.R., and C.L Gibson. 1989. *Contemporary Soviet Military Affairs: The Legacy of World War II.* Crows Nest, Australia: Unwin Hyman.

Al Jazeera. 2009. "Belarus Shuns Moscow Amid Loan Row." www.aljazeera.com/news/europe/2009/05/2009529121949669957.html (accessed January 28, 2015).

Alam, A., P.A. Casero, F. Khan, and C. Udomsaph. 2008. *Unleashing Prosperity: Productivity Growth in Eastern Europe and the Former Soviet Union.* Washington: World Bank.

Amadeo, K. November 7, 2013. "What Is a Currency War?" Retrieved from http://useconomy.about.com/od/tradepolicy/g/Currency-Wars.htm

Andrej Kiska. 2015. "NATO2020: We Need Trust, Solidarity, and Resolve." *News Release*, November 11, www.prezident.sk/en/article/prezident-na-nato2020-potrebujeme-doveru-solidaritu-a-rozhodnost/

Apollo. n.d. "Turpina pieaugt iedzīvotāju atbalsts eiro ieviešanai." Apollo. lv. http://apollo.tvnet.lv/zinas/turpina-pieaugt-iedzivotaju-atbalsts-eiro-ieviesanai/625128 (accessed December 2, 2015).

Aprinķis.lv. March 18, 2014. "Puse Latvijas iedzīvotāju atbalsta NATO militārās klātbūtnes pastiprināšanu [Half of Latvian Citizens Support the NATO Military Presence in the Reinforcement]." Retrieved from www.aprinkis.lv/babites-novads-zinas/latvija/item/16700-puse-latvijas-iedzivotaju-atbalsta-nato-militaras-klatbutnes-pastiprinasanu#

"Apstiprināta jaunā valdība Laimdotas Straujumas vadībā." January 22, 2014 [Approved the new government under management of Laimdota Laimdota], LV portals. http://m.lvportals.lv/visi/galerijas/955-apstiprinata-jauna-valdiba-laimdotas-straujumas-vadiba/.

Aristovnik, A. 2010. *The Determinants & Excessiveness of Current Account Deficits in Eastern Europe and the Former Soviet Union.* Retrieved from http://papers.ssrn.com/sol3/papers.cfm?abstract_id=920507 (accessed August 12, 2015).

Armstrong, W., and J. Anderson. 2007. *Geopolitics of European Union Enlargement: The Fortress Empire.* New York: Routledge.

Arkalgud, A.P. 2011. "Filling 'Institutional Voids' in Emerging Markets." *Forbes Magazine*, September 9. www.forbes.com/sites/infosys/2011/09/20/filling-institutional-voids-in-emerging-markets/ (accessed December 15, 2015).

Axell, A. 2002. *Russia's Heroes, 1941–45*. New York: Carroll & Graf Publishers.

Balmforth, R. 2010. "Yanukovich Vows to Keep Ukraine Out of NATO." Retrieved from www.reuters.com/article/us-ukraine-election-yanukovich-idUSTRE6062P320100107 (accessed January 28, 2016).

Bandeji, N. 2007. "Supraterritoriality, Embeddedness, or Both? Foreign Direct Investment in Central and Eastern Europe." In *Globalization: Perspectives from Central and Eastern Europe,* ed. K. Fábián, 25–63. Amsterdam: Jai Press.

Bandelj, N. 2008. *From Communists to Foreign Capitalists: The Social Foundations of Foreign Direct Investment in Postsocialist Europe.* Princeton, NJ: Princeton University Press.

Bank of Latvia. n.d. "EU and Euro." Retrieved from http://ec.europa.eu/economy_finance/euro/countries/latvia_en.htm (accessed May 04, 2015).

Bartlett, W. 2007. "Economic Restructuring, Job Creation and the Changing Demand for Skills in the Western Balkans." In *Labour Markets in the Western Balkans: Challenges for the Future*, ed. A. Fetsi, 19–50. Turin: European Training Foundation.

Bartlett, W. 2013. "Skill Mismatch, Education Systems, and Labor Markets in EU Neighborhood Policy Countries." European Institute. www.ub.edu/searchproject/wp-content/uploads/2013/09/WP05.20.pdf (accessed January 4, 2016).

BBC News: World Edition. April 30, 2001. "ERM Exchange Rate Method." Retrieved from http://news.bbc.co.uk/2/hi/in_depth/europe/euro-glossary/1216833.stm (accessed 20 July 2015).

BBC. 2006. "Montenegro Vote Result Confirmed." *BBC News,* May 23. Retrieved from http://news.bbc.co.uk/2/hi/europe/5007364.stm (accessed December 20, 2015).

BBC. 2008. "Q&A: Armenian Genocide Dispute." *BBC News.* Retrieved from http://news.bbc.co.uk/2/hi/europe/6045182.stm (accessed January 10, 2016).

BBC. 2012. "EU Leaders Grant Serbia Candidate Status." *BBC News,* March 1. Retrieved from www.bbc.com/news/world-europe-17225415 (accessed January 02, 2016).

BBC. 2013. "EU Set for Serbia Membership Talks." *BBC News*, June 28. Retrieved from www.bbc.com/news/world-europe-23099379 (accessed October 12, 2015).

Beachain, D., V. Sheridan, and S. Stan. 2012. *Life in Post-Communist Eastern Europe After EU Membership: Happy Ever After?* New York: Routledge.

Bevin, A., and S. Estrin. 2004. "The Determinants of Foreign Direct Investment: An Empirical Analysis." *Journal of Comparative Economics* 32, pp. 775–87.

Bibić, B. 2015. "Brain Drain in the Western Balkans." Opendemocracy.net. Retrieved from www.opendemocracy.net/can-europe-make-it/bilsana-bibic/brain-drain-in-western-balkans (accessed August 23, 2015).

Bideleux, R. 1987. *Communism and Development.* Oxford, UK: Routledge.

Bideleux, R., and I. Jeffries. 2007. *A History of Eastern Europe: Crisis and Change.* 2nd ed. London: Routledge.

Bilefsky, D. 2014. "Protests Over Government and Economy Roil Bosnia." *The New York Times*, February 7. Retrieved from www.nytimes.com/2014/02/08/world/europe/protests-over-government-and-economy-roil-bosnia.html?_r=0

Bilsen, V., and J. Konings. 1998. "Job Creation, Job Destruction, and Growth of Newly Established, Privatized, and State-Owned Enterprises in Transition Economies: Survey Evidence from Bulgaria, Hungary, and Romania." *Journal of Comparative Economics* 26, no. 3, pp. 429–45.

BIS: Department of Business, Innovation, and Skills. 2010. "The Benefits and Achievements of EU Single Market." UK Government National Archives. Retrieved from http://webarchive.nationalarchives.gov.uk/+/bis.gov.uk/policies/europe/benefits-of-eu-embership (accessed December 28, 2015).

Bleiere, D. 1996. *Latvija 1985–1996.* Gada: Notikumu hronika, N.I.M.S.

Blejer, M.I., and M. Kreb. 2002. *Transition: The First Decade.* Boston, MA: The MIT Press.

Bornhorst, F., and S. Commander. 2006. "Regional Unemployment and Its Persistence in Transition Countries." *Economics of Transition* 14, no. 2, pp. 269–88.

Brahmbhatt, M., O. Canuto, and S. Ghosh. December 2010. "Currency Wars Yesterday and Today." Economic Premise, The World Bank, Number 43.

"The Bratislava Declaration of the Prime Ministers of the Czech Republic, the Republic of Hungary, the Republic of Poland and the Slovak Republic on the occasion of the 20th anniversary of the Visegrad Group." 2011. Official Web Portal of the Visegrád Group. https://web.archive.org/web/20140824082057/http://www.visegradgroup.eu/2011/the-bratislava (accessed January 02, 2016).

The Breakup of Czechoslovakia. n.d. www.slovakia.org/history-topics (accessed December 12, 2014).

Brunwasser, M. 2013. "After Political Appoint in Bulgaria, Rage Boils Over." *The New York Times*, June 28. Retrieved from www.nytimes.com/2013/06/29/world/europe/after-political-appointment-in-bulgaria-rage-boils-over.html?_r=0

"Bulgaria's 2014 Parliamentary Election: CEC Announces Final Results." October 9, 2014. The Sofia Globe, http://sofiaglobe.com/2014/10/09/bulgarias-2014-parliamentary-election-cec-announces-final-results/.

Bukovskis, K., and A. Sprūds. 2015. "Latvia: Nations in Transit 2015." Freedom House. Retrieved from https://freedomhouse.org/report/nations-transit/2015/latvia

Bulgaria Economic Outlook. January 12, 2016. Focus Economics. Retrieved from www.focus-economics.com/countries/bulgaria

Busky, D.F. July 20, 2000. *Democratic Socialism: A Global Survey*. Santa Barbara, CA: Praeger.

Canuto, O. 2010. "Toward a Switchover of Locomotives in the Global Economy." *Economic Premise*, no. 33. Retrieved from www-wds.worldbank.org/external/default/WDSContentServer/WDSP/IB/2010/09/30/000334955_2010093 0035932/Rendered/PDF/568290BRI0EP330Box353739B01PUBLIC1.pdf

Canuto, O., and M. Giugale, eds. 2010. *The Day After Tomorrow—A Handbook on the Future of Economic Policy in the Developing World*. Washington, DC: World Bank.

Case, K.E., and C. Fair. 2004. *Principles of Economics*. Prentice Hall: Pearson.

CIA. January 15, 2016. "Economy Overview: SERBIA." *CIA World Factbook*. Retrieved from www.cia.gov/library/publications/the-world-factbook/geos/ri.html

"Cloudy Outlook for Growth in Emerging Europe and Central Asia." World Bank Press Release. October 8, 2014. Retrieved from www.worldbank.org/en/news/press-release/2014/10/08/cloudy-outlook-for-growth-in-emerging-europe-and-central-asia

Cornell, S.E. 2010. *Azerbaijan Since Independence*, 165, 284. Armonk, NY: M.E. Sharpe.

"Corruption Perceptions Index: Transparency International." 2012. Transparency International. www.transparency.org/cpi2012/results/ (accessed March 12, 2015).

Costigan, S., and J. Perry. 2012. *Cyberspaces and Global Affairs*. Abingdon, UK: Ashgate Publishing.

Country and Lending Groups, Data. n.d. http://data.worldbank.org/about/country-and-lending-groups#OECD_members (accessed March 12, 2015).

Crampton, R.J. 1994. *Eastern Europe in the Twentieth Century*. London: Routledge.

Crayne, J. 2000. "Publishing in Bosnia and Hercegovina." In *Publishing in Yugoslavia's Successor States*, eds. M. Biggins and J. Crayne, 41–82. New York: Haworth Press.

Croatia Economic Outlook. January 12, 2016. *Focus Economics*. Retrieved from www.focus-economics.com/countries/croatia

"Croatia to Pull Out of Border Dispute Arbitration with Slovenia." 2015. *DW*, July 27. Retrieved from www.dw.com/en/croatia-to-pull-out-of-border-dispute-arbitration-with-slovenia/a-18610325

Cseres, T. 1993. *Titoist atrocities in Vojvodina, 1944–1945: Serbian vendetta in Bácska*. Budapest, Hungary: Hunyadi Pub.

Čumlivski, D. 2012, October 1. "800 let Zlaté buly sicilské (in Czech)." National Archives of the Czech Republic (Národní Archiv České Republiky). Retrieved from www.nacr.cz/zpravy/zlatabula800.aspx (accessed February 22, 2014).

Cunningham, B. 2015. "Slovakia: Nations in Transit 2015." Freedom House. Retrieved from https://freedomhouse.org/report/nations-transit/2015/slovakia

Cuprik, R. 2014. "Pavol Paška of Smer Resigns." *Slovak Spectator*, November 17. Retrieved from http://spectator.sme.sk/c/20052671/pavol-paska-of-smer-resigns.html

Czech News Agency. 2015. "Czech Trade Deficit With China Is Long-Term Problem." *Prague Post*, August 30. Retrieved from www.praguepost.com/economy/49526-czech-trade-deficit-with-china-is-long-term-problem

Czech Republic Economic Outlook. January 12, 2016. *Focus Economics*. Retrieved from www.focus-economics.com/countries/czech-republic

Czech Republic Profile—Leaders. 2015. *BBC News*, December 25. Retrieved from www.bbc.com/news/world-europe-17220320 (accessed December 29, 2015).

Dabrowski, M. December 10, 2014. Central and eastern Europe: uncertain prospects of economic convergence. Brugel. Retrieved from http://bruegel.org/2014/12/central-and-eastern-europe-uncertain-prospects-of-economic-convergence/

Dabrowski, M. February 2015. "It Is Not Just Russia: Current Crisis in the CIS." Bruegel Policy Contribution, no. 1. Retrieved from http://bruegel.org/wp-content/uploads/imported/publications/pc_2015_01_CIS_.pdf (accessed January 10, 2016).

Dalakoglou, D. n.d. "The Road From Capitalism to Capitalism." www.academia.edu/1934474/_The_Road_from_Capitalism_to_Capitalism_Infrastructures_of_Post_Socialism_in_Albania (accessed December 12, 2015).

Dale, G. 2004. *Between State Capitalism and Globalization: The Collapse of the East German Economy.* Oxford: Lang.

Dale, G, ed. 2011. *First the Transition, Then the Crash: Eastern Europe in the 2000s.* London: Pluto Press.

Darvas, Z. December 5, 2014. "Central Bank Rates Deep in Shadow." Bruegel. Retrieved from www.bruegel.org/nc/blog/detail/article/1497-central-bank-rates-deep-in-shadow/

Day, M., and B. Waterfeld. 2014. "Donald Tusk, the New Head of Europe." *The Telegraph*, August 31. Retrieved from www.telegraph.co.uk/news/worldnews/europe/eu/11066174/Donald-Tusk-the-new-head-of-Europe.html

Debating Europe. 2014. "Which Country Should Join the European Union Next?" www.debatingeurope.eu/2014/03/20/which-country-should-join-the-european-union-next/#.Vo6RHTZhUxw (accessed January 03, 2016).

de Crombruggle, A., Z. Minton-Beddoes, and J. Sachs. 1996. *EU Membership for Central Europe: Commitments, Speed, and Conditionality.* Cambridge, MA: Harvard Institute for International Development.

de la Dehesa, G. 2006. *Winners and Losers in Globalization.* Oxford: Blackwell Publishing.

Deloitte. 2012. "Aftershock: Adjusting to the New World of Risk Management." *Forbes: Management and Business Operations.* Retrieved from www.forbes.com/forbesinsights/risk_management_2012/

Derluguian, G. 2005. *Bourdieu's Secret Admirer in the Caucasus: A World System Biography.* Chicago: University of Chicago Press.

Dixon-Kennedy, M. 1998. *Encyclopedia of Russian & Slavic Myth and Legend.* Santa Barbara, CA: ABC-CLIO.

Dobbs, M. 1999. "NATO's Latest Target: Yugoslavia's Economy." *Washington Post*, September 3. Retrieved from www.hartford-hwp.com/archives/62/306.html (accessed September 03, 2015).

Dolan, E. 2012. "What Happened When Poland's Fixed Exchange Rate Experiment Failed: Lessons for a Euro Divorce." *EconoMonitor.* Retrieved from www.economonitor.com/dolanecon/2012/04/13/what-happened-when-polands-fixed-exchange-rate-experiment-failed-lessons-for-a-euro-divorce/#sthash.BGjvEvtE.dpuf

Drahokoupil, J. 2009. *Globalization and the State in Central and Eastern Europe: The Politics of Foreign Direct Investment.* London: Routledge.

Drolc, T. 2015. "Out State Must Become a Promotor of Sustainable Economic Growth and Development." *The Slovenia Times*, December 16. Retrieved from www.sloveniatimes.com/our-state-must-become-a-promotor-of-sustainable-economic-growth-and-development

Du Bois, G., and M. Davidova. 2015. "China and the Czech Republic, a Recent Political Shift." *Nouvelle Europe*, June 29. Retrieved from www.nouvelle-europe.eu/en/china-and-czech-republic-recent-political-shift

Dumbrovsky, T. March 18, 2014. "Constitutional Change through Euro Crisis Law: A Multi-Level Legal Analysis." European University Institute. Retrieved from http://eurocrisislaw.eui.eu/slovakia/

Dzidic, D. 2014. "Bosnia-Herzegovina Hit by Wave of Violent Protests." *The Guardian*, February 7. Retrieved from www.theguardian.com/world/2014/feb/07/bosnia-herzegovina-wave-violent-protests

Eglitis, A. 2009. "Latvian GDP Shrank 18% in First Quarter, EU's Biggest Fall." *Bloomberg L.P.* Retrieved from http://www.baltic-course.com/eng/analytics/?doc=14481 (accessed April 30, 2015).

The Economist. 2011. "Investigating Kyrgyzstan's Ethnic Violence: Bloody Business." Retrieved from www.economist.com/node/18682522 (accessed January 28, 2016).

The Economist. 2012. "Slovenia's Economy: Next in Line." www.economist. com/node/21560567 (accessed November 20, 2015).

The Economist. January 14, 2014. "New Currency, New Leader." Retrieved from www.economist.com/news/europe/21593502-latvias-president-nominates-laimdota-straujuma-prime-minister-new-currency-new-leader   (accessed January 20, 2015).

The Economist's Writers. 2013. "Taking Europe's Pulse." *The Economist*, November 05. www.economist.com/blogs/graphicdetail/2013/11/european-economy-guide (accessed December 13, 2013).

Engjellushe, M. April 29, 2014. "Brussels 'First Agreement'—A Year After." KAS Policy Brief. Retrieved from www.kas.de/wf/doc/kas_37608-1522-1-30. pdf?140429132226

ETF. 2011. *Labour Markets and Employability: Trends and Challenges in Armenia, Azerbaijan, Belarus, Georgia, Moldova and Ukraine.* Turin: European Training Foundation.

The European Union Explained: Economic and Monetary Union and the Euro. 2014. Luxembourg: European Commission Publication.

Europa Publications Limited. 1998. *Eastern Europe and the Commonwealth of Independent States.* Oxford, UK: Routledge.

European Commission. 2015a. "European Neighbourhood Policy and Enlargement Negotiations: Steps Towards Joining." http://ec.europa.eu/ enlargement/policy/steps-towards-joining/index_en.htm

European Commission. 2015b. "Economic and Financial Affairs: Convergence Reports." http://ec.europa.eu/economy_finance/euro/adoption/convergence_ reports/index_en.htm (accessed December 28, 2015).

European Commission. 1993. "Copenhagen Criteria." Retrieved from http:// europa.eu/rapid/press-release_DOC-93-3_en.htm?locale=en

European Commission. 2012. "European Economic Forecast 2012." Retrieved from http://ec.europa.eu/economy_finance/publications/european_economy/ 2012/pdf/ee-2012-1_en.pdf (accessed January 03, 2016).

European Commission. January 21, 2014. "President Barroso Meets Serbian Prime Minister Dačić." Retrieved from http://europa.eu/rapid/press-release_ IP-14-52_en.htm

European Commission. October 19, 2015a. "Country Report: Croatia 2015." Retrieved   from   http://ec.europa.eu/europe2020/pdf/csr2015/cr2015_ croatia_en.pdf (accessed January 09, 2016).

European Commission. 2015b. "Economic and Financial Affairs: Why the Euro?" Retrieved from http://ec.europa.eu/economy_finance/euro/why/ index_en.htm (accessed December 28, 2015).

European Commission. October 19, 2015c. "European Neighborhood Policy and Enlargement Negotiations: Conditions for Membership." Retrieved from http://ec.europa.eu/enlargement/policy/conditions-membership/index_en.htm (accessed December 28, 2015).

European Commission. October 19, 2015d. "The History of the European Union." Retrieved from http://europa.eu/about-eu/eu-history/index_en.htm

European Commission. February 4, 2015e. "Migration and Home Affairs: Lithuania Anti-Corruption Report." Retrieved from http://ec.europa.eu/dgs/home-affairs/what-we-do/policies/organized-crime-and-human-trafficking/corruption/anti-corruption-report/index_en.htm

Eurostat. June 26, 2007. "Taxation trends in the EU." http://ec.europa.eu/eurostat/help/new-eurostat-website (accessed January 02, 2015).

Eurostat. 2010. *Statistical Pocket Book for the Candidate and Potential Candidate Countries*. Brussels: Eurostat.

Eurostar. 2011. "Real GDP Growth Rate." http://ec.europa.eu/eurostat/tgm/table.do?tab=table&language=en&pcode=teilm020&tableSelection=1&plugin=1 (accessed August 23, 2015).

Eurostat. April 12, 2013a. "Industrial Production up by 0.4% in Euro Area and EU27." Retrieved from http://ec.europa.eu/eurostat/help/new-eurostat-website (accessed October 24, 2015).

Eurostat. 2013b. "Tables, Graphs and Maps Interface (TGM) Table." Retrieved from http://ec.europa.eu/eurostat/tgm/table.do?tab=table&plugin=1&language=en&pcode=tps00018 (accessed October 10, 2015).

Eurostat. 2014. *Taxation Trends in the European Union: Eurostat Statistical Books*. Luxembourg: Publications Office of the European Union.

Eurostat. April 28, 2015a. "Growth Rate of Real GDP per Capita." Retrieved from http://ec.europa.eu/eurostat/help/new-eurostat-website (accessed April 28, 2015).

Eurostar. 2015b. "GDP Per Capita in PPS, Eurostat." http://ec.europa.eu/eurostat/tgm/table.do?tab=table&init=1&language=en&pcode=tec00114&plugin=1 (accessed January 2, 2015).

Faber, A. 2009. "The effects of Enlargement on the European Polity: State of the Art and Theoretical and Methodological Challenges." In *Enlarging the European Union: Effects on the New Member States and the EU*, eds. G. Avery, A. Faber, and A. Schmidt, 20–28. Brussels: Trans European Policy Studies Association. Retrieved from www.um.edu.mt/__data/assets/pdf_file/0017/71054/Enlarging_the_European_Union.pdf

Fábián, K., ed. 2007. *Globalization: Perspectives from Central and Eastern Europe*. Oxford: JAI Press.

Feige, E. 1991. "Perestroika and Ruble Convertibility." *Cato Journal* 10, no. 3, pp. 631–53. Retrieved from http://object.cato.org/sites/cato.org/files/serials/files/cato-journal/1991/1/cj10n3-2.pdf (accessed September 12, 2015).

Feige, E. 1994. "The Transition to a Market Economy in Russia: Property Rights, Mass Privatization and Stabilization." In *A Fourth Way?: Privatization,*

Property, and the Emergence of New Market Economics, eds. G. Alexander and G. Skąpska, 57–78. London: Routledge.

Feldstein, M. November 26, 2014. "The Geopolitical Impact of Cheap Oil." Project Syndicate. Retrieved from www.project-syndicate.org/commentary/oil-prices-geopolitical-stability-by-martin-feldstein-2014-11?barrier=true

Fenyvesi, A. 2005. *Hungarian Language Contact Outside Hungary: Studies on Hungarian as a Minority Language.* John Benjamins Publishing Company.

Ferguson, N. 2006. *The War of the World: Twentieth-Century Conflict and the Descent of the West.* New York: Penguin Press.

Filipovic, G. 2012. "IMF Sees Serbian 2012 GDP Up 0.5%, Jobless Rate 'a Concern'." *Bloomberg.* Retrieved from www.bloomberg.com/news/articles/2012-02-10/imf-sees-serbian-2012-gdp-up-0-5-jobless-rate-a-concern-1- (accessed September 20, 2015).

Fox News. 2006. "Turkmenistan's Leader Promises Citizens Free Gas, Electricity and Water Through 2030." Retrieved from www.foxnews.com/story/2006/10/25/turkmenistan-leader-promises-citizens-free-gas-electricity-and-water-through.html (accessed January 28, 2016).

Frankel, J. 2015. "Should Eastern European Countries Join the Euro? A Review and Update of Trade Estimates and Consideration of Endogenous OCA Criteria." Paper Presented at the Dubrovnik Economic Conference (June 2008). Retrieved from www.hks.harvard.edu/fs/jfrankel/EuroEffectsDubrovnikEC08.pdf (accessed December 28, 2015).

Furtlehner, P. 2008. "Slovenia." In *Compliance in the Enlarged European Union: Living Rights or Dead Letters?*, eds. G. Falkner, O. Treib, E. Holzleithner, 126–27. Ashgate Publishing, Ltd.

G.K. 2014. "Romania and Bulgaria: Depressing Reading." *The Economist: Eastern Approaches,* January 22. Retrieved from www.economist.com/blogs/easternapproaches/2014/01/romania-and-bulgaria

Garsoïan, N. 1997. *Armenian People from Ancient to Modern Times*, Vol. 1. New York: Palgrave Macmillan.

Gelazis, N. 2005. *The Tenth Anniversary of the Dayton Accords and Afterwards: Reflections on Post-Conflict State- and Nation-Building.* Washington, DC: Woodrow Wilson International Center for Scholars. Retrieved from www.wilsoncenter.org/sites/default/files/EES_dayton.pdf

Gillet, K., and P. Karasz. 2015. "Victor Ponta, Romania's Premier, Steps Down After Outcry Over Corruption." *New York Times,* November 4. //www.nytimes.com/2015/11/05/world/europe/romania-victor-ponta-resigns.html?_r=0 (accessed December 12, 2015).

Global Edge. n.d. "Serbia: Introduction." Michigan State University. Retrieved from http://globaledge.msu.edu/countries/serbia (accessed November 24, 2015).

Goclowski, M., and P. Florkiewicz. 2015. "Polish President Suffers Shock Reverse in First Round Vote: Exit Poll." *Reuters*, May 10. Retrieved from www.reuters.com/article/2015/05/11/us-poland-vote-president-idUSKBN0NU0RX20150511

Goncalves, M., Jose Alves, Carlos Frota, Harry Xia, Rajabahadur V. Arcot. 2014. "Coping with Political and Economic Risks." *Advanced Economies and Emerging Markets: Prospects for Globalization,* 298–99. New York: Business Expert Press.

Grabbe, H., and K. Hughes. 1998. *Enlarging the EU Eastward.* London: Royal Institute for International Affairs.

Grajewski, M. 2008. "Slovakia Revalues Currency Ahead of Euro Entry." *The Guardian*, May 28. Retrieved from https://web.archive.org/web/20080601034210/http://www.guardian.co.uk/business/feedarticle/7546478 (accessed September 23, 2014).

Green, F., D. Ashton, D. James, and J. Sung. 1999a. "The Role of the State in Skill Formation: Evidence from the Republic of Korea, Singapore, and Taiwan." *Oxford Review of Economic Policy* 15, no. 1, pp. 82–96.

Green, F., D. James, D. Ashton, and J. Sung. 1999b. "Post-School Education and Training Policy in Development States: The Cases of Taiwan and South Korea." *Journal of Education Policy* 14, no. 3, pp. 301–15.

Gros, D., and A. Steinherr. 1995. *Winds of Change: Economic Transition in Central and Eastern Europe.* London: Longman.

The Guardian. May 18, 2014. "Bosnia and Serbia Floods: Thousands Flee as Death Toll Rises." Retrieved from www.theguardian.com/world/2014/may/18/thousands-flee-floods-bosnia-serbia

Guerrera, F. 2013. "Currency War Has Started." *The Wall Street Journal*, February 04. http://online.wsj.com/news/articles/SB10001424127887324761004578283684195892250 (accessed December 13, 2013).

Gulyas, V. 2014. "The US Cancels Visas for Hungarians Involved in Corruption." *Wall Street Journal*, October 17. Retrieved from http://blogs.wsj.com/emergingeurope/2014/10/17/the-us-cancels-visas-for-hungarians-involved-in-corruption/

Guyader, M. 2009. "Accession Effects on Cohesion in the New Member States." In *Enlarging the European Union: Effects on the New Member States and the EU,* eds. G. Avery, A. Faber, and A. Schmidt, 101–3. Brussels: Trans European Policy Studies Association. Retrieved from www.um.edu.mt/__data/assets/pdf_file/0017/71054/Enlarging_the_European_Union.pdf

Harizanova, T. June 17, 2010. "Inter-Company Debt—One of Bulgarian Economy's Serious Problems." Bulgarian National Radio. Retrieved from https://web.archive.org/web/20121101112308/http://bnr.bg/sites/en/Economy/Pages/1706compandebts.aspx (accessed October 10, 2015).

Haynes, M., and R. Hasan. 1998. "The State and Market in the Transition Economies: Critical Remarks in the Light of Past History and the Current Experience." *The Journal of European Economic History* 27, no. 3, pp. 609–46.

Heinisch, R., and C. Landsberger. (2012). "Returning to Europe: East Central Europe's Complex Relationship with European Integration and its Repercussions." In *The Routledge History of East Central Europe Since 1700,* eds. A.S. Klimo and I. Livezeanu. Retrieved from www.uni-salzburg. at/fileadmin/multimedia/Politikwissenschaft%20und%20Soziologie/documents/Heinisch-Landsberger_East_Central_Europe%E2%80%99s_Complex_Relationship_with_European_Integration.pdf

Hellman, J. 1998. "Winners Take All: The Politics of Partial Reform in Postcommunist." *Transitions: World Politics* 50, no. 2, pp. 203–34.

Hinsburg, H., J. Matt, and R. Vinni. 2015. "Estonia: Nations in Transit." Freedom House. Retrieved from https://freedomhouse.org/report/nations-transit/2015/estonia

Hirsch, D., J. Kett, and J. Trefil. 2002. *The New Dictionary of Cultural Literacy.* Boston: Houghton Mifflin Harcourt.

Hoogvelt, A. 1997. *Globalization and the Postcolonial World.* Basingstoke: Macmillan.

HRW. 2014. "World Report 2014: Turkmenistan." Retrieved from www.hrw. org/world-report/2014/country-chapters/turkmenistan (accessed January 28, 2016).

Human Rights First. October 17, 2014. "U.S. Sanctions Target Corrupt Hungarian Officials."

Human Rights Watch, World Report. 2015. "Kazakhstan." Retrieved from http://www.humanrightsfirst.org/press-release/us-sanctions-target-corrupt-hungarian-officials (accessed January 28, 2016).

Humer, Ž. 2007. "Europeanization and the Equal Opportunities Policy in Slovenia." In *Globalization: Perspectives from Central and Eastern Europe,* ed. K. Fábián, 305–26. Oxford: JAI Press.

Iglicka, K. (Center for International Relations, Warsaw). 2008. "Poland: Waiting for Immigrants. But Do We Really Want Them?" CeSPI Centro Studi di Politico Internazionale. Retrieved from http://www.cespi.it/WPMIG/Country%20mig-POLAND.pdf (accessed October 12, 2015).

IMF. 1997. *World Economic Outlook.* Washington, DC: International Monetary Fund. Retrieved from www.imf.org/external/pubs/ft/weo/weo1097/weocon97.htm

IMF. 1998. *World Investment Report.* Washington, DC: International Monetary Fund. Retrieved from http://unctad.org/en/Docs/wir1998ch3_en.pdf

IMF. 2006. "Advanced Economies." www.imf.org/external/pubs/ft/weo/2009/01/weodata/weoselco.aspx?g=110&sg=All+countries+%2f+Advanced+economies (accessed November 11, 2015).

IMF. 2010a. *World Economic Outlook.* Washington, DC: International Monetary Fund. Retrieved from www.imf.org/external/pubs/ft/weo/2010/01/index.htm

IMF. 2010b. *Global Financial Stability Report.* Washington, DC: International Monetary Fund. Retrieved from www.imf.org/external/pubs/ft/gfsr/2010/01/index.htm

IMF. 2012a. *Unemployment, Around 40% of the Population, Is a Significant Problem that Encourages Outward Migration and Black Market Activity.* Washington, DC: International Monetary Fund. Retrieved from www.imf.org/external/pubs/ft/scr/2012/cr12100.pdf

IMF. July 16, 2012b. *IMF Executive Board Concludes First Post-Program Monitoring Discussions with the Republic of Latvia.* Public Information Notice (PIN) No. 12/76 by IMF. Washington, DC: International Monetary Fund. Retrieved from www.imf.org/external/np/sec/pn/2012/pn1276.htm (accessed October 24, 2015).

IMF. 2014. *Central, Eastern, and Southeastern Europe: Regional Economic Issues Update.* Washington, DC: International Monetary Fund. Retrieved from www.imf.org/external/pubs/ft/reo/2014/eur/eng/pdf/erei1014.pdf

IMF. 2015a. "Report for Selected Countries and Subjects." Retrieved from www.imf.org/external/pubs/ft/weo/2015/01/weodata/index.aspx (accessed January 28, 2016).

IMF. 2015b. *Romania and the IMF.* Washington, DC: International Monetary Fund. Retrieved from https://www.imf.org/external/country/ROU/index.htm

Index of Economic Freedom: Estonia. 2015. "The Heritage Foundation." Retrieved from www.heritage.org/index/country/estonia

The Independent. January 28, 1994. "The UNICEF Annual Report." Retrieved from www.unicef.org/about/history/files/unicef_annual_report_1994.pdf

IndustryWeek. April 9, 2008. "Slovak Car Industry Production Almost Doubled in 2007." Industryweek.com. Retrieved from www.industryweek.com/global-economy/slovak-car-industry-production-almost-doubled-2007   (accessed October 10, 2015).

Inotai, A. 2009. "BUDAPEST—Ghost of Second-Class Status Haunts Central and Eastern Europe." *Europe's World.* Retrieved from www.europesworld.org/NewEnglish/Home_old/Article/tabid/191/ArticleType/articleview/ArticleID/21480/language/en-US/Default.aspx

INSTAT. 2015. "Population Of Albania, Republic of Albania Institute of Statistics." Retrieved from www.instat.gov.al/en/publications/press-releases/press-release-population-of-albania-1-january-2015.aspx (accessed January 02, 2016).

International Energy Agency. 2012. "Oil Market Report." Retrieved from https://web.archive.org/web/20120518015934/http://omrpublic.iea.org/omrarchive/18jan12sup.pdf (accessed January 28, 2016).

Iossifov, P. 2015. "Disinflation in Non-Eurozone EU Nations." VOX CEPR Policy Portal. Retrieved from www.voxeu.org/article/disinflation-non-eurozone-eu-nations (accessed January 10, 2016).

Iossifov, P., and J. Podpiera. 2014. "Are Non-Euro Area EU Countries Importing Low Inflation from the Euro Area?" Retrieved from www.imf.org/external/pubs/ft/wp/2014/wp14191.pdf (accessed January 10, 2016).

"ISO Currency—ISO 4217 Amendment Number 159." n.d. Currency Code Services—ISO 4217 Maintenance Agency. SIX Interbank Clearing. Retrieved from www.currency-iso.org/en/shared/amendments/iso-4217-amendment.html (accessed November 11, 2015).

Jacoby, W. 2004. *The Enlargement of the European Union and NATO: Ordering from the Menu in Central Europe.* Cambridge, UK: Cambridge University Press.

Jahan, S. March 28, 2012. "Inflation Targeting: Holding the Line." Finance & Development.

Janzen, J., and T. Taraschewski. 2009. *Shahshahānī, Suhaylā, ed. Cities of Pilgrimage.* Iuaes-series 4. Germany: Münster: LIT Verlag. https://books.google.com/books?id=0T7DAJqAN7wC&pg=PA11&lpg=PA11&dq=Cities+of+Pilgrimage&source=bl&ots=xKP899LEnG&sig=Grbyt3l1vXSKfz4wWncIB9yfCzQ&hl=en&sa=X&ved=0ahUKEwj8sM3R7NbMAhVBGqYKHZk8CQUQ6AEIMDAC#v=onepage&q=Cities%20of%20Pilgrimage&f=false, Retrieved December 21, 2012.

Jean-Phillippe Pourcelot. November 11, 2015. "GDP Growth Eases in Q3." Focus Economics. Retrieved from www.focus-economics.com/countries/estonia/news/gdp/gdp-growth-eases-in-q3

Jense, N. October 2008. "Political Risk, Democratic Institutions, and Foreign Direct Investment." *The Journal of Politics* 70, no. 4, pp. 1040, 1052.

Jones, M. 2015. "Central Europe Looking Tranquil Port in Emerging Markets Storm." *Reuters,* August 10. Retrieved from http://finance.yahoo.com/news/central-europe-looking-tranquil-port-124848904.html;_ylt=A0LEVrciwMhV52gAqLMnnIlQ;_ylu=X3oDMTByMjB0aG5zBGNvbG8DYmYxBHBvcwMxBHZ0aWQDBHNlYwNzYw

Jurkynas, M. 2015. "Lithuania: Nations in Transit 2015." Freedom House. Retrieved from https://freedomhouse.org/report/nations-transit/2015/lithuania

K.S. 2013. "Resignation Amid Scandal." *The Economist: Eastern Approaches,* June 18.

Kajne, S. 2009. "The Effects of EU Enlargement: Slovenia." In *Enlarging the European Union: Effects on the New Member States and the EU,* eds. G. Avery, A. Faber, and A. Schmidt. Brussels, Belgium: Trans European Policy Studies Association.

Khanna, T., and K.G. Palepu. 2010. *Winning in Emerging Markets: A Roadmap for Strategy and Execution*. Boston: Harvard Business School Publishing.

Kapacki, R., and M. Prochiniak. 2009. "The EU Enlargement and the Economic Growth in the CEE New Member Countries." European Commission, Brussels. Retrieved from http://ec.europa.eu/economy_finance/publications/publication14295_en.pdf (accessed January 10, 2016).

Karasinka-Fendler, M. 2009. "The Effects of Accession on Poland." In *Enlarging the European Union: Effects on the New Member States and the EU,* eds. G. Avery, A. Faber, and A. Schmidt. Trans European Policy Studies Association.

Katzenstein, P.J. 1997. *Mitteleuropa: Between Europe and Germany*. Berghahn Books.

Kaza, J. 2015. "Latvia's Prime Minister Laimdota Straujuma Steps Down." *Wall Street Journal*, December 5. Retrieved from www.wsj.com/articles/latvias-premier-laimdota-straujuma-steps-down-1449480185

Kieser, H.-L., D.J. Schaller. 2002. "Der Völkermord an den Armeniern und die Shoah [The Armenian genocide and the Shoah] (in German)." Chronos.

King, D.C. 2006. *Azerbaijan, Marshall Cavendish*, 99. Tarrytown, NY.

Knight, A. n.d. *Beria: Stalin's First Lieutenant*, Princeton, NJ: Princeton University Press.

Kolev, A., and C. Saget. 2005. "Understanding Youth Labour Market Disadvantage: Evidence from South-East Europe." *International Labour Review* 144, no. 2, p. 161.

Kolyako, N. 2009. "Rimsevics: Failing to Bail Out Parex Banka Would Result in Closing Down of Four Banks in Latvia." The Baltic Course. Retrieved from www.baltic-course.com/eng/finances/?doc=22011 (accessed November 12, 2014).

Kornecki, L. 2010. "Foreign Direct Investment and Macroeconomic Changes in CEE Integrating In To The Global Market." *Journal of International Business and Cultural Studies*. Embry-Riddle Aeronautical University. Retrieved from www.aabri.com/manuscripts/09222.pdf (accessed January 08, 2016).

Kowalik, T. 2011. *From Solidarity to Sell-Out: The Restoration of Capitalism in Poland*. New York: Monthly Review Press.

Krassimir, N.Y., and S.D. Kaloyan. 2009. "The Effects of EU Accession on Bulgaria." In *Enlarging the European Union: Effects on the New Member States and the EU,* eds. G. Avery, A. Faber, and A. Schmidt. Trans European Policy Studies Association.

Kubilius, K. 2016. "Map of Eastern Europe." Retrieved from http://goeasteurope.about.com/od/introtoeasteuropetravel/ig/Maps-of-Eastern-Europe/Map-of-Eastern-Europe.htm

Kunštát, D. November 2015. Důvěra stranickým představitelům [Confidence in Party Representatives], Centrum pro výzkum veřejného mínění [Public Opinion Research Center] (Prague: CVVM). http://cvvm.soc.cas.cz/en/

politicians-political-institutions/confidence-in-constitutional-institutions-and-satisfaction-with-political-situation-in-november-2015

Kuruvilla, S., C.L. Erickson, and A. Hwang. 2002. "An Assessment of the Singapore Skills Development System: Does It Constitute a Viable Model for Other Developing Countries?" *World Development* 30, no. 8, pp. 1461–76.

Lankes, H.P., and A. Venables. 1996. "Foreign Direct Investment in Economic Transition: The Changing Pattern of Investments." *Economics of Transition* 4, pp. 331–47.

"Latvia Economic Outlook." 2016. *Focus Economics*, January 12. Retrieved from www.focus-economics.com/countries/latvia

Latvian Economy in Rapid Decline. 2009. *BBC News,* May 11. Retrieved from http://news.bbc.co.uk/2/hi/business/8043972.stm (accessed May 10, 2015).

Latvian Institute. 2011. "Latvia in Brief." Retrieved from www.li.lv/en (accessed November 05, 2014).

Leconte, C. 2010. *Understanding Euroscepticism.* Basingstoke, MD: Palgrave MacMillan.

Lejour A.M., and R. Nahuis. 2004. "EU Accession and the Catching Up of the Central and East European Countries." In *The Past, Present and Future of the European Union*, ed. A. Deardorff, IEA Conference Volume, no. 138. New York: Palgrave Macmillan.

Levinson, A. 1994. "Bulgaria's Transition to a Market Economy." Sofia University. Archived from the Original (PDF) on August 12, 2011. Retrieved from https://web.archive.org/web/20110812095458/http://www.demokratizatsiya.org:80/bin/pdf/DEM%2003-1%20Levinson.PDF (accessed October 03, 2015).

The Lithuania Tribune. 2005. "Western Union Opens Centre in Vilnius." www.alfa.lt/straipsnis/11255175/western-union-opens-centre-in-vilnius (accessed November 12, 2015).

"Lithuanian Minister of Interior Resigns." 2015. *Delfi*, November 20, http://en.delfi.lt/lithuania/politics/lithuanian-minister-of-interior-resigns.d?id=69631766.

Lonely Planet. n.d. "Lonely Planet's Bosnia and Herzegovina Tourism Profile." https://www.lonelyplanet.com/bosnia-and-hercegovina (accessed January 02, 2016).

Lsm.lv. July 2014. "Budžeta komisija apstiprina aizsardzības finansējuma pieauguma grafiku" [Budgetary Commission approves defense funding growth schedule]. www.lsm.lv/lv/raksts/latvija/zinas/budzheta-komisija-apstiprina-aizsardziibas-finansejuma-pieauguma.a90189/

Lukowski, J., H. Zawaszki. 2001. *A Concise History of Poland*. 1st ed. University of Stirling Libraries—Popular Loan (Q 43.8 LUK): Cambridge University Press.

Lumans, V.O. 2006. *Latvia in World War II (World War II: The Global, Human, and Ethical Dimension)*. New York: Fordham University Press.

Malcolm, N. 1996. *Bosnia: A Short History Updated Edition*. New York: NYU Press.

Mardiste, D. 2015. "Pro-Russian Estonia Mayor Arrested for Bribery." *Reuters,* September 22. Retrieved from www.reuters.com/article/us-estonia-arrest-idUSKCN0RM1R820150922

McKinnon, R.I. 1973. *Money and Capital in Economic Development*. Washington, DC: Brookings Institution.

Medrano, J.D. 2003. *Framing Europe: Attitudes toward European Integration in Germany, Spain, and the United Kingdom*. Princeton, NJ: Princeton University Press.

Meyer, K. 1995. "Foreign Direct Investment in the Early Years of Economic Transition: A Survey." *Economics of Transition* 2, pp. 301–20.

Meyer, K. 1998. *Direct Investment in Economies in Transition*. Massachusetts: Edward Elgar.

"MIT Observatory of Economic Complexity." n.d. http://atlas.media.mit.edu/en/profile/country/cze/ (accessed January 02, 2016).

Mlsna, P., F, Šlehofer, and D. Urban. 2010. "The Path of Czech Constitutionality" (PDF). 1st ed. (in: (Bilingual)—Czech and English). Praha: Úřad Vlády České Republiky (The Office of the Government of the Czech Republic). pp. 10–11. Retrieved from www.vlada.cz/assets/udalosti/vystavy/Cesty-ceske-ustavnosti.pdf (accessed March 28, 2015).

Moghadam, R., R. Teja, and P. Berkmen. 2014. "Euro Area Deflation Versus Lowflation." iMFdirect blog. Retrieved from http://blog-imfdirect.imf.org/2014/03/04/euro-area-deflation-versus-lowflation/ (accessed January 10, 2016).

Mojzes, P. 2000. *Religion and the War in Bosnia*. Oxford University Press. "Medieval Bosnia was founded as an independent state (Banate) by Ban Kulin (1180–1204)."

Monstat. 2011. "Census of Population, Households and Dwellings in Montenegro 2011." Retrieved from www.monstat.org/userfiles/file/popis2011/saopstenje/saopstenje(1).pdf (accessed December 20, 2015).

Moore, J.B. 1969. *Social Origins of Dictatorship in Democracy*. Harmondsworth: Penguin.

Mühlberger, M., and K. Körner. 2014. "CEE: Fit for the next decade in the EU." EU Monitor, Deutsche Bank. Retrieved from www.dbresearch.com/PROD/DBR_INTERNET_EN-PROD/PROD0000000000333559/CEE%3A+Fit+for+the+next++decade+in+the+EU.pdf (accessed January 03, 2016).

Naimark, N.M. 1995. *The Russians in Germany: A History of the Soviet Zone of Occupation, 1945–1949.* Cambridge, MA: Harvard University Press.

Nardelli, A, D. Dzidic, and E. Jukic. 2014. "Bosnia and Herzegovnia: The World's Most Complicated System of Government?" *The Guardian*, October 8. Retrieved from www.theguardian.com/news/datablog/2014/oct/08/bosnia-herzegovina-elections-the-worlds-most-complicated-system-of-government

National Democratic Institute for International Affairs. December 4, 2014. "Bosnia and Herzegovina's 2014 Elections: Post-Election Analysis." Retrieved from www.ndi.org/node/22226

Newell, A., and F. Pastore. 2006. "Regional Unemployment and Its Persistence in Transition Countries." *Economics of Transition* 14, no. 2, pp. 269–88.

The New York Times. November 1, 2010. "Romania to Get Next Installment of Bailout." Retrieved from www.nytimes.com/2010/11/02/business/global/02romecon.html?_r=0 (accessed January 07, 2016).

Novinite. November 22, 2010. "Ireland Stays in Bulgaria-Led Club of Low Corporate Taxes, Ups Income Levy." Retrieved from www.novinite.com/view_news.php?id=122395 (accessed March 25, 2015).

Novinite.com. November 21, 2013. "Bulgarian Protests: Students Determined to Overthrow System." Retrieved from www.novinite.com/articles/155746/Bulgarian+Protests%3A+Students+Determined+to+Overthrow+System

Novinite.com. January 16, 2015. "Bulgaria to Follow Romanian Example in Fighting Corruption – Deputy PM." Retrieved from www.novinite.com/articles/166000/Bulgaria+to+Follow+Romanian+Example+in+Fighting+Corruption+%E2%80%93+Deputy+PM

O'Connor, K. January 1, 2003. *The History of the Baltic States.* Westport, Connecticut: Greenwood Publishing Group.

OECD. 1998. "Survey of OECD Work on International Investment." Organization for Economic Co-Operation and Development. Working Paper. https://www.oecd.org/investment/investment-policy/WP-1998_1.pdf

OECD. 2015. "Central and Eastern Europe, the Caucasus and Central Asia." Retrieved from www.iea.org/newsroomandevents/pressreleases/2015/april/iea-reviews-energy-policies-countries-in-eastern-europe-caucasus-central-asia.html (accessed September 12, 2015).

"OECD Established Roadmap for Membership with Lithuania." 2015. *OECD News Release,* October 27. Retrieved from www.oecd.org/newsroom/oecd-establishes-roadmap-for-membership-with-lithuania.htm

Özsagir, A., and Y. Bayraktutan. 2010. "The Relationship Between Vocational Education and Industrial Production in Turkey." *International Journal of Economic Perspectives* 4, no. 2, pp. 439–48.

Outhwaite, W. 2010. "What Is Left After 1989?" In *The Global 1989: Continuity and Change in World Politics,* eds. G. Lawson, C. Armbruster and M. Cox. Cambridge: Cambridge University Press.

Pacek, N., and D. Thorniley. 2007. *Eastern Europe Markets: Lessons for Business and the Outlook for Different Markets.* 2nd ed. London: The Economist and Profile Books.

Parliament of Ukraine. 2007. "Declaration of State Sovereignty of Ukraine." Verkhovna Rada of Ukraine. Retrieved from https://web.archive.org/web/20070927224650/http://gska2.rada.gov.ua:7777/site/postanova_eng/Declaration_of_State_Sovereignty_of_Ukraine_rev1.htm (accessed January 28, 2016).

Pavel, M. 2015. "Reforming the Czech Civil Service: An Unfinished Journey." *Post.* Retrieved from http://postnito.cz/reforming-the-czech-civil-service-an-unfinished-journey/ (accessed December 29, 2015).

Petrolongo, B., and C. Pissarides. 2001. "Looking Into the Black Box: A Survey of the Matching Function." *Journal of Economic Literature* 39, pp. 390–431.

Pitas, C. 2015. "Jaguar Land Rover Plans New Plant in Slovakia." *Reuters,* August 11. ed. J. Merriman. Retrieved from www.reuters.com/article/jaguar-lnd-rover-slovakia-idUSL5N1033QE20150811#bW9TkFRo3BsYJTmT.97 (accessed September 20, 2014).

Pleso, S. 2014. "Fico's Suprising Defeat." *The Economist* March 31. Retrieved from www.economist.com/blogs/easternapproaches/2014/03/slovakias-election-0

Pllumi, Z. November 28, 1948. *Live to Tell: A True Story of Religious Persecution in Communist Albania.* Bloomington, IN: iUniverse.

Pogany, I.S. 1997. *Righting Wrongs in Eastern Europe.* Manchester University Press ND.

"Police Search Home of Former Slovenian Premier." 2015. *Daily Mail,* March 11. Retrieved from www.dailymail.co.uk/wires/ap/article-2989681/Police-search-home-former-Slovenian-premier.html

Portes, R. November 4, 2010. "Currency Wars and the Emerging-Market Countries." VoxEU.

Prauser, S., and A. Rees. 2004. "The Expulsion of 'German' Communities from Eastern Europe at the End of the Second World War." EUI Working Paper HEC No. 2004/1. San Domenico, Florence: European University Institute.

Press Service of the President of the Republic of Belarus. 2004. "Section V: Local government and Self-Government." Constitution of Belarus, Archived from the original on December 17, 2007. Retrieved from https://web.archive.org/web/20071105204240/http://president.gov.by/en/press19333.html (accessed January 29, 2016).

R.P. April 3, 2015. "A New State Body to Fight Corruption in Bulgaria." CEE Insight. Retrieved from www.ceeinsight.net/2015/04/03/new-state-body-fight-corruption-bulgaria/

Radka Minecherová. 2014. "Slovakia Improves on the Corruption Index." *Slovak Spectator*, December 3. Retrieved from http://spectator.sme.sk/articles/view/56140/10/slovakia_improves_in_the_corruption_index.html

Reinhard, S. 2000. *A Modern History of the Islamic World*. New York: I.B. Tauris.

Reinhart, C.M., and J.F. Kirkegaard. 2012. "Financial Repression: Then and Now." Voxeu. Retrieved from www.voxeu.org/article/financial-repression-then-and-now (accessed April 23, 2012).

Reporters Without Borders. 2012. "Press Freedom Index 2011–2012." En.rsf. org. Retrieved from http://en.rsf.org/press-freedom-index-2011-2012,1043. html (accessed April 12, 2014).

Resolution of the European Council on the Stability and Growth Pact Amsterdam. June 17, 1997. *OJ C 236, 2.8.1997, p. 1–2 (ES, DA, DE, EL, EN, FR, IT, NL, PT, FI, SV)*. Retrieved from http://eur-lex.europa.eu/legal-content/EN/ALL/?uri=CELEX:31997Y0802%2801%29

Rettman, A. 2015. "Donbas: A New 'Black Hole' in Europe." EU Observer. Retrieved from https://euobserver.com/foreign/128618 (accessed November 12, 2015).

Reuters. 2013. "OECD Sees Economic Rebound in CEE, Russia in 2015." Retrieved from www.reuters.com/article/oecd-economy-east-idUSL5N0J33P820131119 (accessed January 02, 2016).

Rieber, A.J. 2000. *Forced Migration in Central and Eastern Europe, 1939–1950*. London: Routledge.

Ristic, M. 2012. "Serbia, Bosnia Rank Low on Economic Freedom Index." *Balkan Insight*. Retrieved from www.balkaninsight.com/en/article/serbia-bosnia-rank-low-on-economic-freedom-index (accessed January 10, 2016).

Roaf, J., R. Atoyan, B. Joshi, and K. Krogulski. October 2014. "25 Years of Transition: Post-Communist Europe and the IMF." *International Monetary Fund*, p. 15.

"Romania Economic Outlook." 2016. *Focus Economics*, January 12. Retrieved from www.focus-economics.com/countries/romania

"Romania Supports Sanctions Against Russia Until Full Implementation of Minsk Agreements." 2015. *Unian,* March 17. Retrieved from www.unian. info/politics/1056476-romania-supports-sanctions-against-russia-until-full-implementation-of-minsk-agreements.html

Robert, M. 1992. *Revolution and Genocide: On the Origins of the Armenian Genocide and the Holocaust*. Chicago, IL: University of Chicago Press.

Rodrik, D. 2009. "Growth after the Crisis." Commission on Growth and Development Working Paper No. 65.

Roisman, J., and I. Worthington. 2011. *A Companion to Ancient Macedonia*. John Wiley & Sons, 135–38, 343–45.

Romanian National Institute of Statistics. 2007. "GDP in 2006." (in Romanian). www.insse.ro/cms/files/statistici/comunicate/pib/pibr06.pdf (accessed August 30, 2015).

Romer, P.M. 1994. "The origins of endogenous growth." *Journal of Economic Perspectives* 8, no. 1, pp. 3–22.

Rossi, M. 2014. "Five More Inconvenient Truths About Kosovo." TransConflict. Retrieved from www.transconflict.com/2014/10/five-inconvenient-truths-kosovo-300/ (accessed December 12, 2015).

"RosBusinessConsulting—News Online." n.d. Rbcnews. www.rbcnews.com/free/20070403193147.shtml (accessed January 10, 2016).

Rothschild, J. 1974. *East-Central Europe Between the Two World Wars*. Seattle: University of Washington Press.

Rozmahel, P., L. Kouba, L. Grochová, and N. Najman. 2013. "Integration of Central and Eastern European Countries: Increasing EU Heterogeneity?" European Commission, WWWforEurope, Working Paper no. 9, Retrieved from www.foreurope.eu/fileadmin/documents/pdf/Workingpapers/WWWforEurope_WPS_no009_MS77.pdf (accessed January 10, 2016).

Russia Pushes Peace Plan. 1999. *BBC News*, April 29. Retrieved from http://news.bbc.co.uk/2/hi/europe/331036.stm (accessed December 17, 2015).

Sachs, J. 1994. *Poland's Jump to the Market Economy*. Cambridge, MA: M.I.T. Press.

Schabnel, A., and R. Thakur. 2001. *Kosovo and the Challenge of Humanitarian Intervention: Selective Indignation, Collective Action, and International Citizenship*. New York: The United Nations University.

Schadler, S., P. Drummond, L. Kuijs, Z. Murgasova, and R. Van Elkan. 2005. *Adopting the Euro in Central Europe: Challenges of the Next Step in European Integration*. Washington, DC: International Monetary Fund.

Schmidt, K.D. 1995. "Foreign Direct Investment in Eastern Europe: State-of-the-Art and Prospects." In *Transforming economies and European Integration*, eds. R. Dobrinsky and M. Lndesmann, 268–89. Aldershot, UK: Edward Elgar.

Schwab, K. n.d. "The Global Competitiveness Report 2013–2014." World Economic Forum, p. 27 (41/516). http://www3.weforum.org/docs/WEF_GlobalCompetitivenessReport_2013-14.pdf (accessed November 12, 2015).

SEB Bank. December 2014. "Lithuanian Macroeconomic Review No. 58." Retrieved from www.seb.lt/sites/default/files/web/document/lietuvos_ekonomikos_apzvalga_LMR/lmr58_0.pdf (accessed May 22, 2015).

"Serbian Prime Minister Vucic Pledges Millions to Srebrenica." 2015. *DW,* November 11. Retrieved from www.dw.com/en/serbian-prime-minister-vucic-pledges-millions-to-srebrenica/a-18843982

Serbos, S. 2008. "European Integration and South Eastern Europe: Prospects and Challenges for the Western Balkans." *UNISCI Discussion Papers* 18, p. 97.

Shields, S. 2011. "Poland the Glaobal Political Economy: From Neoliberalism to Populism (And Back Again)." In *First the Transition, Then the Crash: Eastern Europe in the 2000s,* ed. G. Dale, 169–86. London: Pluto Press.

Sinani, N. 2013. "Will the EBRD Do the Right Thing for Kosovo, Its Newest Member?" Retrieved from http://neurope.eu/article/will-ebrd-do-right-thing-kosovo-its-newest-member/ (accessed January 10, 2016).

Sjöberg, Ö., and M. Wyzan, eds. 1991. *Economic Change in the Balkan States.* London: Pinter.

Skrpec, D. September 11, 2015. "Playing the Field in Serbia." Foreign Affairs. Retrieved from www.foreignaffairs.com/articles/serbia/2015-09-11/playing-field-serbia

"Slovenia Prime Minister Alenka Bratusek Resigns." 2014. *DW,* May 5. Retrieved from www.dw.com/en/slovenia-prime-minister-alenka-bratusek-resigns/a-17612637

Smith, A. 2000. *The Return to Europe: The Reintegration of Eastern Europe into the European Economy.* London, UK: Palgrave MacMillan.

Smith, H. 2015. "7 Years of Kosovo, Geelong." Retrieved from http://hsog.tk/2015/03/7-years-of-kosovo/ (accessed January 01, 2016).

Smith-Doerr, L., and W. Powell. 2005. "Networks and Economic Life." In *The Handbook of Economic Sociology*, eds. N. Smelser and R. Swedberg, 379–402. 2nd ed. Princeton, NJ: Princeton University Press.

Sobczak, P., and A. Barteczko. 2015. "Polish President Concedes Election Defeat to Conservative Challenger." *Reuters* May 24. Retrieved from www.reuters.com/article/2015/05/24/us-poland-election-idUSKBN0O900A20150524

"Šogad Krievijas bruņoto spēku lidmašīnas un kuģi Latvijai pietuvojušies vairāk nekā 250 reizes." December 1, 2014. [This Year, the Russian Military Planes and Ships Have Approached Latvia More Than 250 Times], LETA/Tvnet.lv. Retrieved from www.tvnet.lv/zinas/latvija/537513-sogad_krievijas_brunoto_speku_lidmasinas_un_kugi_latvijai_pietuvojusies_vairak_neka_250_reizes

Sommers, J., and J. Bērziņš. 2011. "Twenty Years Lost: Latvia's Failed Development in the Post-Soviet World." In *First the Transition, Then the Crash: Eastern Europe in the 2000s,* ed. G. Dale, 119–42. London: Pluto Press.

Sondergaard, L., and M. Murthi. 2012. *Skills, Not Just Diplomas: Managing Education for Results in Eastern Europe and Central Asia.* Washington: The World Bank.

SPI. 2015. "SPI Progress Index 2015." www.socialprogressimperative.org/data/spi (accessed November 11, 2015).

Stastny, D. 2010. "Czech Economists on Economic Policy: A Survey." *Econ Journal Watch* 7, no. 3, pp. 275–87.

"Stirring the Pot." 2015. *The Economist,* March 3. Retrieved from www.economist.com/news/europe/21645522-leader-ethnic-polish-party-tries-broaden-his-appeal-reaching-out-ethnic

Stockholm International Peace Research Institute. 2014. "Trends in International Arms Transfer, 2014." Retrieved from http://books.sipri.org/product_info?c_product_id=495 (accessed January 28, 2016).

Stoian, C. April 8–9, 2005. "Multinationals in Emerging Markets: Making the Best of the Good Side: Comparative Evidence from Poland and Romania." Paper at the Academy of International Business Conference. UK Chapter, Bath.

Stokes, G., ed. 1991. *From Stalinism to Pluralism.* Oxford: Oxford University Press.

Storobin, D. 2005. "Estonian Economic Miracle: A Model for Developing Countries." Global Politician. Archived from the original on June 28, 2011. Retrieved from https://web.archive.org/web/20110628230137/http://www.globalpolitician.com/2614-baltic-eu-expansion-estonia (accessed November 18, 2015).

Stringer, M.D. 2005. *A Sociological History of Christian Worship.* Cambridge: Cambridge University Press.

Svensson, L.E.O. 2008. "Inflation Targeting." In *The New Palgrave Dictionary of Economics*, eds. S.N. Durlauf, and L.E. Blume. 2nd ed. New York: Palgrave Macmillan.

Swietochowski, T. 1995. *Russia and Azerbaijan: A Borderland in Transition.* New York: Columbia University Press.

Szakacs, G. 2014. "U.S. Ban Hungarians From Entry Over Corruption Charges." *Reuters,* October, 18.

Szemler, T. 2009. "The Effects of Accession in Hungary." In *Enlarging the European Union: Effects on the New Member States and the EU,* eds. G. Avery, A. Faber, and A. Schmidt. Brussels, Belgium: Trans European Policy Studies Association.

Taagepera, R. 1997. "Expansion and Contraction Patterns of Large Polities: Context for Russia." *International Studies Quarterly* 41, no. 3, pp. 475–504. doi:10.1111/0020-8833.00053

Taggart, P. 1998. "A. Touchstone of Dissent: Euroscepticism in Contemporary Western European Party Systems." *European Journal of Political Research* 33, no. 3, pp. 363–88.

Tamás, G.M. 2011. "Marx on 1989." In *First the Transition, Then the Crash: Eastern Europe in the 2000s,* ed. G. Dale, 21–48. London: Pluto Press.

Tanner, A. 2009. "Montenegro's Leader Sees Slow Economic Recovery." *Balkans Business News*. Retrieved from http://balkans.com/open-news.php?uniquenumber=43059 (accessed December 10, 2015).

Taras, R., ed. 1992. *The Road to Disillusion: From Critical Marxism to Postcommunism in Eastern Europe*. Armonk, NY: M.E. Sharpe.

Taylor & Francis Group. 2004. *Europa World Year, Book 1*. Brussels, Belgium: Europa Publications.

Terenzani-Stankova, M. 2014. "Still No Deal on Reporting Property." *Slovak Spectator*, October 6. Retrieved from http://spectator.sme.sk/articles/view/55446/2/still_no_deal_on_reporting_property.html

Thomann, A. 2006. "Skype, a Baltic Success Story." Retrieved from www.credit-suisse.com/us/en/news-and-expertise/economy/articles/news-and-expertise/2006/09/en/skype-a-baltic-success-story.html,   02/24/2008 (accessed December 12, 2015).

Thomas, E. 2014. "Serbia, Bosnia-Herzegovina Slammed by Worst Flooding in Over a Century." *The Huffington Post* 15 May. Retrieved from www.huffingtonpost.com/2014/05/15/balkan-region-floods-serbia-bosnia-herzegovina_n_5333581.html

Today.Az. 2009. "GDP Growth Makes 3.4% in Azerbaijan in 2009." www.today.az/news/business/51114.html (accessed January 12, 2016).

Transparency International. 2014. "*Corruption Perceptions Index 2014*." Berlin. Retrieved   from   www.transparency.org/country#SVK_DataResearch_SurveysIndices

"Treaty of Maastricht on European Union." n.d. *European Union Law*. Retrieved from http://eur-lex.europa.eu/legal-content/EN/TXT/?uri=URISERV:xy 0026 (accessed July 7, 2015).

Tupy, M.L. September 2003. "EU Enlargement: Costs, Benefits, and Strategies for Central and Eastern European Countries." *Policy Analysis Review* 489. p. 4.

Ummelas, O. 2011. "In Eastern Europe, Cold Feet About Joining the Euro." *Bloomberg Business*, June 23. Retrieved from www.bloomberg.com/bw/magazine/content/11_27/b4235017725502.htm

UNCTAD (United Nations Conference on Trade and Development). 1998. *World Investment Report*. Washington, DC: United Nations Conference on Trade and Development.

UNCTAD. 2001. "Top Investor Countries from 2001 (As Measured by FDI Outward Flows)." http://unctadstat.unctad.org/wds/TableViewer/tableView.aspx

UNCTAD. 2006. http://unctadstat.unctad.org/wds/TableViewer/tableView. aspx

UNDP. 2014 "2014 Human Development Report." Retrieved from http:// hdr.undp.org/en/media/HDR_2011_EN_Complete.pdf (accessed July 07, 2015).

United Nations. 1992. "A/RES/47/121. The Situation in Bosnia and Herzegovina." Retrieved from www.un.org/documents/ga/res/47/a47r121. htm (accessed December 20, 2015).

United Nations. 1993. "General Assembly." Retrieved from www.un.org/ documents/ga/res/47/a47r225.htm

U.S. Department of State. 2015. "Background Note: Croatia." http://m.state. gov/md3166.htm (accessed January 02, 2017).

U.S. State Department. 2014. "U.S. Relations With Belarus." www.state.gov/r/ pa/ei/bgn/5371.htm (accessed February 01, 2016).

van Brabant, J.M. 1989. *Economic Integration in Eastern Europe.* London: Harvester Wheatsheaf.

V.V.B. 2013. "Breaking up With Peevski." *The Economist: Eastern Approaches,* September 20.

Velinger, J. 2006. "World Bank Marks Czech Republic's Graduation to 'Developed' Status." Radio Prague. Retrieved from www.radio.cz/en/section/ curraffrs/world-bank-marks-czech-republics-graduation-to-developed-status (accessed June 23, 2015).

Vuk Dirnberk, V., and T. Valantič. n.d. "Statistični portret Slovenije v EU 2011 [Statistical Portrait of Slovenia in the EU 2011] (in Slovenian and English)." Statistical Office of the Republic of Slovenia. Retrieved from www.stat.si/doc/ pub/00-RP-909-1103.pdf (accessed February 12, 2015).

"Vyriausybės Naujienlaiškis." June 2, 2014. [Government Newsletter Nr. 125 (22)]. Retrieved from http://lrv.lt/naujienos/savaites-naujienos/?nid=14508

Walker, C.J. 1980. *Armenia: The Survival of A Nation.* London: Croom Helm.

Walton, J., and D. Seddon. 1994. *Free Markets and Food Riots: The Politics of Global Adjustment.* Oxford: Blackwell.

Wandycz, P.S. 2001. *The Price of Freedom: A History of East Central Europe from the Middle Ages to the Present.* Hove, UK: Psychology Press.

White, J. 2006. "Czech Republic to Join Schengen." The Prague Post, December 13. Archived from the Original on 25 February 2008. Retrieved from https://web.archive.org/web/20080225173344/http://www.praguepost. com/articles/2006/12/13/czech-republic-to-join-schengen.php (accessed December 12, 2015).

Whitefield, S., and R. Rohrschneider. 2006. "Forum Section. Political parties, Public Opinion and European Integration in Post-Communist Countries. The State of the Art." *European Union Politics* 7, no. 1, pp. 141–60.

Wolchik, S.L., and J. L. Curry. 2011. *Central and East European Politics: From Communism to Democracy.* Lanham, MD: Rowman & Littlefield Publishers.

World Bank. 2014. worldbank.org. Retrieved from http://data.worldbank.org/about/country-and-lending-groups#High_income (accessed April 25, 2015).

World Bank. 2015a. "Doing Business in Macedonia 2016." Retrieved from www.doingbusiness.org/data/exploreeconomies/macedonia,-fyr/ (accessed January 02, 2016).

World Bank. 2015b. "Doing Business: Georgia is This Year's Top Reformer." Retrieved from www.worldbank.org/en/country/georgia/overview (accessed January 28, 2016).

World Bank. 2015c. "Doing Business: Measuring Business Regulations" www.doingbusiness.org/rankings (accessed March 01, 2016).

WTO Staff Working. November 2000. *International Trade and the Position of European Low-Skilled Labour.* St. John's, Canada: Economic Research and Analysis Division. ERAD-2000-01.

WTO. 2012. "Accessions: Belarus." Retrieved from www.wto.org/English/thewto_e/acc_e/a1_belarus_e.htm (accessed January 28, 2016).

WTO News. 2013. "Serbia a Few Steps Away From Concluding WTO Accession Negotiations." www.wto.org/english/news_e/news13_e/acc_srb_13jun13_e.htm (accessed November 10, 2015).

Zaman, G. 2008. "Economic Effects of CEE Countries Integration into the European Union." *Journal Annales Universitatis Apulensis Series Oeconomica* 2, pp. 10, p. 2.

Zarakhovich, Y. 2006. "Kazakhstan Comes on Strong." *Time.* Retrieved from http://content.time.com/time/world/article/0,8599,1539999,00.html (accessed January 28, 2016).

Zolo, D. 2002. *Invoking Humanity: War, Law and Global Order.* Continuum International Publishing Group.

Index

OTHER TITLES FROM THE ECONOMICS COLLECTION

Philip Romero, The University of Oregon and
Jeffrey Edwards, North Carolina A&T State University, Editors

- *Monetary Policy within the IS-LM Framework* by Shahdad Naghshpour
- *What Hedge Funds Really Do: An Introduction to Portfolio Management* by Philip J. Romero and Tucker Balch
- *Advanced Economies and Emerging Markets: Prospects for Globalization* by Marcus Goncalves, Jose Alves, and Harry Xia
- *Comparing Emerging and Advanced Markets: Current Trends and Challenges* by Marcus Goncalves and Harry Xia
- *Learning Basic Macroeconomics: A Policy Perspective from Different Schools of Thought* by Hal W. Snarr
- *The Basics of Foreign Exchange Markets: A Monetary Systems Approach* by William D. Gerdes
- *Learning Macroeconomic Principles Using MAPLE* by Hal W. Snarr
- *Macroeconomics: Integrating Theory, Policy and Practice for a New Era* by David G. Tuerck
- *Emerging and Frontier Markets: The New Frontline for Global Trade* by Marcus Goncalves and Jose Alves
- *Doing Business in Emerging Markets: Roadmap for Success* by Marcus Goncalves, Jose Alves, and Rajabahadur V. Arcot
- *Seeing the Future: How to Build Basic Forecasting Models* by Tam Bang Vu
- *Global Public Health Policies: Case Studies from India on Planning and Implementation* by KV Ramani
- *U.S. Politics and the American Macroeconomy* by Gerald T. Fox

Announcing the Business Expert Press Digital Library

Concise e-books business students need for classroom and research

This book can also be purchased in an e-book collection by your library as

- a one-time purchase,
- that is owned forever,
- allows for simultaneous readers,
- has no restrictions on printing, and
- can be downloaded as PDFs from within the library community.

Our digital library collections are a great solution to beat the rising cost of textbooks. E-books can be loaded into their course management systems or onto students' e-book readers.
The **Business Expert Press** digital libraries are very affordable, with no obligation to buy in future years. For more information, please visit **www.businessexpertpress.com/librarians**. To set up a trial in the United States, please email **sales@businessexpertpress.com**.